D0088352

THE DANGER FROM STRANGERS

Confronting the Threat of Assault

THE DANGER FROM STRANGERS

Confronting the Threat of Assault

James D. Brewer

Foreword by
Judge William S. Sessions
Former Director
Federal Bureau of Investigation

 **INSIGHT BOOKS**

Plenum Press • New York and London

Library of Congress Cataloging-in-Publication Data

Brewer, James D.
    The danger from strangers : confronting the threat of assault /
James D. Brewer ; foreword by William S. Sessions.
       p.   cm.
    Includes bibliographical references and index.
    ISBN 0-306-44642-1
    1. Self-defense. 2. Assault and battery--Prevention of. 3. Rape-
-Prevention of. 4. Victims of crimes. 5. Crime prevention--Citizen
participation.   I. Title.
GV1111.B69 1994
362.88--dc20   93-50220
                                                                CIP

ISBN 0-306-44642-1

© 1994 Plenum Press, New York
A Division of Plenum Publishing Corporation
233 Spring Street, New York, N.Y. 10013-1578

An Insight Book

Printed in the United States of America

To those who have so unselfishly supported
my quest for a safer society:

My instructors;
The victims of criminal assault who so generously
shared their stories;
and
My patient, indulgent family

FOREWORD

The last decade of the twentieth-century in America has the unfortunate probability of being the most violent in post-Civil War America. From coast to coast and border to border, in the country's metropolitan regions, as well as its small towns and rural areas, crime has become the principal concern of Americans. From kindergartners to the elderly, they feel and express similar concerns about the dangers lurking just beyond the front doors of their homes. Law enforcement officials, from the local police station to the Department of Justice in Washington, D.C., are searching for effective approaches to reduce violence on the streets of the cities, towns, and suburbs, all of which are struggling to find solutions to these seemingly intractable problems.

Violence has now created a fear of injury or death that is viewed by teenagers as the primary concern in their lives, with concern about drugs coming in a close second. James Brewer, in *The Danger from Strangers*, has taken a positive approach to helping concerned people think through their own personal circumstances in order to find the means and methods that will help them reduce their exposure to violence and assault.

The Danger from Strangers is chock-full of facts and figures supported by Brewer's thoughtful analysis of what they will mean to the reader. There are exercises that will help the reader think through and prepare to confront potentially dangerous circumstances with a confidence that will reduce the fear that can be immobilizing. The book can serve as a supplemental reference in schools, colleges, and service organizations and can provide a basic, thought-provoking format for discussion among people who want to restore their ability to cope with violence in their lives and avoid harm.

This book, therefore, is a very timely publication, coming just after the passage of the 1993 crime bill by the United States Congress—legislation that includes the extremely important "Brady Bill," which I view as an important first step in reducing the means so often used to obtain handguns and other assault weapons. *The Danger from Strangers* has a clear message to the reader that violence from crime is not inevitable in one's life and that one can do something about it.

Brewer guides the reader through discussions about "who the criminals are and what they look for in a victim." *The Danger from Strangers* will help the reader understand "the principles of confrontation avoidance" and will enhance the reader's confidence in "his or her ability to handle a situation," enabling the reader to move "beyond fear" to confront the problems of crime in his or her life. *The Danger from Strangers* provides guidance for community-based support groups in order to put a stop to the victimization that plagues America. Brewer's thoughtful analysis and discussion will make a meaningful contribution to helping us find ways to not only cope with violence but also to find ways to reduce that violence.

JUDGE WILLIAM S. SESSIONS

Former Director,
Federal Bureau of Investigation

ACKNOWLEDGMENTS

Without the open, direct testimony of crime victims—people willing to share their pain so that others might be spared—this book would not exist.

Without the hours of meticulous research by victimologists and criminologists, many of whom are cited herein, we would all be unable to quantify the dangers that confront us.

Without the writers, journalists, and security theorists who put it on the line by offering solid advice for average citizens, we would still be grasping for responses to the threat of criminal assault.

Without the editorial skills of Frank Darmstadt and Curtis Epstein, this book would have been infinitely less well defined and useful to the reader.

I would like to specifically acknowledge the outstanding research support I received from the libraries at the University of South Carolina, Columbia, South Carolina, and the United States Military Academy, West Point, New York.

CONTENTS

THE DANGER FROM STRANGERS

Confronting the Threat of Assault

Introduction

THE THREAT OF ASSAULT

• Robert lives in fear. He travels to and from his job in the city and wonders every day if he will be the victim of a criminal assault. Fear did not always plague this 39-year-old professional man. Once Robert felt confident and safe in his daily activities, but something happened on March 18, 1987, that has forever changed his outlook on life. He was a victim of what is commonly called a mugging, or assault. It was 9:30 P.M. when Robert locked his office and started across the street for the parking lot. He had worked late and was looking forward to going home to a cold supper and a few quiet moments with his wife. Since Robert was a bright, successful office manager, it was not uncommon for him to be the last to go home when the workload was heavy, and this particular week had been horrible. As he locked the building Robert was still preoccupied with business, so, with his overcoat over his arm, he started across the street, paying little attention to a man standing in the vicinity of the parking lot less than a city block away from the office door. His was the only car left in the lot, and he fumbled for his keys as he approached the door. With his mind on how fast he could get home, he never noticed that the individual he had seen a moment earlier did not continue to move down the street. As he put his key in the door lock, Robert felt a hand on his shoulder. The stranger jerked him around, pushed him against the car, and stared into Robert's face. His breath smelled of beer.

"You got any money?" the stranger said.

Robert's throat tightened as he tried to speak.

"Get away from me!" he said. The man slapped him across the face with the back of his hand and again demanded money.

Robert was no stranger to physical contact. He had faced 250-pound linebackers in high school and held his own. But for the first time in his life, he was frozen with fear. The assailant used the hesitation to drive his knee sharply into Robert's abdomen. Doubled over with pain, Robert heard the man demand his wallet, but before he could reach his back pocket, the stranger knocked him to the pavement with a crushing blow from a powerful right hand. Robert lost his wallet that night and a lot of his dignity. The money, credit cards, and family photos can eventually be replaced. The dignity is much harder to recover.

• Sharon is a tall, attractive, single woman in her early thirties. She works at a suburban hair salon as a stylist. Dating has been sporadic for her during the last four years, but she does occasionally visit a local night spot with some of the girls from the salon. About six months ago she was enjoying a long-awaited Friday night happy hour with her friends when a man began to harass her. She told him nicely that she would rather sit with her friends and asked him to leave her alone, but he persisted. Sharon did not want to create a scene, but the man was making a nuisance of himself and ruining her evening, so she spoke to the manager of the club. The manager asked him to leave. One hour later, when Sharon walked out of the club with her friends, she encountered the man again. He was waiting for her. He became verbally abusive and when she tried to walk away he grabbed her sleeve. Her blouse tore as she pulled away. A friend went inside to get help. Before help could arrive, the man pushed her against the wall of the building, causing her to hit her head; then he ran to his car and drove away.

Sharon's injury was not serious. She was lucky. Still, she had never before experienced anything like that, and she just could not figure out what she had possibly done to deserve it. Had she said the wrong thing? Did she behave in some way to provoke the attack? The bruise on her head has gone away, but the questions have continued to bother her.

Every 21 minutes someone is murdered, according to the *Uniform Crime Reports for the United States*, printed annually by the Federal Bureau of Investigation. A rape occurs every five minutes, and before you finish reading this chapter, four citizens will be victims of a robbery and nearly a dozen others will be assaulted (4). When you consider that this may represent only half the actual crime rate (up to 50% may go unreported), it is little wonder that people are worried. Lois Herrington wrote in the final report of the President's Task Force on Victims of Crime (1982): "Every citizen of this country is more impoverished, less free, more fearful, and less safe, because of the ever-present threat of the criminals" (218).

One of the most frightening and frequent manifestations of this criminal activity is the stranger assault, or the intentional attack upon a citizen by a person, or persons, unknown to the victim. Using a specific legal and research definition, this book will focus specifically upon the crime of assault, examining the people and situations involved. Other crimes—robbery, homicide, stranger rape, and acquaintance rape—will be discussed to the extent they are precipitated by assault, qualify as extreme forms of assault, or where they shed light on the overall crime threat. But beyond a mere cataloging of criminal acts, the reader will find an analysis of the perpetrators and the victims of specific assaults, highlighting those behavioral and environmental factors that make a person more vulnerable to a criminal act. Once we know what enhances our chances of being assaulted, we can then apply the confrontation avoidance behaviors described in Chapter 4 to protect ourselves. Along with a discussion of the physical and psychological ramifications of fighting back, we will examine the specific threats to children and the elderly, and offer a strategy for handling potential assault situations.

Instances like those of Robert and Sharon occur at an alarming rate throughout the nation. With anywhere from 2.5 to 2.9 million stranger assaults in the United States each year, the average citizen becomes increasingly concerned that someday he or she may at any time be the next victim (*Sourcebook—1991* 265). Public assurances by politicians and government officials have done little to alleviate the mounting concern, causing many citizens to sense that the criminal justice system is failing. As Willie L. Williams, Los Angeles Commissioner of Police, points out:

> The worst thing is that the situation creates a climate of fear that the government can't control criminals, that the police can't control the criminals, that the courts can't control the criminals, and that there is no hope (Pater & Pater 60).

"The fear of crime holds people hostage in their own homes," says Louis R. Mizell, Jr., a security consultant in Bethesda, Maryland. "[Fear] creates unsettling anxiety and definitely reduces the quality of life" (Miller 12). According to the *Washington Post*, as cited by Miller,

> In Annandale, Lina Johnson is so uneasy, she won't answer her door after dark. In Cleveland Park, Laura Goodin, a part-time self-defense instructor, gets by on pocket change in the evening instead of getting cash at an automatic teller machine because she fears becoming the target of a robber. "Before it was easy to know what was safe and what wasn't," said Goodin, an editor at the World Bank. "There aren't as many rules anymore" (Miller 12).

Each year the Bureau of Justice Statistics interviews approximately 3,200 victims of assaultive violence. They tell their own horror stories about their encounters with assault, which is the most frequent crime involving physical contact between victims and offenders. These interviews create the National Crime Survey (NCS), from which we learn about the nature and actual threat of criminal assault.

For the purpose of this study, I shall adopt a definition of assault used by the Bureau of Justice Statistics, clarifying where necessary the legal aspects of the issue. Of course, any subject that attracts the interesting combination of academic types and lawyers trying to define critical words is bound to end up being couched in some long, detailed, hair-splitting, mind-clouding definitions. Let me simplify if it is possible. In legal terms, the word assault is usually linked with battery, although both refer to different acts. Battery is the more severe offense from the point of view of the legal community, requiring the attacker to have made physical contact with the victim, and to have acted with an intent to injure or through criminal neglect. The victim must have also suffered a bodily injury to meet the criteria for battery (Kadish 88). So a person intentionally striking another person with his or her fist would clearly be guilty of battery. As with any legal term, there are many fine points for argument; for example, poisoning someone would also constitute battery, but in this book I will focus primarily upon the acts of physical confrontation.

Assault, on the other hand, is considered the lesser offense, and is defined as either an "attempted battery or an intentional frightening of another person" (Kadish 89). Again, the assailant must have intent to cause injury, but what is interesting here is that no physical attack need take place for someone to be guilty of assault, as it is defined legally. In most states, an act that is designed to frighten another person—"causing reasonable apprehension of immediate bodily harm"—is enough ground for a charge of assault (Kadish 89). This becomes more significant as we later examine the psychological effects of an encounter with a criminal, for legally, the culprit is guilty of assault the moment he or she terrorizes a citizen in the initial confrontation. Aggravated assault is frequently defined in state statutes as the intent to kill or rape, and it most often carries with it the use of a deadly weapon.

While all those legal definitions make for some interesting discussion, it is the more direct version of assault, as defined by the Department of Justice, that will guide our examination and keep us focused. We will look at techniques for anticipating, avoiding, or reacting to what Department of Justice surveys call *assault*, *simple assault*, and *aggravated assault*.

- *Assault*:   Unlawful intentional inflicting, or attempted or threatened inflicting, of injury upon the person of another.
- *Simple assault*:   Unlawful intentional inflicting, or attempted or threatened inflicting, of less than serious bodily injury without a deadly or dangerous weapon. This generally consists of all assaults not specifically defined as serious.
- *Aggravated assault*:   Unlawful intentional inflicting of serious bodily injury, or unlawful threat or attempt to inflict bodily injury or death, by means of a deadly or dangerous weapon, with or without actual infliction of any injury. This encompasses the earlier legal notion of battery, but also includes assault with intent to commit manslaughter or murder (*Sourcebook—1991* 745).

AN EGALITARIAN THREAT

During your lifetime, the chances that you will suffer a simple or aggravated assault are greater than the chance that you will be injured in a motor vehicle accident ("Fear of Crime" 24). No one, regardless of age, race, sex, or economic status, is safe from the threat of physical attack. That attack may come in the form of a mugging, rape, robbery, drive-by shooting, or any number of equally disturbing invasions of human rights, up to and including the ultimate violation of civil rights—murder. In the three years that I was living just 50 miles from New York City, scarcely a day passed that I did not hear on the evening news of a homicide, a rape, a kidnapping, or some equally heinous crime. If a priest was not being robbed for the contents of the church's offering plate, then a stock-market worker on lunch break was the unwitting victim of stray bullets from a drug dealers' shoot-out.

"It's just the big city," some might argue, and to an extent they are correct; the drug problem and poverty of urban areas, coupled with the dense population, do tend to spawn a high crime rate. But when I recently returned to my hometown in Tennessee to visit ailing relatives in the local hospital, I had not been there five minutes when the EMS workers brought in four males who suffered gunshot and stab wounds. Crime is not new, nor is it limited to large cities, but it does seem to have escalated and become more sophisticated. As John Townsend, chief of the detective bureau, Chicago Police Department, said:

> Years ago gang members used to ride on bicycles and have fist fights. Now they drive Buicks and Cadillacs and have gunfights with high-priced weapons (Pater & Pater 60).

In reporting on crime in the Washington, D.C. area, Bill Miller wrote in the *Washington Post*:

> Dozens of people interviewed in recent weeks said they now believe their suburban neighborhoods are potentially as dangerous as urban streets. They are not cowering in their homes, but anxious local residents are buying handguns, burglar alarms, and Mace; taking self-defense courses; attending classes on how to avoid carjacking; and changing their habits.

While crime statistics portray some groups as having a higher risk of victimization, *everyone* must face the potential threat of physical or emotional injury at the hands of the criminals in our society. If you have never been victimized on our nation's streets, or in your home, the chances are good that you know someone who has been victimized. The resulting suffering, degradation, and rage often alter that person's personality and outlook on life. Recently, victim assistance groups have emerged to counsel and support citizens who have suffered attack. These groups provide a valuable service in helping sort through the maze of financial, emotional, and legal difficulties that confront victims. But surely there is more to be done. While victim assistance after a crime is critical to recovery, does it not make sense to assist citizens in avoiding the assault situation in the first place? People want answers to tough questions.

- How can I avoid becoming a victim of assault?

- If I am confronted by a criminal, what do I do?

In the following chapters we will answer not only these two important questions but we will also find out:

- Who is committing these crimes of assault, robbery, rape, and murder?
- Who are being victimized most, and what are they doing to contribute to their circumstances?
- What are some commonsense ways to recognize potential attackers *before* they strike?
- What are the techniques I can use to avoid confrontation or diffuse a potential attack?
- If attacked, should I fight back?
- Under what circumstances should I submit to an attacker?
- How do I keep fear from ruling my life?

Between the volumes that have been written to morally and legally support the unfortunate victim and the physical techniques of the self-defense manuals, I offer you a common sense approach to self-protection based upon facts. There is a clear and present danger of crime facing every citizen. Depending upon your age, sex, occupation, and place of residence, you run a particular risk of being victimized. As we shall see, there are steps you can take to minimize your vulnerability, but you cannot remove it entirely. This book is designed to help *people* reduce their risk of being victimized. The word *people* is important here. This is not a book designed specifically for one racial group or a particular sex. Yes, there are certain risks of crime that vary by race, sex, and/ or behavior, but the actions that can get a Hispanic homosexual assaulted are generally dangerous even for a white heterosexual male. Black males make themselves vulnerable in ways similar to Asian females—what is foolish and dangerous for one to do, is foolish and dangerous for the other. And yes, there are crimes that occur predominantly against women: We shall look at the most significant of those crimes—rape. Then, too, there are the frightening instances of hate crimes grounded in racism, as well as the disturbing phenomenon of gay-bashing that is apparently on the increase. But this book will specifically attempt to deemphasize race, sex, or sexual orientation because, quite simply, there are enough unavoidable discriminators that keep our nation divided without enhancing those divisions along racial, sexual, or personal lines. So, unless an instance of assault is specifically tied to a particular race or element of society, it is more meaningful to talk about people avoiding criminals rather than classes of people. The tenets of confrontation avoidance and mental alertness that we will learn about in the next several chapters can work to keep you safe regardless of your sex, race, income, or sexual preference.

CRIME: INCREASING OR DECREASING?

The period from 1960 through 1970 saw the United States struggle through a crime wave, with increases in both violent and nonviolent crime (Karmen 47). From 1970 through 1980, the rapid increase did not continue, but the crime continued. In the 1970s one might have taken an optimistic view and pointed to the lack of significant increase in crime rates as a positive sign that the whole law and order problem was being brought under control. But that would be grossly misleading. Unless crime is decreasing, it's not being controlled. People were still being robbed and raped during the 1970s, and people are still being mugged and beaten today. The lack of an increase in such behavior is not very comforting, particularly if you are a victim.

Those who thought that crime was coming under control in the seventies had to admit they were wrong during the decade of the eighties, since from 1984 to 1988 aggravated assault was up 33%, increasing some 6% just between 1987 and 1988 (*Uniform Crime Reports* [UCR] 23, 24). But making sense out of the statistics from various crime panels, surveys, and reports is a difficult business. It is like cutting one's way through a dense jungle using a dull machete. The government and police agencies produce the

National Crime Survey with its set of figures. The Uniform Crime Reporting Program involves various agencies and a different set of crime figures, and there are many subelements to each of these reports, for example, the Supplementary Homicide Report. Large cities, as well as the Department of Justice, produce their own statistics. We also have victimization surveys done by criminologists and victim support groups, which offer yet another quantification of criminal activity. All these different groups are producing statistics, each using a slightly different form of measurement, and each looking for a different emphasis from their findings. Reacting to this flood of information, and sometimes adding to the chaos, is a group of politicians and professors trying to analyze the data to make it support their contentions. They are having a round-robin in which everyone is questioning everyone else's data and thinking he or she knows more about the subject than the next person. You, the average citizen, are the loser in all this. Scholars are too busy enlightening each other to bother with enlightening you, and all that scholastic debate gives you little you can *use* to avoid becoming a victim of crime. This book offers you the raw information in a straightforward, no nonsense manner, using only enough statistics to illustrate the problem. Do not get bogged down worrying whether you have a .005 or a .006 chance of someone hitting you on the head with a baseball bat. (Sadly, the baseball bat has become the weapon of choice among drug dealers on the street. Why? It's legal to carry and it generally gets the wielder less prison time since it's not considered a deadly weapon.) Just pay close attention to the actions and attitudes of both the criminals and the victims, as described in the following pages, and you will stand a better chance of avoiding an unhealthy confrontation with a stranger.

In regard to personal crimes per 1,000 people, Table I.1 shows your chances of being on the losing end of a criminal encounter for three selected years. While the chances didn't significantly increase during this period, they didn't appreciably decrease either. And although crime may not have skyrocketed between these years, neither has it quietly gone away. The 1989 figure of 23

TABLE I.1. Victimization Chances
for Selected Years

	1973 (%)	1981 (%)	1989 (%)
Rape	.01	.01	.01
Robbery	.07	.07	.05
Assault	2.5	2.7	2.3
Aggravated	1.0	.09	.08
Simple	1.5	1.7	1.5
Personal larceny			
With contact	.03	.03	.03
Without contact	8.8	8.2	6.6

SOURCE: *Sourcebook—1990* 252.

assaults per 1,000 people does not sound very threatening, unless you are one of the 23. Most of the 23 would probably have read such a statistic and felt rather safe, and I am confident that not one of the 23 ever intended to be the victim of an assault, or perhaps even thought that he or she would someday be a victim. But who is to say that *you* will not be a part of next year's statistics?

Examining the period 1989–1990, we encounter conflicting reports. The Justice Department claimed in its National Crime Victimization Survey that the overall national crime rate (excluding murder) had fallen by 4% (*Facts on File—1992* 615). But Table I.2 shows trends in the FBI's Uniform Crime Report that reflect a 2.7% increase in the overall crime rate for the period 1990–1991, and a 10.1% increase between 1987 and 1991. What is particularly disturbing in the FBI statistics for 1989–1990 is the continuing upward trend in homicide—the most extreme form of assault—which increased by 44% from 1965 to 1985 (Martinez-Schnell 287).

Let me digress a moment and talk about homicide, which, while not the focus of the book, is nonetheless the notion of assault carried to its ultimate conclusion. Though not legally defined as assault, or measured among assault reporting, homicide frequently has its genesis in even simple assault. What starts as a

TABLE I.2. Trends from the FBI Uniform Crime Report

	1990–1991 (%)	1987–1991 (%)
Rape	up 3.9	up 17.0
Robbery	up 7.6	up 32.8
Aggravated assault	up 3.6	up 27.8
Larceny	up 2.5	up 8.6
Violent crime (murder, assault, robbery, and rape)	up 5.0	up 28.8
Crime Index Total	up 2.7	up 10.1

SOURCE: *Uniform Crime Reports for the United States—1991* 58.

shoving match or perhaps an argument over a poker game, if not properly controlled, can quickly escalate to lethal violence. Homicide is the nation's third leading cause of premature mortality (dying before you statistically should) from injury, topped only by motor vehicle accidents and suicides (Martinez-Schnell 288). During the period when homicide increased by 44% (1965–1985), it effectively doubled the years of potential life lost in the United States. Homicide frequency is important to the person concerned about assault not only because of the potential for assault to lead to homicide but also because the growth of homicide is itself an indicator of how bad the threat of assaultive violence actually is.

> Mortality is the tip of the interpersonal violence iceberg. The rate of nonfatal injuries from intentional interpersonal violence is estimated to be at least *100 times greater* than the rate of homicide. (Martinez-Schnell 292; italics added)

So, is crime increasing? It depends upon the crime. The FBI says that while the number of reported murders and robberies decreased for 1990–1991, forcible *rapes* and *aggravated assaults* rose by 4% and 6%, respectively, for the same period. And while the Bureau of Justice Statistics maintained that the overall crime rate varied little during 1990–1991, even that organization admitted that violent crimes had jumped 7%, "mainly because of a sharp rise in *simple assaults*" (Rubin 9A; italics added). Even if you believe the Justice Department and are satisfied that crime has somehow leveled off, crime researchers Steffensmeier and Harer point out that any decrease researchers denote in crime may be directly tied to the aging of our society. It seems that the crime rate festered as the baby-boom generation passed through adolescence and young adulthood, but as this group moves into middle age, they take with them the large percentage of the population that commits most of the crimes (23). Look at it this way: The bad news is we're all getting older; the good news is we're robbing fewer liquor stores.

Just because a crime occurs does not mean it occurs successfully. The Bureau of Justice Statistics indicates that from 1973 through 1979 only 38% of the attempted rapes were completed, only 61% of the attempted robberies were completed, only 30% of the attempted assaults (aggravated) were completed, and only 21% of attempted simple assaults were completed. Why were those who perpetrated these crimes unsuccessful? What did the victims do, or not do, that inhibited their assailants? The answers to these and other questions will be covered in the following chapters to help you develop a personal strategy for dealing with the threat of a face-to-face confrontation with a criminal.

Chapter One

PROFILE OF AN ATTACKER

Who are the bad guys? How can you recognize them before it's too late? If there were easy answers to these questions you would not be reading this book. But criminals do not wear black hats, as they do in the movies, you cannot count on hearing that certain kind of bad-guy music when they approach, and those characteristic beady eyes are just not beady enough anymore.

Criminologists and psychologists in the early and mid-twentieth century spent much time and money trying to figure out how to recognize criminals by their protruding foreheads or their bushy eyebrows or some other telltale feature. The method was called phrenology; it enabled one to study how the conformation of the skull is indicative of character and mental capacity. These phrenologists, such as Cesare Lombroso and Gina Lombroso Ferrero in *The Criminal Mind* (1911), sought a relationship between the tendency toward certain behaviors and the shape of the exterior of the skull. Skull shape equaled brain shape, so would not the varied shapes of the skull also offer insight into specific character traits? If your skull was thicker or unusually shaped in certain places, you might have a tendency toward combativeness or destructiveness; thus phrenologists like Lombroso could conclude "a predominance of acquisitiveness [leads] to theft and gambling, and . . . combativeness [leads] to manslaughter and murder" (Ziegenhagen 12).

After the phrenologists produced far less than definitive results, researchers looked at broader physical characteristics to figure out who was likely to become a criminal. Lombroso saw criminal activity as a sign of less than perfect evolution; and while anyone who has been attacked by a mugger or a rapist might agree that the culprit behaved like a neanderthal, Lombroso actually went about the business of identifying physical features—slanting forehead, jutting jaw, large, bony ridges above the eyes— characteristic of what he called a throwback in the evolutionary process. Criminals were, therefore, simply abberations or "biological reversions to an earlier form of man . . . incapable of dealing with the complexities of modern life" (Ziegenhagen 12). While Lombroso and other phrenologists admitted that this evolutionary flaw might be only one cause of criminal behavior, and that socialization might also be a contributing factor, such research does not help the average citizen anticipate an assault. There is neither time nor opportunity to measure the skull of a likely assailant.

Others continued to study inmates at correctional facilities for biological indicators of criminal potential; but as crime and behavior researcher Eduard A. Ziegenhagen points out, "inmates of prisons [represent] only criminals who were inept practitioners of their trade" (12).

From phrenology and evolution, the quest to identify the bad guys moved toward glandular and chromosomic links to criminality. Explanations ranged from "his glands made him do it," to "he's genetically flawed," to "he's evil because that is his natural tendency, which if left unchecked, will result in crime." The latter sounds strangely like the Calvinistic doctrine of the Depravity of Man, which shows just how far afield so-called scientific examinations of criminality can drift. Of course the psychiatrists are not to be outdone, offering their varied views and research to indicate that criminality is really just a form of mental illness; thus it becomes the "task of the psychoanalyst then to help persons cope with [criminal] drives in a manner acceptable to others" (Ziegenhagen 13). While that may be true, we do not need a psychiatrist to tell us, *after* criminals have murdered or molested, that people like Jeffrey Dahmer are crazy. We need criteria to help us *anticipate* who will likely commit a criminal act against us, and in that respect, science has failed to produce.

What do the bad guys look like? They look like YOU. They are tall–short, fat–thin, white–black–yellow individuals who blend into the surroundings like a chameleon. They are male and female, they are old and young. They have bushy eyebrows and no eyebrows at all. Much of their success is dependent upon melting into a crowd, avoiding suspicion, and catching their victim off-guard. Although they hide among the law-abiding citizens, enough of them have been caught to provide us a reasonably accurate picture of their overall makeup. According to the NCS figures, most of the offenders who commit assault are 21 years of age or older. This group accounts for about 65% of assaults whereas attackers under 18 account for only 17% (*Sourcebook—1990* 276). We know that most assault offenders act alone. I am not suggesting that group assaults do not exist, or that cities have no gang-related crime problems, but when considered in the total statistics for assault, these incidences account for a small portion. The important question is, "Who is most likely to attack *you*?"

In the crime of robbery, 25% of offenders are under the age of 21 and 66% are over 21 (276) (see Table 1.1). But the older the offender in a robbery, the greater the chance that he or she will be carrying a knife or a gun. It would be ideal if we could predict that on September 15, 1996, you will be accosted at 10:05 P.M. by a blond-haired, green-eyed, white male, six feet tall, weighing 177 pounds, near the corner of 2nd and Wilshire. As he pulls the pearl-handled knife from his left jacket pocket you will see a "snake" tatoo on his forearm. He will demand your wallet. Unfortunately, the business of victimology has not yet achieved such a level of specificity, so you will have to settle for some generalities that can help you identify potential offenders. While it is interesting to review the demographics of the criminal population, and it is nice

TABLE 1.1. Who Are the Assailants? Characteristics
of Lone Offenders

	Percent distribution (rounded off)[a]								
	Age				Sex		Race		
Type of crime	15–17	18–20	21–29	30+	male	fem	wh	bl	oth
Violent crimes	10	13	44	31	87	12	67	25	6
Rape	6	12	40	31	96	4	53	34	7
Assault	9	13	33	33	86	13	72	21	6
Robbery	11	13	44	22	93	6	40	50	8

[a]Totals may not equal 100% because of cases where the race or sex of the attacker could not be
determined. Only selected age categories are included in this chart.
Source: *Sourcebook—1991.*

to know such information, the best way to show what criminals
are like is to look at some examples of how they work.

IN ANSWER TO THE BOOZE

Warren Martin is doing three to five years in the South
Carolina Prison System for assault. But Warren is no social drop-
out or weak-minded pawn of society. He is a smart guy. He
graduated from high school with a B average and attended junior
college for a year. He is not into illegal drugs, but he does have a
weakness for alcohol. When I recently interviewed him, he told
me that alcohol made him do something he regretted.

I was drinking with a couple of friends on Labor Day
weekend in 1985. We'd been downing sixpacks all afternoon
and we were heading for the beach. Jeff, the guy who was
driving, pulled into this service station for gas and I went to
get something to eat at this minimarket next door. I was
pretty loaded when I went in, and I said some pretty raunchy
things to the woman that was running the cash register. The

Figure 1.1. Yes, many Americans drink responsibly. But the link between *alcohol consumption, criminal activity, crime victimization,* and *early mortality* is statistically solid and undeniable. Just remember that a creature who may be stronger than you lurks in each of these bottles; and once you remove the top and let it out, you may or may not be able to put it back in.

> manager came out and asked me to leave. I guess I just got pissed. I called him a bunch of names and told him I wasn't going to leave and he couldn't [expletive deleted] make me.

At this point the manager of the minimarket picked up the telephone and called the police while Warren stood there ranting and raving in a drunken rage. A customer came in behind Warren and accidentally bumped into him with the door. Warren explained:

> I turned around and shoved the door back at him and told him to stay the [expletive deleted] away from me. He said something and I pushed him against a rack of fried pies or something. It knocked him down.

Warren went out the door with the manager following close behind. When he got to the gas station his friends were ready to leave, but Warren hadn't had enough. When he saw the manager following him, he ran inside the garage and picked up a piece of metal from the mechanic's bay, then came back outside to meet the manager of the minimarket. Warren continued:

> I told him he better stay away from me, or I'd bust his head. I was drunk, you know, I didn't really know what I was doing. When the guy said he'd called the cops, I guess I just snapped. I started swinging at this guy and I hit him in the head. He was bleeding pretty bad, and I was going to hit him again, when a couple of guys from the service station grabbed me.

Warren took some swings at them, too, and managed to break one man's ribs before the bystanders finally subdued him. Warren's story is an example of incidental assault. He never set out to find a victim that day, and the manager of the minimarket never expected to be one, but the two managed to get together anyway. The criminal justice system tried and convicted Warren of his crime. He is paying the price. But the manager is paying a price, too. Five years have passed and he still suffers from migraine headaches that are directly related to the assault. He has also changed jobs, and like many crime victims, he suffers from psychological stress that even his closest friends cannot appreciate.

How should that store manager have recognized Warren as a potential attacker? Was there something about his age, his mannerisms, or his demeanor that could have foreshadowed this tragedy? In this particular instance there probably was little that would have distinguished Warren from hundreds of other customers who came in the store that day. But Warren did display one aspect of behavior that is common to many offenders. He was *under the influence of alcohol or other drugs*. When the manager recognized Warren was intoxicated and asked him to leave, as he had every right to do, the situation escalated.

When a confrontation develops, no matter how minor it may seem, between you and someone who is under the influence of drugs, you should prepare yourself for the worst. There is simply no way to predict the behavior of a stranger who is intoxicated. Alcohol, marijuana, cocaine, heroin, or crack make behavior extremely unpredictable; and they make it unwise to take risks with potential attackers. Fights have even occurred because someone could not get to a cigarette quickly enough! Anytime an attacker is under the influence of a chemical substance he or she will be (1) more difficult to reason with, (2) more prone to violence, and (3) more difficult to avoid or control.

Even in the nineteenth century, American writers and thinkers recognized the link between alcohol and criminal behavior. Businessman and showman P. T. Barnum said, "three-fourths of all crime and pauperism existing in our land are traceable to the use of intoxicating liquors" (Room 36). Early studies by Samuel Chipman (1834), who examined the physiological action of alcohol, and subsequent studies of crime causation and alcohol by John Koren (1899), were the first in a series of attempts to empirically determine how alcohol changes behavior. Alcohol researcher Kai Pernanen, in "Alcohol and Crimes of Violence" for *Social Aspects of Alcoholism* (1976), describes a "disinhibition theory"— that alcohol works pharmacologically on the parts of the brain that would normally inhibit a person's antisocial or criminally violent actions. More recent studies have attempted to weigh the types of criminal offenses, the sex and age of perpetrators, the ethnic and cultural differences, and varied situational factors to determine how and to what degree alcohol and other drugs influence behavior toward crime. This is a complicated issue, as the effect of alcohol and other drugs on crime is often a function of the type of crime; but if you look at disinhibition as an open gateway for crime—not a guarantee that crime will occur, but at least one less failsafe of human judgment—it only seems logical that a crime becomes more likely with the presence and use of intoxicants. Keep in mind that it is a misnomer to talk about "alcohol and drugs," because alcohol *is a drug*. It is more accurate to say alcohol and *other* drugs. Since it is a drug, alcohol is frequently the trigger mechanism that pushes people into crime. Actions they might not otherwise take—actions that with a clear mind and conscience they might find morally repugnant—suddenly become acceptable, or even desirable, under the influence of alcohol. (See Table 1.2.)

As a person's Blood Alcohol Content (BAC) rises, there are some predictable responses in his or her behavior. At a BAC of about .05 percent . . . *thought, judgment and restraint may be more lax; the individual is freed from many ordinary anxieties and inhibitions* and may feel more at ease socially (*Alcohol Topics* 1; italics added).

TABLE 1.2. Alcohol Use and Criminal Behavior

Did you know that alcohol misuse is blamed in
   64% of the murders in the United States?
   41% of the assaults?
   34% of the rapes?
   29% of other sex crimes?
   30% of suicides?
   56% of the fights or assaults in the home?
   69% of child abuse?
Add to those figures
   50% of all road fatalities
   53% of fire deaths
   45% of drownings
   22% of home accidents
   36% pedestrian accidents
   55% of arrests
   37.4% of admissions to state and county mental hospitals

SOURCE: *Chicago Tribune*, July 8, 1984, Sec. 6.

Once Warren had refused to leave, and was beginning to threaten the safety of other customers, the manager wisely chose to call the police. Since the bystander was apparently uninjured, and since it appeared that Warren was leaving of his own accord, there was no need for the manager to physically intervene. Yes, Warren and his friends might have been gone by the time the police arrived. That is the justification that the store manager used in following Warren to the gas station. Getting the license number of the vehicle seems like a reasonable action. Perhaps if he had stopped there, without confronting Warren outside the service bay, the police could have overtaken the vehicle and returned Warren to the scene of his actions.

"I should have never gone in that gas station after him," the store manager admitted. By following an intoxicated stranger with whom he had already had a verbal altercation, he placed himself in needless danger and further provoked Warren's anger.

Recognize when someone is out of control and keep a safe distance. The cost of the manager's not-so-effective apprehension of Warren was much greater than the satisfaction of the capture. By staying conscious of one's surroundings and closely observing people for signs of substance abuse, one can be on guard for potential attack.

IN SEARCH OF A ROUTINE

In July of 1984, Albert R. Pagley accosted a woman in broad daylight in a suburban park. For several months the woman, who we will call Julie, had been going to this park during her lunch break. Each day, at 1:00 P.M. she walked from her office in a nearby building and sat at a table near the edge of the park. Julie was not Albert's first victim, but she shared something with his others— something Albert, in my 1988 interview with him, called a dependable routine. "I always watch people before I hit'em," explains Albert. "I'm very patient. Sometimes I'll watch for two or three days before I make my move. I got to be sure. I got to know what to expect."

Offenders like Albert take comfort and security in the consistency of their victims. Criminals don't like surprises. Another way they feel more secure is by working close to home. The reason is simple. If someone tries to apprehend them, it is easier to get away when they know the terrain. Albert does not work the inner city. He prefers to stay near residential areas where he can blend in easily. He says:

> If I want to do a purse (purse-snatch) or shake somebody down, I stay away from downtown. Women are holding on to their purses for dear life, and always looking out when they're downtown. But you get just a little ways from the block, over where there's lots of houses, and they aren't watching too close.

Street robberies frequently occur in residential areas adjacent to commercial districts. Residential areas used for parking are a favorite target of criminals. As Albert explained:

> I knew she didn't meet nobody, cause I seen her there a lot. I just walked right up to her and told her I had a knife, and to give me her wallet. I didn't want no purse. You can't walk around with a purse, so I told her to hand me her wallet. I never did show a knife or nothing, I just told her I'd cut her if she didn't do what I said.

At this particular crime scene there were people sitting two tables away from the victim, but she was probably afraid to scream for fear of the knife. There is no guarantee that anyone would have come to her aid even if she had screamed for help. Albert remembers that she was shaking as she reached into her purse to retrieve the wallet. He stuffed the wallet in his pocket and walked away calmly. He was counting upon his victim being in shock and delaying long enough to buy him some time. In this case he was right. Albert claims he was never caught for this particular crime, but fortunately he is presently doing time for two similar robberies.

What was it about Albert that made him stand out as a potential adversary? Was there any clue immediately available to Julie that might have alerted her to an impending crime? What might she have done differently?

Given the complete surprise that Albert achieved, there is little doubt why Julie behaved as she did. It could be easy to second-guess what Julie should or should not have done. Some people will suggest that she should not have surrendered so easily, that she should have physically struggled against her attacker, but we shall see later that this course of action can have some serious side effects. Others might argue that she should have screamed or tried to draw attention to the crime, thus frightening her attacker away. But the threat of the knife she could not see, coupled with her complete surprise, committed her to a role of capitulation. She might have come out of the situation much worse than losing her wallet. Still, it is not unreasonable to suggest that her failure to be aware of her surroundings and her failure to recognize any hints that the attacker might have offered could have contributed to her vulnerability. Although criminals have habits and behaviors that send signals to their victims, it takes a careful eye and a somewhat suspicious nature to pick up those signals and anticipate a confrontation.

Criminals repetitively work the same locations. It goes back to the need for security and confidence in their operation. They get comfortable with a particular site and fall into patterns and routines (*modus operandi*) just as surely as their victims. The problem is that while they are watching for *our* routines, we are not watching for *theirs*, and we are unaware of our own. Julie never expected to get robbed in a public park in the middle of the afternoon, and that worked to Albert's advantage. By achieving the element of surprise, he caught her completely off-guard and used her shock to assist him. Like most offenders, Albert shaped the situation in his favor and chose a target who was dependable and predictable. To the casual observer, Albert looked every bit as much in place in that park as Julie did. He sat at a table and appeared to be enjoying the sunshine and the view. He said that Julie had seen him a couple of days before but she paid no attention to just another bystander. The fact that he never ate lunch, like most of the other visitors, must not have seemed unusual to her. The fact that he always left the park shortly after she left her table never caught Julie's attention. She apparently did not notice that he seemed particularly interested in what was happening at her table. She must not have thought it odd that he never spoke to others and always sat by himself. Albert says that she even saw him walking toward her the day of the robbery but she apparently thought nothing of it. I am not saying that Julie did anything wrong by simply going to the park to have her lunch. But wherever she is now, she might agree that perhaps she could have been more observant. As a result of this encounter, she is likely to be more suspicious of strangers, even when she has no cause to be. Julie epitomizes the feelings that victimologists M. Bard and D. Sangrey described in their seminal work on victimization, *The Crime Victim's Book* (1979):

> The crime may be a murder or a rape, a robbery or a burglary, the theft of an automobile, a pocket-picking or a purse snatching—but the essential internal injury is the same. Victims have been assaulted—emotionally and sometimes physically—by a predator who has shaken their world to its foundation (xii).

I chose to narrow the focus of this book to stranger assault because most assaults are committed by strangers. So you might say that one way to recognize the bad guys is to not recognize them at all. According to the *Sourcebook of Criminal Justice Statistics* (1990), 57% of all rapes, robberies, and assaults involve strangers. Recent victimization surveys tell us that strangers were the most frequent offenders in robberies (77%), and strangers were responsible for 52 to 56% of all rapes, aggravated assaults, and simple assaults (Riedel 234). The only positive note in these figures is that there has been a tiny decline in stranger involvement. The period 1973–1979 had 59% stranger involvement, while the 1982–1984 period had 57% stranger involvement. Whereas that narrow

period showed some decrease in stranger assault, the data col-
lected from seven different studies in six cities suggested that
there is an *increase* in the proportion of homicides involving
strangers.

IN SEARCH OF A NEARBY TARGET

Most criminals are homebodies. The nature of the crime will
frequently determine how far criminals will travel from their
home. They go further to commit crimes against property than to
commit crimes against people. What that means to you is that if
someone you do not know takes a swing at you, they probably live
closer to you than they would if they were going to rob you. This
illustrates the point that if you routinely visit high-crime areas (the
place where most of the bad guys live) you are more subject to
confrontation than if you avoided such areas.

James L. LeBeau, in "The Journey to Rape" for the *Journal of
Political Science Administration*, cites a mid-1980s study in Indianapolis that found rapists traveled an average of 1.25 miles to get
to their victims (131). He also indicates that in Chicago studies,
87% of the rape offenders lived in the neighborhood or precinct of
their offense (131). When we say that a criminal lives in the "area"
or vicinity of the crime he commits, we are talking about approximately a five city-block area. LeBeau also cities a 1976 study by
noted rape researcher M. Amir (author of *Patterns in Forcible Rape*)
that found 65% of the known rape offenders lived in the vicinity of
both the victim and the scene of the offense. Again, this argues for
choosing carefully where you will live and where you will spend
your time (131).

IN THE GUISE OF THE HARMLESS

Offenders do not all fall under a singular description, nor do
they always have a potential to harm you that is readily discern-

ible. Appearance alone is not an adequate method of determining how dangerous a stranger may be. As Mack Barnhouse, a young construction worker in South Carolina, found out, it is wise to treat all potential offenders as a serious threat. Mack stopped in a supermarket one afternoon to talk to a friend who worked there as a checkout clerk. Business was slow so they had a few moments to chat. While they were talking, the clerk called Mack's attention to a young girl who had been browsing through the paperbacks and magazine rack.

"Did you see that?" the clerk asked.

"What?"

"She put a book under her shirt," the clerk said. "We've got another klepto, and no one's working security right now."

"Are you just going to let her get away?" Mack asked.

The clerk tried to explain to Mack that he could not leave his register unattended and there was no one else free to confront her once she stepped outside the store. He had to let her get outside the store with the book or else she would claim she was going to pay for the item. Mack took another look at the girl and figured that she could not be more than 5'2" and probably did not weigh more than a hundred pounds. She was sixteen or seventeen at the most, and certainly no match for a grown man. (Mack was 6'3" and very muscular.)

"I'll confront her for you," Mack offered.

"I don't know, Mack, I'm not sure if that's legal."

"It sure ain't legal to steal a book," Mack argued.

"Well, I guess it would be okay if you don't touch her or anything, I mean, as long as you can just scare her into staying outside until I can get hold of our security man.

Mack waited until the girl started out the front door of the store without paying for the book, and feeling proud of his role as citizen-guardian, he followed her out the door and confronted her. He stepped up to the girl and gently held out his hand to one side.

"Just a minute," he said sternly. "I believe you've taken a book from the store without paying for it. You'll either have to show me a receipt or wait here until security arrives."

The girl looked at him for a moment and appeared completely unmoved by his speech. She acted neither frightened nor angry. She simply executed a swift kick to Mack's groin before he ever saw it coming. He slumped to the pavement and she disappeared, never to be seen again. The checkout clerk watched the ambulance take his friend away and learned later that afternoon that the blow the girl delivered to Mack's testicles had injured him for life.

In this particular situation the offender appeared to represent no threat to the victim. Mack, who thought he has doing his community a good deed, ran squarely up against a vicious attacker who could just have easily passed for the girl next door. He was taken in, as are many crime victims, by the seemingly innocent nature of the stranger, and what he perceived as the stranger's inability to cause him any serious harm.

There are some strong arguments for Mack not placing himself in such a compromising situation in the first place, but assuming that he was already in the confrontation, it is absolutely critical that he regard her as a threat, and keep plenty of defensible space between them. The role of personal and defensible space will be fully discussed in the chapter on resistance to assault.

IN THE COURAGE OF A GROUP

In most instances of stranger assault, the offender acts alone. But there are instances of multiple attack every day. Some of these crimes are gang related, but many are not. Peer pressure often acts to compel people to commit crimes that they might not otherwise commit, if acting alone. This group courage is frequently a contributing factor in multiple assailant crimes.

In 1986 a man and his wife (seven months pregnant) and another male friend were leaving the movie theater in a large suburban mall. The other stores in the mall had closed about 45 minutes earlier, and only the cars of the moviegoers remained in the lot. As they walked toward their car they were assaulted by five unknown men. The offenders popped up from behind the few cars still remaining in the lot and began to beat them with short pieces of rubber hose. The woman was not severely injured, due primarily to her own ferocity and the valiant efforts of her escorts. The two men required out-patient medical attention at a nearby hospital.

None of the victims had ever seen any of the attackers before, and they could offer the police no reason as to why they were singled out for attack. About two months later the police arrested six suspects involved in a similar incident at the same shopping mall. In the course of questioning they discovered that the group, although not a gang, was regularly conducting these raids. The raids originated as a series of personal challenges among the offenders, as to who could lead the most successful attack and dish out the most punishment. They always chose targets who appeared least able to protect themselves. These offenders were not kids. They were a mixed racial group ranging in age from 17 to 23, and one was even married with a child of his own.

That's the way it is, sometimes, when attackers materialize out of nowhere and seem to prey upon total strangers with no apparent motive. This kind of stranger assault cannot be anticipated, it can only be reacted to. The chapter on resistance will discuss what form those reactions may take, and it will examine the legal implications of going to the defense of others.

Chapter Two

PROFILE OF A VICTIM

For every crime there is a victim. The criminal may or may not be caught and punished, but the victim is always punished. Who are these victims? Who are the people who are suffering at the hands of criminals, and what do they endure? The victims of crime, specifically stranger assault, cut across social, economic, racial, and sexual boundaries. According to the 1988 U.S. Bureau of Justice Statistics, if crime continues at the current rate, some 83% of children 12 years of age will become victims of actual or attempted violence during their lifetime (*Victims* 16). Once assaulted, victims must then wander through a maze of police and court proceedings based upon the English tradition of jurisprudence—a view of law that insists "justice is best served when the legal clash is between the defendant and the state rather than the defendant and the victim" (16). After rejecting a Charles Bronson/*Death Wish* approach to dealing with those who violate him, the victim quickly discovers that the system is geared more to the needs of the criminal than to those of the victim.

Victimologists and criminal justice scholars have spent years jousting with one another over the definition of a victim. Some have argued from a criminal's viewpoint, that is, a victim is the person a criminal "wishes to damage," regardless of whether or not any actual injury takes place (Ziegenhagen 6). Other researchers talk of victim "constituencies," and take the broad view that beyond the person actually suffering at the hands of the criminal, one must consider "friends . . . family . . . [and] those who can imagine the same injury being done to them" (7). But when you get to the heart of the matter, a victim is anyone who has been placed at a disadvantage as a result of a criminal act. That disadvantage may range anywhere from mild inconvenience to loss of life; and it certainly must encompass the family of a homicide victim as surely as it does the victim.

J. Salasin, in *Evaluating Victim Services* (1981), defines victimization as a "situation that produces a break in the human lifeline, when someone is assaulted, damaged for a long time" (Siegel, 1268). And calling upon other evaluations of victim services, Max Siegel of the American Psychological Association, couples being a victim with the concept of stress, saying that victims are people who have received threats, either to the body, to self-image, or to life itself. Victims have a stress reaction that manifests itself in physiological symptoms (1268). Strip away the scientific jargon and you can see that victims are people who have been *frightened*, and they are worried about the frightening situation happening again.

Recognizing the trauma of crime victims and appreciating their challenge has been a popular enterprise only for the past decade. Up until the last few years society had basically disregarded its crime victims. The money and influence were directed to the criminal's rights, rehabilitation, and return to society. The victim was frequently stigmatized, as much of society viewed them as losers. Victims were seen as people who somehow "lost" in a competitive society, and were thus responsible for their own fate. Although we will see that behavior can increase the chances of becoming a crime victim, there need not be a stigma of culpability attached to people unfortunate enough to be confronted by criminals.

CALLING EVIL GOOD

We have a strange habit of misdirecting our compassion in this country. A prime example of that misdirection is the way our culture has served up murder and assault as entertainment. Books, television, and motion pictures generate huge profits by offering heavy helpings of criminal activity in graphic detail, occasionally turning criminals into cult heroes, such as Bonnie and Clyde, Thelma and Louise, and the ever-present Amy Fisher. *Time* magazine referred to the various programs about Amy Fisher as "six hours of vidiocy," and reported that "the NBC movie producers forked over $80,000 toward Fisher's bail," while CBS was offering the Buttafuocos $300,000 for their story. But society is cleaning the plate and clamoring for second servings. Unfortunately, not too many crime victims are signing six-figure movie deals and seeing 70,000–80,000 copies of their stories in print. Their heartache and misery just do not make for good business or good entertainment. Meanwhile, we sit white-knuckled through movies like *Cape Fear* or *The Hand that Rocks the Cradle*, wondering if we could be the next victim, while the evening news cannot resist the urge to portray graphically the latest brutal murder. Consider the case of the Florida man who gunned his wife down right in front of the television camera in January of 1993. As the victim's cemetery visit was being covered by a local television affiliate, her estranged husband's brutal act was captured on videotape. While some networks, such as CNN and ABC used restraint and chose not to air the horrifying footage, still others could not resist the ratings temptation, all the while masquerading their proliferation of violence as the public's so-called right to know. George Gerbner, professor emeritus of communications at Annenburg School of Communications in Philadelphia, called these terrifying video messages "Mean World Syndrome," the idea that some horror lurks just around the corner and everyone is just a victim waiting for his or her turn to be had. Gerbner says, "Television shows are full of violence, and news programs dole out risk information without comparison, context, perspective or other relative values" (Peden 74).

The rampage of Ted Bundy and the so-called Son of Sam killer were the subjects of national attention, while the plight of their victims was virtually unchronicled. Recently, however, some 7,000 groups have appeared to provide psychological and financial support to crime victims. Concerned psychologists, scholars, doctors, and criminologists have teamed up to form victims' rights groups throughout the country, and they have been influential in giving victims not only monetary compensation, but also a role in determining the sentence for the individuals who violated their lives. According to the Washington-based National Organization for Victim Assistance, over 1,500 laws have been enacted in different states to empower victims and allow them to participate in making the case against their assailants (*Victims* 17). Some states allow victims or their families to make a courtroom statement prior to sentencing. Other states grant monetary compensation to victims and/or their families. This is a step in the right direction. But even with improved efforts at representing victims' interests, it is not uncommon for crime victims to feel tremendous anger and a sense of guilt over their involvement in a criminal act. Many still sense a lack of legitimate concern on the part of law enforcement, the criminal justice system, and their neighbors. They get the impression that they have been deceived all their lives, being led to believe that someone really cares about them, when in fact, no one cares at all.

FACING FEAR AND LOSS

Experiencing a stranger assault is kind of like having a bug hit your car windshield at 60 miles per hour. The wipers can get the big pieces, but you always end up streaking your view for the rest of the trip. The moment you are confronted by a criminal, you are a victim, even if the assailant is unsuccessful in his crime against you. Just because someone threatens to rob you and does not succeed does not insulate you from the feeling of violation. In my conversations with people who have been forced to confront an attacker I have noticed some important after-effects. Whether someone tries to punch you during a friendly softball game, or tries to rob you at gunpoint in your driveway, or attempts to relieve you of your stereo tape deck, there is still a sense of loss associated with the crime. That sense of loss develops further to a sense of violation. You feel that you or your home or your car has been defiled by a stranger. Whether it is property or dignity that was lost, the loss endures. Once compromised, your basic trust in people takes a long time to return, if it ever does. A victim's fundamental psychological sense of security, a base element in the hierarchy of human needs, has been threatened and will not easily recover.

When 27-year-old New York City resident Bill Dyer was robbed on Park Avenue while using an automatic teller machine, he suffered a bullet wound that shattered the bone in his thigh. After months of painful rehabilitation, he eventually was able to walk with the aid of a knee brace and crutches. The money he lost was the least of his problems, and he was even able to reschedule his wedding and eventually begin the job he had taken just before the robbery. But Dyer was a changed man—a man whose emotional scars came to influence his daily life. "I'm constantly looking over my shoulder to see who's there," Dyer said. "I'm so aware now of where I go and what I do. I check around corners. I look behind me" (Mills 1A). It is unfortunate that it took such an encounter to put Dyer, and millions of others like him, on guard to the threat around them.

Nowhere is this sense of fear and loss more present than in the instance of rape. The statistics the government uses to measure crime do not include rape as an assault, but give it a separate category due to its nature as a sex crime. Information about rape, however, appears in this book because of the crime's frequency and heinous nature. The psychological effects of rape—humiliation, isolation, guilt—can be devastating for both the victim and the victim's family. To the internal struggle, society often adds the burden of suggesting that the victim somehow "asked for the crime," or the conclusion that the victim really suffered little physical trauma. How much psychological damage a crime like rape does to the victim is dependent upon how the particular assault took place, the past mental health of the victim, and how the victim's support network responds. But, using rape as an example, we can see psychological processes that occur as well in the reactions to many other crimes. Even minor crimes, like a backyard burglary, may impel the victim through these processes.

LOSING CONTROL

Each of us has a certain basic, primitive sense of our own omnipotence. We like to believe we are in control of our lives and the activities around us. If you're a student of psychology you might recognize this as one of pioneer psychology researcher A. H. Maslow's security needs. But for the average person it means that people would like to affirm the idea that they are in charge of their own future. A major psychological effect of crime is that it destroys or seriously inhibits the notion that the victims are still in control of their lives. The feeling of being in control is necessary for a healthy self-image. In the case of rape, the victim frequently maintains a sense of fear or annihilation long after the crime. Rape victims commonly generalize their fear and suspicion toward all men. It is hard for either rape victims or robbery victims to regain that element of trust, or to recover their sense of control in their lives.

If you are robbed at knifepoint on the way to the bowling alley, and you have to surrender your last dollar to a criminal who disappears into the night, you will experience a sense of loss that, while certainly not as traumatic as that of the rape victim, is just as real. That sensation of being overpowered will be accompanied by a sense that someone else took control of your life. All of this has an impact on how you feel about yourself.

A businesswoman who has her purse snatched on the way to a meeting experiences a sense of loss in her ability to accomplish daily tasks.

"Is there no place I can go that I will be safe?" she asks.

A crime victim's fear is frequently accompanied by the sense that the system has let him or her down. In 1988 a 48-year-old Pittsburgh bartender named McGrogan was brutally beaten with a baseball bat and robbed of $70 while walking home through his residential neighborhood. Permanently blinded and suffering hearing loss as a result of the attack, McGrogan was further horrified to learn that one of the men who beat him had been released pending trial for an earlier assault ("Victims" 17). "If the system had worked right, he wouldn't have been out on the street and I wouldn't be blind," McGrogan rightfully argues (17).

The July 31, 1989, issue of *U.S. News & World Report* reveals the sad quandary of a Queens, New York, couple who sought justice after their 16-year-old son was stabbed while trying to settle a quarrel. By the time prosecutors finished plea bargaining, their son's attacker had the potential of being out on parole in four years. "He [the judge] had more sympathy for the murderer than for us," the father said. "We have been victimized twice—by the killer and the system," his wife added ("Victims" 17).

Victims will often blame the law enforcement community for what they perceive as their inability to keep a lid on crime. According to *U.S. News and World Report*, police solve only one out of five major crimes. Crowded court dockets drag cases out as much as a year; for instance, the average disposition time in Newark, New Jersey, is 308 days. While free on bail, one out of six defendants is arrested for fresh crimes ("Victims" 16). Law enforcement has its share of problems, but considering the limited funds and manpower available, they do about as well as can be expected. The American citizen must recognize and accept the fact that the largest part of the responsibility to protect oneself from criminals falls upon *the individual*.

EXPERIENCING GUILT

A companion to the feeling of loss of control in a crime situation is the feeling of guilt. This feeling is often also accompanied by a sense of rage against the attacker, who may remain at large. Eventually, these feelings take their toll on the victim's emotional health. Guilt increases as the victims begin to question themselves. The sense of "I wish I had . . ." begins to outweigh the sense of "I'm glad I did . . ."

"Could I have fought back better?"

"Maybe I should have tried harder to get away?"

Max Siegel, 91st President of the American Psychological Association, in a 1985 article in *American Psychologist*, offers a gripping analysis of some of the feelings victims must endure. Once their world has radically shifted from secure to violent, the victims have heaped upon themselves more humiliation, and they feel reduced to standing by and watching as their empowerment erodes.

> Doctors dominate, lawyers and judges dictate, creditors agitate and the victim suffers helplessly. Vulnerable, angry, insecure, selfless, the victim who survives observes a criminal who is fed, housed, given legal, medical, psychological and psychiatric aid, even education and vocational training. The victim, perhaps with a murdered spouse or child, a loss of job, a loss of economic security, a destroyed career, suffers alone in isolation (1269).

Bard and Sangrey, in *The Crime Victim's Book*, compare the experiences of a crime victim to the experiences of individuals who confront the death of a loved one. They describe three stages through which a crime victim will pass. Phase One is the impact-disorganization phase, where the victim is plagued with feelings of fear and inadequacy, of isolation. Phase Two is the recoil phase, where the question of "Why me?" is the predominant issue in the victim's life. In Phase Three the individual tries to reorganize and resume a normal role in society, yet this individual knows he or she will never be the same.

One thing that many crime victims will never forget is the face of their attacker. About 93% of the victims of violence had a face-to-face encounter with their offender. You may occasionally forget an appointment, or even your spouse's birthday, but you will never forget the face of an individual who threatens you with a weapon. But in the instance of personal theft only about 49% of the victims actually get a good look at their attackers, due largely to the fact that purse-snatching and pocket-picking comprise most of this category of crime, and these fleeting types of crime make it very difficult to see the assailant.

CONSIDERING FACTORS OF VICTIMIZATION

We have heard much about the experiences of victims, but let us now focus upon the demographics of stranger violence, by examining who comprises the high-risk groups and what constitutes high-risk behavior. Table 2.1 shows victimization rates for assault and for all crimes of violence. Noted criminology researcher Robert J. Sampson, in an "extension and test of the opportunity model of predatory victimization," published in *The Journal of Criminal Law and Criminology* (1987), found that if you are a man, your risk of violent victimization by a stranger is more than three times greater than a woman's risk. Single, separated, or divorced persons have a risk that is 2.5 times greater than a married person. And depending upon how often you go out at night, your risk of violent confrontation with a stranger will increase. If you go out five to seven nights per week, then your risk is four times higher for stranger violence than if you remained at home (Sampson 342).

Age is a factor of victimization that you cannot control. Because of lifestyle and associations, the younger you are the greater your risk. Young persons are at a risk that is 7.7 times

TABLE 2.1. Who Are the Victims? Rate of Personal
Victimization per 1,000 Persons for 1989

| | | | All crimes of violence | | | |
| | Assault | | White | | Black | |
Age	Male	Female	Male	Female	Male	Female
12–15	**65.9**	38.1	**81.8**	46.7	**81.5**	31.2
16–19	**77.4**	45.3	**95.1**	**52.5**	**82.0**	**68.0**
20–24	**60.5**	43.2	**72.1**	46.3	**78.9**	36.0
25–34	33.0	21.3	39.7	27.2	**56.3**	34.1
35–49	18.1	13.5	22.7	17.9	39.8	15.3
50–64	6.5	4.6	9.7	6.0	14.3	5.1
65+	3.4	1.5	5.3	2.9	8.7^a	0.0^a

Note: Boldface type indicates a higher risk (over 50/1000 rate) or a danger
zone. Note that black males from age 12 through 34 run a significantly
higher risk of violent crime than the rest of society; age 12 through 24 is the
high-risk period for white males; and women seem at greatest risk between age 16 and 19.
^{a}Estimate based upon 10 or fewer samples.
SOURCE: *Sourcebook—1990*.

higher than the risk for older adults. Just as age is a factor that may
incline you to a particular risk, your sex exposes you to different
types of crimes. Women, for example, are much more likely to
experience stranger theft than are men, since purse-snatching is
one of the primary means of personal theft.

The risk of stranger assault is directly related to the lifestyle
and routine activities of the victim and the opportunity of the
criminal. Daily activities, guardianship (the presence of someone
to protect you from crime), target attractiveness and lifestyle, all
work together to affect your risk of victimization. For example,
young people are more likely to visit night clubs and social
establishments during high crime hours. They are more likely to
be outside the home and away from the guardianship of fellow
family members, thus their risk of exposure to crime increases.
But by the time they reach their mid- or late twenties, these same

people are more likely to be involved in home-centered activities. Their risk goes down.

What criminologists refer to as the Opportunity Model assumes that your risk increases when you are exposed to criminals in the absense of capable guardians, who might otherwise intervene on your behalf. Robert J. Sampson puts it this way:

> The general hypothesis is that younger persons, males, single/divorced people, and those who spend leisure time in public places, suffer a higher risk of stranger victimization than do older persons, females, married persons, and those who confine their activities to home situations (331).

In his 1987 article for *The Journal of Quantitative Criminology*, Michael G. Maxfield cites a 1979 study by Cohen and Felson to highlight three minimum elements of a crime:

1. A motivated offender
2. A suitable target
3. The absence of guardians

Your daily or routine activities determine how those three elements will converge; and since it is reasonable to assume motivated offenders are already in proximity, then your behavior must constitute the single most important factor in keeping these elements from combining (Maxfield 276). Whether or not you recognize the threat of crime in your daily activities will determine your vulnerability. And even though our lives will always contain certain unavoidable risks (e.g., going to school or work, where we live—given that poverty can limit one's choice of neighborhood), we can learn adaptive behavior to reduce our risk. We shall see that a significant percentage of our exposure to crime is not as much forced on us by fate as it is created by our lifestyle choices.

This opportunity model is easily understood when you consider the plight of the single person. If you live alone, you are more likely to do things alone, such as going to work, going out to dinner, etc. Since you spend so much time alone, you are more vulnerable to rape or robbery than would be a middle-aged, married woman. To that threat, you must add the fact that your residence remains unguarded during the day when you are at work or in the evenings when you are socializing, so you also run a greater risk of suffering a property crime. Since many singles tend to live in apartment dwellings with other singles, the opportunity for mutual guardianship is decreased. It is no secret that a community that has a high percentage of single-person households is a much more attractive environment to a criminal than one that has a high percentage of families. This is not an advertisement for marriage, but it is an illustration that shows that when you combine the ingredient of a suitable target with the absence of a guardian against crime, you can end up with a dangerous concoction.

Some of the most prominent and consistent findings in the study of stranger offenses involve alcohol use, reinforcing the idea that lifestyle and routine activity determine the risk of assault. Many assaults stem from confrontations between individuals in a bar or a night club, where strangers congregate to consume alcohol. If you spend much of your time in a drinking establishment among strangers who are consuming alcohol, you should not be surprised when you eventually become a victim of assault. James R. Lashley and Jill Rosenbaum of California State University at Fullerton found a strong relationship between alcohol consumption and *multiple* crime victimizations. Using the 1982 British Crime Survey, they argue that as your drinking increases so does your risk of being victimized (Table 2.2). Medium- to high-level drinkers (eight ounces and up per week) showed a high risk, while those who abstained showed a much lower risk (48).

Spending both Friday and Saturday night out on the town also increased the risk of multiple victimization, as did being out of work (Table 2.2). This is further evidence that lifestyle determines vulnerability; and while we cannot always help it when we are unemployed or reduced to part-time work, we certainly can control how much we drink and where we go to party. "Routine activities centered about steady work and home reduced the

TABLE 2.2. Lifestyle Characteristics of Multiple Victims

	Single victims (%)	Multiple victims (%)
Hours worked		
30+	73	27
10–30	66	34
Occasional/unemployed	63	37
Retired	80	20
Housewife	81	19
Student	64	36
Nights out		
Neither Friday nor Saturday	79	21
Either Friday or Saturday	71	29
Both Friday and Saturday	61	39
Alcohol use		
Abstainer (0 oz./wk)	78	22
Infrequent (0.1–3.9 oz./wk)	74	26
Occasional (4.0–7.9 oz./wk)	74	26
Moderate (8.0–11.9 oz./wk)	72	28
High (12.0+/wk)	60	40

SOURCE: Lashley & Rosenbaum 49–50.

probability of suffering multiple personal crimes" (Lashley & Rosenbaum 48). Not only does going to bars increase your chances of being assaulted, but Ichiro Tanoika, in *Sociology and Social Research* (1986), shows that smoking also correlates to victimization. He points to responses on the 1978 and 1983 General Social Survey that indicate "32.3% of smokers had experienced assault victimization, compared to 17.0% of nonsmokers." Tanoika argues that the threat of assault for single females aged 18–49 who smoke is even more prominent—43.5% of these smokers were victimized compared with 20.0% of nonsmokers of the same age and sex (58). One cigarette company likes to show a svelt, well-dressed lady delicately balancing a cigarette between her fingers, and would have women believe they have come a long way. But crime statistics and social/behavioral research tell us they do not have much farther to go until they meet a criminal. If the threat of cancer is not enough to deter smokers, consider the increased threat of assault as an added bonus for the privilege of lighting up.

So you may better understand how age, lifestyle, and activities can combine to make you vulnerable to criminals, Chapter 3 will help you determine your "V-Factor," or vincibility.

DETERMINING YOUR OPTIONS

So what choices do citizens have for dealing with the very real threat of assault? Several actions initially appear as viable options, and while some are more desirable than others, you should examine all the alternatives to choose the response that is right for you. Only you can ultimately decide how you will deal with potential adversaries. To stare into the face of a determined criminal and make a response to that threat is a highly individual decision based upon many factors. Still, there are certain options that must be reasoned through to make the informed, intelligent choice that may ultimately determine your personal health and welfare.

Do Nothing

Some criminal and psychological research seems to suggest that, in certain situations, submission to an attacker may be the wisest choice. Such a decision is largely based upon either (1) your faith in humankind, (2) some deeply held religious convictions, or (3) confidence that the statistics will come out in your favor. In any case, by not responding to the attacker you are hoping for the best from the situation, rather than actively trying to influence it. If you opt for this response you will be in the minority, for in 1989 only 30% of the victims of violent crime (assault, rape, and robbery) took no self-protective measures. As a response to assault alone, even fewer chose to do nothing—26% (*Sourcebook—1990* 268). I will show in the next chapter the consequences of a pacifist response to assault and the risks attendant to it.

Depend upon Law Enforcement

Our nation is blessed with a generally well-trained, efficient, law enforcement network. It is made up of many skilled, dedicated individuals who excel in catching criminals after they commit a crime, and bringing them eventually to justice. The key word is *after*. The police certainly have a deterrent effect upon criminals as long as they are reasonably near the scene of a potential crime. The problem comes when the police are not around. Being limited in number and resources, the law enforcement agencies cannot be everywhere. Even Gerald Arenberg, director of the National Association of Police Chiefs, admits "there are fewer police on the street than there were ten years ago" (Rossi 68). So if you are depending upon the police to keep you from being attacked, you must not plan on going anywhere very often.

Carry a Weapon

Some Americans have chosen this option as their best response to potential attack. The weapons of choice vary from person to person, as does the level of expertise in using a weapon. Varying in type from handguns to handheld spray repellants, weapons offer some inherent problems. The first factor that you must consider when electing to carry a weapon is the legal implication of such possession. The law differs somewhat from state to state, but on the whole, carrying a concealed weapon such as handgun or knife can buy you some hard time, if you are caught with it. Some will say that the threat of attack is so great as to warrant any potential penalties you might face when caught with an illegally carried weapon. Bernhard Goetz received six months in jail and narrowly avoided a murder or manslaughter conviction. Was it worth it? Only Goetz can answer that question. Only you can make the decision in your own situation.

One problem with weapons is getting adequate training in their use. A gun or knife in the hands of an untrained person is more dangerous than no weapon at all. Not only will the untrained person be less effective with a weapon, but he or she may lose that weapon to the attacker. It brings to mind the old saying, "Never choose a personal weapon that you aren't willing to face yourself."

The Old West is often cited as an example of a place where people carried guns for self-protection. But the major difference between the Old West and our society is not that we are somehow more civilized, for we have just as much murder and assault as they did in 1880 Dodge City, if not more. The difference is that in the old West everyone who wanted to carry a gun could do so, therefore, the question of survival at least came down to who was fastest or most accurate. Today, only the bad guys get the guns. The average citizen doesn't want to be a law-breaker, so he or she doesn't carry an illegally concealed weapon. The possibility of being charged with a weapon violation doesn't phase the criminal who is intent on robbery or assault, so he has his weapon anyway. Today the question of survival doesn't rest upon who is fastest or best with his or her weapon; it rests upon whether or not the attacker wants to use that weapon on you, who are defenseless.

Change Your Lifestyle

If you fear going from your car to your aerobics class at the health club, stop going to the health club. It is always an option to stop doing those things that you think might place you at risk to assault, rape, or mugging. The good news is that no one can make you endanger yourself. The bad news is that unless you like being a hermit, or crave loneliness as a character-building experience, this approach makes little sense. To what extent are you willing to allow the thugs of this world to control your very existence? What are you willing to sacrifice to keep criminals from having a shot at you? Even if you stay at home and lock the doors, what is to keep them from coming to you? Can you afford to give up your job because it happens to take you into a rough section of town? In Chapter Six, "Fear, Self-Defense, and Weapons," we will see how this idea of radically altering your lifestyle can actually help to promote crime, in what is called the crime-causes-crime model.

Adopt a Realistic Skepticism

This concept goes with the techniques of awareness already discussed under the subject of confrontation avoidance. It deals with training yourself to be aware not only of potentially threatening situations, but also of your own mental and physical skills at resistance or retaliation to attack. Put simply, it means to keep your eyes open, your mouth shut, fight back when you should, submit when you must, and learn to know the difference—that is a tall order. But it can mean the difference between living to see your children grow up and meeting an untimely death.

Chapter Three

VINCIBILITY

Criminal opportunity and victim behavior combine to determine vincibility. Vincibility is a measure of your attractiveness to a criminal. We already know from the statistics that people of a particular sex, age, and lifestyle have a greater risk of being attacked. In this chapter you will learn how to calculate your own level of risk (the *V-Factor*), using the vincibility scale. The vincibility scale ranges from 0 through 10, with 0 being the theoretical position of having no risk and 10 being the maximum risk. By examining your routine behavior and lifestyle, and by considering the circumstances that surround a particular behavior, you can assess your V-Factor for that behavior. Sitting home, watching television with your family will reflect one factor, while going alone into a high-crime area at 2:00 A.M. will provide a different factor. As your V-Factor increases, so does your risk of being victimized by a stranger.

To understand the extremes on the vincibility scale, consider these representative descriptions. A V-Factor of 0 might be represented by a 6′4″ bodybuilder wearing a police uniform and armed with two 44-Magnums, a machete, and a two-way radio. He is walking his two dobermans down a crowded street at noon, wearing his bullet-proof vest and talking to two of his friends.

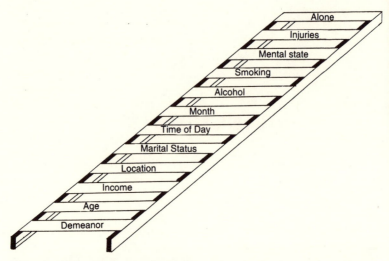

Figure 3.1. The ladder of vulnerability. The higher you climb the ladder of vulnerability, the more likely you are to fall.

Most of us would agree that such an individual is probably not a very lucrative or safe target for a criminal. Most criminals are smart enough that if given a choice between this individual and an easier target, they will choose the easy target. The person who characterizes the V-Factor of zero is what might be called a hard target. This is a target who will require more time, effort, and risk to overcome. When the bad guys see a zero on the vincibility scale they start looking for another victim.

On the other end of the scale is the 10, the soft target, or a target who is attractive to a criminal. A good example of a 10 might be a trusting, soft-hearted community service volunteer, who is frail-looking, nervous, distracted, and limping through a dark parking lot at night. He is fumbling for his car keys and sporting a blood-alcohol content of 0.08% or higher.

When you determine your V-Factor you are simply doing

what the criminal is going to do before he has the chance to do it. Offenders take a look at an individual and rapidly assess that person's vulnerability, deciding whether he or she is a hard or a soft target. Should they attack that person or move on to someone who is more defenseless and vulnerable? Although criminals do not use this process in all instances of assault—for example, assaults done on impulse—it is a common technique for choosing a victim. The offenders want to gather an overall impression of their potential victim. They want to get in quickly and get out quickly, and they want nothing to delay or call attention to themselves. "We're looking for quick and easy," says convicted mugger Jim McCann. "[People] who appear frail, timid or preoccupied [make good targets]" (Wheeler 64).

DETERMINING YOUR OWN VINCIBILITY

Each individual's vulnerability to assault is different, yet there are some common behavioral, lifestyle, and psychological traits that increase everyone's risk. If people realize they are making themselves attractive to a criminal or easier for a criminal to victimize, they can take action to minimize that vulnerability. Not all aspects of vulnerability can be changed. Some characteristics, such as age and physical handicaps, will be with us regardless of our actions; but it is the very fact that we have irreversible risk factors that makes it so important for us to recognize and modify those characteristics we *can* control. Remember, we saw earlier that the "chance of being a violent crime victim, with or without injury, is greater than that of being hurt in a traffic accident" (Bureau of Justice Statistics, "The Fear of Crime," 1988). If it makes sense to fasten your seatbelt, or purchase a car with an airbag to lower your risk for injury in a traffic accident, doesn't it make even more sense to lower your risk for the even more likely occurrence of violent crime victimization?

The vincibility scale offers a simple way to emphasize how behavior, lifestyle, and natural disposition can combine to make a person more or less vulnerable in a given situation. Based upon your age, your sex, and the specific circumstances of your environment, you add vulnerability points to arrive at your V-Factor. Your goal in the exercise is akin to golf—try to keep your score as low as possible. A 1 is ideal, but it is also unrealistic, so if you can maintain your V-Factor at a 3 or less, you are doing well. If your factor reaches 4 or 5 you should consider yourself to be at a moderate risk of assault. A factor of 6 or 7 is getting dangerous, and if your V-Factor hits 8 or higher on the scale, consider yourself at high risk of assault. You can refer to Figure 3.2 to determine your own V-Factor. Here are the general rules. Give yourself a point if:

- You are an adult male, 18–21 years of age.
- You are over 60 and you show it.
- You are traveling alone (particularly if you are female).
- You are out of shape and cannot run, or you have a physical handicap that limits your ability to flee.
- You live in a major metropolitan area (population > 700,000).
- You are consuming alcohol or other drugs.
- You are mentally preoccupied.
- You are single or divorced.
- You earn less than $10,000 per year.
- You are a smoker.
- You are out between 6:00 P.M. and 3:00 A.M.
- It is either July or August.

Using these basic guidelines, which have been developed by assessing the varied lifestyle and situational factors that correlate with increased victimization risk, you can calculate the V-Factor for a hypothetical situation prior to ever leaving home. Since your V-Factor is subject to change based upon time, location, and behavior, you should constantly reevaluate your risk, and choose behaviors that reflect a reduced risk.

Alice is a 43-year-old electrician, who is divorced, with one

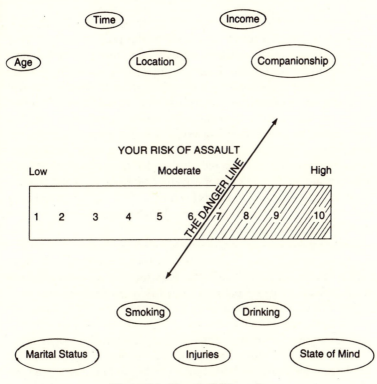

Figure 3.2. The vincibility scale.

child (presently spending the weekend with his father). She is going shopping at a mall approximately three miles from her home, in her hometown of some 60,000 people. It is 4:30 P.M. on an April afternoon, and she is going alone. Calculating Alice's V-Factor is very simple. Since she is divorced, she gets one point. Being female and alone gets her another point. With a V-Factor of 2 she is at a low risk of victimization, providing she remains mentally alert, is aware of her surroundings, and carries herself with confidence and purpose.

Chuck is a 20-year-old male. He twisted his ankle two days ago and had it taped and wrapped to the point that he cannot move very quickly. He and two friends are going to McGregor's Pub this evening to drink beer, eat popcorn, and watch Monday Night Football. If the evening proceeds as it has in the past, he will consume the equivalent of a sixpack and return home sometime after midnight. Chuck gets one point for being an adult male 18–21, and another point for being single. He gets a third point for his temporary handicap, a fourth for consuming alcohol, and a fifth point for being out between 6:00 P.M. and 3:00 A.M. With a V-Factor of 5 he is at a moderate risk for assault. Still, if he pays attention to what he is doing, stays with his friends, and chooses a route home that bypasses the high-crime neighborhoods, he has a good chance of avoiding trouble.

Harold is a 63-year-old, overweight, single male who lives in a large midwestern city. He lost his part-time job yesterday (just before Christmas) and spent the past four hours drowning his sorrows with 90-proof bourbon. On his way home at 11:00 P.M., Harold is alone; and a breathalyzer right now would show him at a 0.09% BAC, just below the point of being legally drunk in most states. He gets one point for being under the influence of alcohol, another point for being preoccupied and mentally out of focus, a third point for being over 60, another point for being alone, a fifth point for being single, another for his low income, another for being out at 11:00 P.M., still another for where he lives, and a final point for being out of shape and unable to run if the situation required it. With a V-Factor of 9, Harold is at high risk of criminal assault.

CONSIDERING OTHER INFLUENCES

While the V-Factor gives you an indication of your level of risk, there are other issues that figure into your vincibility. The location of your activities is directly related to the offender's sense of security in choosing you as a target. The presence of bystanders, or on-lookers, at a potential crime scene gives the criminal another factor to consider before choosing you as victim. Yet we often have little or no choice in where we must go or whether or not by-standers will be present. We can lose our personal control over these factors of assault. But the vincibility scale consists of factors that are either constantly with us, for instance, age or sex, or factors that we can control, for instance, physical condition, mental attitude, and the like.

One of the intangible, yet most influential, aspects of your attractiveness to criminals is your *demeanor*. Your behavior can create just enough uncertainty in the mind of a potential attacker to make the difference between survival and disaster. How you carry yourself, or the overall impression you give the criminal as to your ability to protect yourself, will influence how that criminal determines your vincibility. If you slink down the street and give the appearance of being vulnerable, the offender will most likely assume you *are* vulnerable and will choose you over someone who presents a positive, self-controlled manner. In the book, *How to Prevent Street Assault, Mugging and Rape* (1984), Hofstra University professor Betty Grayson videotaped random pedestrians moving along a New York City street. She first showed her tapes to prisoners at Rahway State Penitentiary in New Jersey, where the inmates rated each pedestrian's walk and manner on a ten-point scale of vulnerability, viewing each pedestrian for only about seven seconds—the time muggers claim it takes to evaluate a target. Those rated an "easy rip-off" were again showed to a dance choreographer who was quick to identify several flawed motions these easy targets had in common. Among the commonalities were exaggerated strides (either too short or too long) and a lack of flowing motion in their walk, that is, moving more in a lifting than in a smooth heel-to-toe action. "They moved unilaterally, not col-laterally, that is, they swung the left arm and left leg together, rather than the left arm with the right leg" (Castleman 63). In short,

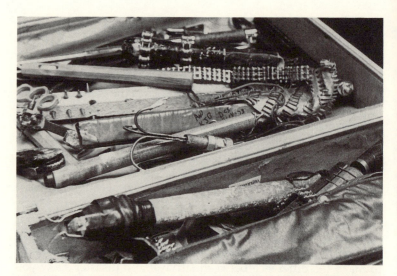

Figure 3.3. Tools of the criminal's trade. In a story for a national magazine in 1985, I interviewed Officer Arthur N. Sapp, an instructor with the Police Training Academy in Colorado Springs, Colorado. Art took me to a storeroom at the police station and produced a large suitcase containing street weapons he and other officers had taken off thugs over the past year. The photo above shows some of the horrifying homemade bludgeons and cutting instruments assailants are likely to carry. Is it any wonder that we assess our vincibility—so that we may in turn Reduce our vulnerability to such weapons? The photo below is a close-up of a set of brass knuckles Officer Sapp obtained.

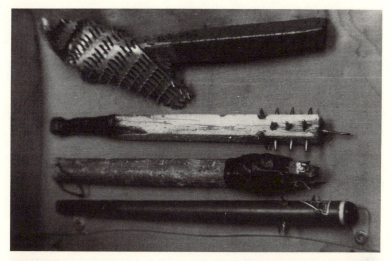

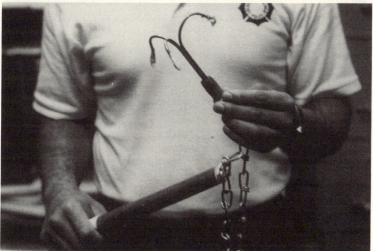

Figure 3.4. The criminal mind does not lack imagination. The photo above shows several battering instruments made from stakes or pool cues, often augmented with bullets imbedded into the shaft. The damage one of these instruments could cause to the head of a citizen is enough to keep all of us watching over ourshoulders. The photo below is one of the most mystifying, yet potentially dangerous, of the weapons in Sapp's collection. Some enterprising hoodlum has attached three shark hooks to the end of a chain, which in turn has been attached to a sawed-off pool cue. How would you like to have been the police officer who disarmed the person wielding this weapon?

> the prime difference between assault victims and nonvictims
> . . . revolves around "wholeness" of movement. Nonvictims
> have organized movements [that] come from the body center.
> In contrast, victim's movements come from the body's periph-
> ery, and communicate inconsistency (Castleman 63).

Grayson is convinced that when people understand *how* to move
confidently, they can "be taught to walk that way and substantially
reduce their assault risk." Many people lack confidence, but while
they may be as vulnerable as a newborn calf, they should at least
look like they know what they are doing. Just appearing to be
confident and in control is often enough to make the criminal look
elsewhere for a victim. Having "gunfighter eyes" is a term Brian
Hemsworth, editor of the magazine *Home & Auto Security*, shared
with me one day. It is a certain look on the face of an individual—a
look that, while not appearing to threaten or incite someone else
to action against you, will let them know in a glance that you mean
business and you will not be easily intimidated or surprised.
Consider Figures 3.3 and 3.4 if you are wondering whether or not
all this attention to vincibility is really important.

   By being aware of your V-Factor and remaining constantly
alert to your surroundings, you can control your vincibility and
minimize your attractiveness to criminals. Carrying a concealed
weapon does nothing to decrease your V-Factor, since the factor is
a measure of your *appearance* to the criminal and your perceived
vulnerability. If the bad guy cannot see your Bowie Knife, it will
not inhibit his actions; and if you brandish your weapon, you will
probably find yourself in jail. Even advanced students of self-
defense and skilled martial artists have very little outward appearance that will influence their V-Factor. A martial arts protegé of
mine actually believed having a black belt was some kind of
insurance against an assailant confronting him on the street.
Much to his surprise and dismay, the slightly inebriated father of
the young man living next door came after him one summer
evening with a baseball bat. His self-defense skills may have saved
his life, but they were useless as a deterrent. Unless you wear a

sign that advertises your skill, the criminal will not recognize that you are a hard target.

Once you are aware of the activities that impact upon your vincibility, you can make a conscious decision as to whether or not your risk of exposure to crime is acceptable. When you have managed your V-Factor as low as you can get it, and you have made the decision that you have an acceptable level of risk, then you are ready to adopt the techniques of confrontation avoidance outlined in the next chapter, to further insure that the bad guys choose someone else for their criminal activities.

Chapter Four

AVOIDING CONFRONTATION

Once you have some insight into how a criminal is likely to behave in a potential assault situation, you can take some reasonable, logical steps to protect yourself. When you understand what actions or reactions can contribute to the chances of becoming a victim of assault, then you can take these steps to guard against unknowingly assisting your attacker. Chapters One and Two presented profiles of both criminals and victims, and Chapter Three discussed how to assess our vulnerability to stranger assault. Now let us consider what actions we can take to avoid assailants and keep ourselves out of the statistics.

Confrontation avoidance is commonsense behavior that helps you head off trouble before it arrives, or that diffuses a situation before it explodes into a crime. It is dependent upon a good understanding of the criminal, the situation, and yourself. Confrontation avoidance is not foolproof. Sometimes, in spite of your best efforts, you are unable to prevent a physical or verbal confrontation from leading to assault. There is no such thing as producing a risk-free environment in which to live. But you can *reduce the risks* you take by carefully monitoring your behavior and being aware of the messages you are sending others with your actions. I am not talking about radically altering your lifestyle, but I am suggesting that you can establish in your own life a level of acceptable risk. You can learn to recognize what behaviors and situations are likely to make you a victim of crime, and you can take steps to bring your risk into an acceptable range.

By observing some simple rules you can remove a criminal's opportunity to strike. While there will always be certain thugs who will attack no matter what, most potential assailants are going to look for the easy mark. Following the rules of confrontation avoidance makes that criminal look for someone else. Again, our emphasis is upon what researchers call stranger-to-stranger assault, or assault in which the parties involved do not know each other. This is distinguished in crime and victim research from nonstranger assault, which is characterized by domestic disputes, brawls between so-called drinking buddies, and other such altercations where the participants are in some manner acquainted with one another. The factors that lead to nonstranger assault situations are numerous, and are deserving of a separate discussion, which cannot be reasonably attempted in this volume. As such, we will restrict our observations on avoiding confrontation to the concept of stranger crime.

According to the *Sourcebook of Criminal Justice Statistics—1991*, of the more than 2.5 million stranger assaults that occur yearly in the United States, most of the victims are young males (69%) in their twenties or younger. When you add the percentages for older males, and allow for race considerations, you discover that 76% of stranger assault victims are males, and 92% are white males. That does not mean that black males do not get assaulted; but the incidents of assault involving black males are predominately nonstranger (263).

The systematic application of the common sense techniques I will describe in this chapter has helped many people dodge disaster. By carefully applying these concepts, you can lessen the chance that you will become a victim of criminal assault. The methods I recommend are not costly, physically difficult, or beyond the grasp of the average citizen. But it is not enough just to read them and give intellectual assent. Agreeing with the principles of confrontation avoidance will not protect you on the street. Only through application of these tenets will you gain an added sense of security in your daily life. Pay careful attention and commit them to your daily routine. They could save you a lengthy, costly hospital visit, or worse.

MENTAL ALERTNESS

The most important aspect of confrontation avoidance is mental alertness. This is the driving force behind successfully protecting yourself in our crime-ridden society. It certainly sounds simple enough, but the consistent practice of mental alertness demands tremendous effort. Mental alertness keeps us from doing something stupid and placing ourselves in a compromising situation. If we do allow ourselves to get in difficult circumstances, mental alertness can help us escape to safety. If we cannot free ourselves from a threatening situation, our alertness can help us choose the proper response to the degree of threat.

> Kirk Robert Kinsey, 38, works nights as a waiter in Silver Spring [Maryland]. He takes the Metro home to Takoma Park and uses a rather elaborate strategy for eluding potential muggers. He said he usually dresses in dark clothes, walks on the dark side of the street, and tries to blend into the shadows. If something doesn't look right, he said, he doesn't hesitate to run the two blocks.
> "I'm more aware of what's going on around me. For that five-minute walk, I have to be really focused," Kinsey said. "It reminds me, I guess, of the wild kingdom. You have the animals looking for prey. It's pretty sad right now" (Miller 12).

While Kinsey's approach may be a bit extreme, being unaware of a potential threat is a recipe for disaster. It is easy to get lulled into a sense of complacency and false security. The day-to-day grind becomes routine and we find ourselves developing a pattern of behavior that becomes comfortable and familiar to us. We get up at a certain time. We drive to work along a certain route, park in our assigned space, and do our specific job. We go to lunch, return to work, leave work at a certain time, and return home. If there is any time left, we enjoy a social life, then it's off to bed—only to start all over the next day. It is precisely when they are caught up in the daily routine that people are most likely to mentally relax or at least go into some kind of programmed mode of operation. This is when many citizens fall victim to crime. A 24-year-old Denver woman, Susan Mills (a pseudonym), can tell you the price of complacency. Mills not only had her purse snatched, but also suffered a dislocated shoulder in the process.

"I was daydreaming," she says. "If I'd been paying attention, I'd have heard the thief running up behind me—and I might have at least avoided injury" (Wheeler 63). It is the element of surprise that street criminals are counting on for success, and it is citizen carelessness that convicted rapist Don Jackson calls the critical factor in assault, rape, and abduction.

"I easily stalked and attacked one of my victims because she was distracted by her portable headset," Jackson claims (Wheeler 63). Another of his victims he describes as "blankly staring into space." The momentary dropping of the guard can result in a confrontation that could actually be avoided. Ask a victim of assault and he will tell you that Murphy's Law is on the side of the criminal. It is uncanny how crime seems able to find the exact time when you are least able to deal with it.

Ron and Margie are avid baseball fans who live in a major eastern city. Their idea of a great evening out is leaving the kids with a babysitter and slipping away for a twi-night double-header. They crept through traffic for half an hour as they approached the baseball stadium one summer evening. It was the championship playoff game and was sure to draw the largest crowd of the year. From the gridlock, Ron figured most of the fans were on this street. Radiators and blood pressures were heating up as the sluggish traffic crawled toward the stadium parking lot. Fed up with the wait, and anxious not to miss the first two innings, Ron saw an opportunity to beat the delay. He pulled out of the flow of traffic and parked in an alley near an out-of-business gas station. It was five blocks from the stadium, but he knew they could walk the distance faster than he could drive there in traffic. He locked the car and they hurried to the game.

Ron and Margie saved some time and got to their seats in time to see them throw out the first ball. They enjoyed the game. What they did not enjoy was filling out all those forms at the police station that evening after the game. They enjoyed even less being accosted at knife-point. They certainly got no pleasure out of handing over every penny they were carrying. Some hoodlum was spending their hard-earned money while they were describing the ordeal to the police.

What went wrong? Were they doomed to be robbed that night? Could the incident have been avoided?

Ron did several things wrong, but primarily he failed to remain mentally alert. He allowed the frustration of the traffic and the possibility of being tardy for the game to distract his attention from the threatening situation he was about to place his wife and himself in. He took the easy way out and unfortunately he had to pay for it. The place he chose to park was several blocks from the stadium in a poorly lighted area that had a reputation as being crime ridden. He knew that, he just forgot. The game started in daylight, but ended after dark. That made it risky to walk back to the car. He knew that, too, he just let it slip his mind. Parking in an alley forced them to walk into an area that was out of public view. He knew that was dangerous, he just forgot. By carrying a bundle of cash into a high-crime area, he certainly pleased his attacker. Ron will tell you that was dumb. But he just forgot.

All this forgetfulness is a symptom of mental laziness; and while it will get you into trouble quickly, it is hard to realize this at the time that you are setting yourself up for a fall. Ron thought he was saving time, and if there had been no robbery, then he would have saved time. What makes mental laziness such an easy trap to fall into is that you often get away with it. The chances of your being victimized as compared with any other citizen seem small. It is easy to take shortcuts, to take chances; after all, you haven't been victimized—yet. When it happens to you, then all the percentages and odds go out the window. When it happens to you it is 100%.

TIME AND LOCATION

Understanding the relationship of time and location to assault is critical in adopting protective measures to minimize your risk. The risk of personal attack is greatest during the late night and early morning period (Table 4.1 and Figure 4.1). Victimologist Michael Hindelang, in his *Victims of Personal Crime* (1978), found the period of greatest danger was the six-hour stretch from 6 P.M. until midnight, when 40% of the crimes he studied took place. Wesley G. Skogan, crime researcher and professor of political

TABLE 4.1. The Risk of Being Raped,
by Time and Location (for the period 1979–1987)

Location	Risk (%)	Time	Risk (%)
Home	35	Dawn	1
Near home	8	Day	31
Friend's home	15	Dusk	3
On the street	20	Night	65
In commercial building	4	Before midnight	34
On public transit	0	After midnight	30
Parking lot or garage	6	Don't know	1
On school property	4		
In a park	3		
Other places	5		

Note: While this table deals specifically with rape, it represents a pattern of similarity with assault, that is, the crime of assault most often takes place between the hours of 6:00 P.M. and 3:00 A.M. It is not just a matter of chance that this period coincides with what I call the *party window* for most adults. Again, we see the lifestyle-routine activities theory of crime confirmed. If you are out and about during the time that criminals are working, you drastically increase your risk of victimization.
SOURCE: *Sourcebook—1990*.

Figure 4.1. If you must walk alone, try to stay in well-lighted areas, such as this mall parking lot. Pick a parking space under the light, even if it means waiting a few moments for one to clear, or perhaps having to walk a bit farther to get to the entrance. The trade-off in light versus walking distance is worth the effort, since the presence of light acts as a deterrent—a form of guardianship to the lone shopper.

science and urban affairs at Northwestern University, along with coauthor Richard Block, professor of sociology at Loyola University in Chicago, indicate in their research that 38% of robberies occur between 8 P.M. and 2 A.M. These findings tell us we had better remain mentally alert especially during this high-crime period. We cannot and should not avoid activities during this period, but we must be vigilant and constantly aware of our surroundings. To let down our guard during this time just increases our chance of being victimized.

Not only is night a factor in criminal attack, location plays an important role as well. The evidence indicates that public places, most often open, outdoor areas, are the most common scene of crime. In terms of assault, 53% occurred in this environment. If you think that the presence of onlookers will keep you safe, you are in for a surprise. Some 60% of assault victims report that there were other people around them when they were attacked. While the chance of witnesses may certainly inhibit potential attackers, it will not necessarily stop them. This reinforces the importance of mental alertness. Just because you are walking through a park in the middle of the afternoon, and just because there are other people in the park, there is no guarantee that you will not be accosted. Keeping a sharp eye out for unusual behavior among strangers is just good common sense.

A survey of the *Sourcebook of Criminal Justice Statistics—1990* shows that women are more likely to be attacked during the day than at night, and they are more likely to be approached by a lone offender. The classic image of the lone female attacked by a gang of thugs in a dark alley is not necessarily the usual case. While gang assaults have surely happened, the more common type of assault is often a one-on-one situation, during the day, in a relatively public location. Knowing this fact is in itself a deterrent, for it helps us avoid the mental laziness that lulls us into victimization.

Knowing when and where most assaults take place can either help us to avoid that time and location entirely, or keep us on our toes when we have to be in the danger zone during the danger period. We have already seen that offenders often choose their victims based upon their appearance and what they perceive to be their vincibility. This tells us that how we walk, talk, and behave can make the difference in whether or not we are singled out for attack. If you stroll down the street, oblivious to your surroundings and distracted, you invite an assault.

Criminals may be mean, but they are not fools. When they are given the choice between attacking an alert, confident target, and a weak, distracted target, which one do you think they will choose? You do not have to creep down the street like a warrior, expecting attack from behind every parking meter. But you can walk briskly to your destination, with good posture, your handbag or briefcase held firmly, and visibly aware of the actions of the people around you. This kind of behavior sends the message, "I'm in control of my life and the situation," and can effectively make a mugger look elsewhere for his prey. If you add to this a healthy concern for avoiding high-crime areas and an awareness of when most crimes take place, you have the beginning steps of confrontation avoidance. But understanding the when and where of crime is only a start. We must now refine the subtleties of making yourself less attractive to the criminal.

COMPANIONSHIP

Being alone makes you at a greater risk of assault than traveling with a group, but simply being *aware* of a fact does not insulate you from becoming a statistic of it. Young males are particularly at risk to assault when alone, for they often have a false sense of confidence about their ability to handle a given situation. Part of this is a function of the macho approach to life and the perceived invincibility common to most young males. Regardless of how tough you think you are, there is always someone who is a little bit tougher. Meeting that person in a dark alley, one-on-one, is not as glamorous as you may think. Being in the company of others will decrease the chance of encountering a criminal attack, but it will not eliminate it. As Merri Pearsall, a

crime prevention specialist with the New York City Police Department, says, "Having a companion—male or female—is not a sure
way of avoiding an attack. It might dissuade someone, but it
doesn't guarantee safety" (Frankel 112). This is all part of the
vincibility concept that criminals use to choose their victims. The
presence of bystanders who will be potential witnesses makes a
criminal think twice before attacking. If you know that you are
going into a high-crime area, particularly during the danger
period, you are smart to find some company. To travel with others
does not mean you are weak or cowardly. It means you are smart
enough to avoid trouble whenever you can.

Prompted by an increase in assaults and menacing behavior
in cities across the country, many gay Americans have begun
using companionship and the strength of numbers to inhibit
assault. In January of 1993, a group known as the Pink Panthers
began weekend patrols of the Dupont Circle area in Washington,
D.C. They walk what is known as the "Pink Triangle"—an area
frequented as a gathering place by homosexuals—to deter would-
be gay bashers from attacking isolated individuals. This strength-
in-numbers approach, while helping to decrease assaults against
gays in the area, is not lauded by everyone. Captain Ross Swope of
the D.C. Police, who works the area of the Pink Panther patrols,
says, "I'm concerned that they will be confrontational . . . that an
untrained person may take the law into his own hands" (Reilly
C14). While the police are rightly concerned that groups like the
Pink Panthers—now with organizations in San Francisco and
New York—do not provoke an assault, the group's efforts accurately demonstrate the deterrent effect of companionship.

LIGHT AND DARK

Stay in well-lighted areas. That sounds simple enough, but it
is amazing how many people will compromise their security to
save a few steps or a few seconds. If a shortcut through a dark alley
will save you two minutes, as opposed to a slightly longer walk

along a lighted street, you may initially save the two minutes. But what you save will be more than cancelled out by a two-week stay in the hospital after an assailant clubs you in the back of the head. If you are a gambler at heart, you may say, "The chances are slim that I will be attacked." While that may be true, what if you *are* attacked? Will it be worth it? Why take such a needless risk? Confrontation avoidance is based upon reducing or eliminating needless risks.

The very nature of our existence demands that we take certain unavoidable risks. We have to live our lives with a certain measure of freedom, or it is not really living at all. But do we have to *create* opportunities for the criminals in our society? Recall what the criminals look for in a victim (as discussed in Chapter Three) and choose your routes so that you do not saunter into their hands.

INSTINCTS

To successfully avoid trouble you must trust your instincts. When you observe a situation that looks unsafe, strange, or awkward, it probably is. A young downtown worker in Denver was attacked as she walked to her car, but fortunately she defeated her assailants and sent them fleeing with a spray-burst of cayenne pepper (chemical sprays will be discussed in Chapter Six). "I heard some people behind me, and I had a bad feeling," she said (Seipei C10). Calm, quick action thwarted her assailants.

Hundreds of people have indicated after being victimized that they had a "bad feeling" about the situation before it happened. If your mind is telling you that the stranger in the doorway is out of place, or acting bizarre, *trust your intuition*. The stranger probably is. Unfortunately, in our modern, empirically oriented society we have gotten away from trusting our so-called gut instincts. We have been led to believe that without specific, measurable evidence, it is unkind or unfair to be suspicious of people and actions that we have every right to question.

If you are walking alone down a street at 9:30 P.M., with only one other person in sight, you should try to be aware of what that person is doing (Figure 4.2). If the person is walking toward you, on the opposite side of the street, and he or she suddenly crosses (for no apparent reason) to your side of the street and is now approaching you directly from the front, that should make you suspicious. Why did he cross the street? What is he up to?

Perhaps that person is tired of walking on the other side. That person certainly has every right to cross the street. But you also have a right to wonder why! If the person passes you and does not harm you, then all is well, and your suspicion has caused no difficulty. But if the person intends to harm you, you have at least alerted yourself to the potential threat and can better deal with it. I suggest to my self-defense students that if such a situation occurs, they should cross the street to the side the stranger left. This puts

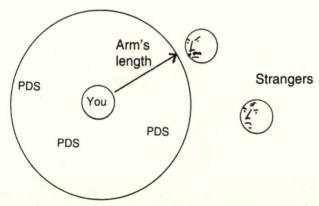

Figure 4.2. Personal defensible space (PDS) is the distance you maintain between yourself and a stranger. Usually, it means keeping just beyond arm's reach. PDS buys you valuable time in the event someone tries to assault you. The split-second it takes for you to realize someone is grabbing for you or taking a swing at you is purchased by the few feet your attacker must cover before making contact. Maybe it is only enough time to lift your hands in self-defense, or maybe it is enough time to get a headstart if your attacker chases you; but without PDS, you risk being surprised and overwhelmed.

the two of you on opposite sides of the street again. If he or she crosses back to the side you are now on, you know you have trouble and you can react accordingly.

Avoiding unnecessary contact with strangers is not rude, it is smart. If your instincts are telling you that something is not quite right, *listen to them*! You should not be ashamed to be suspicious of strangers. Suspicion alone never hurt anyone. When you have had time to evaluate the situation and can determine that the person means you no harm, there is plenty of time for being trusting and friendly.

"I don't like . . . having to be suspicious," says Dana Collier, 42, an Army Intelligence Officer and mother of two children. Yet she recognizes that it is precisely her suspicion—her on-guard behavior—that reinforces her safety. A resident of a Washington, D.C., suburb, Collier says, "I still go to the mall at night, but I do all the tricks. I go to the car with my keys out and I only walk out when other people are walking out" (Miller 12A). She holds her head high and moves confidently to warn potential assailants to look elsewhere for a victim.

There is an old saying, "If something looks too good to be true, it probably is." That applies equally to strangers who are overly helpful. Your instincts may tell you something isn't quite right. Pay attention! Convicted rapist Craig Henry says, "The guy who offers to help carry your bags may be setting you up. We'll offer whatever you seem to need or want" (Wheeler 123). Convicted armed robber Frank Hill points out a confidence scheme in which your instincts are likely to warn you in advance—if you only listen.

> A helpful thief offers a woman correct change for a locker in a train station, airport, or bus terminal. He even inserts the coins and helps put in her luggage. Finally he closes the door and gallantly hands her the key—but it's the key to a different locker (Wheeler 123).

Guess who ends up with the woman's belongings?

Wendy Brown, a 20-year-old Heidelberg College student in Triffin, Ohio, wishes she had trusted her instincts. Walking home from a local tavern one winter evening in 1976, she noticed a man following her up an alleyway (note the V-Factors: night, alone, in an alley, probable alcohol involvement). Her instinct told her something was wrong but she failed to trust it.

"I kept saying, 'It's all in my imagination; I'm blowing this out of proportion'" (Wozencraft 66).

She was raped.

Today Brown, along with martial artist Cotton Batte, runs a monthly self-defense workshop for women. Her colleague, Batte, offers this advice: "Women have good intuition, but society teaches them to doubt themselves. Women must be reeducated to trust their senses of smell, touch, hearing, and sight. In short, they must learn to be more aware" (Wozencraft 66).

Another good example of trusting your instincts involves elevators. If you are riding an elevator and you suspect that someone is standing unnecessarily close to you, or you think that he might possibly have more in mind than an elevator ride, you probably have good reason to think so. Your intuition is talking. Move away and create some personal space. If you are waiting on your floor for an elevator, pay attention to the occupants when it arrives. If the elevator stops and the lone occupant suddenly decides he isn't getting off, you are smart if you ask yourself why. Why did he suddenly change his mind? Perhaps he got the wrong floor. That is certainly possible, and innocent enough. But what if he is thinking of something else? Being alert to the possibilities is half the battle. If you suspect trouble, trust your intuition. Do not take that elevator. Either use the stairs or wait for another elevator.

PERSONAL SPACE

Elevators illustrate the importance of creating personal space. Criminals choose to attack people in confining quarters, like elevators, because they restrict observation and offer the victim minimal defensible space. When there is no place to run and your attacker is practically standing in your face, you have lost many of your options. It is easier for the criminal to overpower you and strike before you have a chance to react. But by creating *personal defensible space*, you buy time—either escape time or reaction time if you must fight (Figures 4.3, 4.4, and 4.5).

Psychologists have known for a long time that the immediate area around a person's body is directly linked to the person's attitudes and actions. Nowhere is this more true than in a self-defense situation. When you allow people you do not know to violate your personal space, you create conditions in which you are easily

- intimidated
- frightened
- restrained
- attacked
- subdued

In the realm of self-protection, personal, defensible space is defined as the distance just beyond arm's reach of an assailant. The importance of maintaining personal space in a confrontation with a stranger cannot be overemphasized. That split second of time purchased by the distance is often just enough time to allow you to avoid catastrophe.

A self-defense student of mine, Steve, told me of being confronted one evening after class. He was walking down the street toward his car when a man called to him. He said the man stepped up close to him, not more than a foot away, and asked directions to a nearby street. Outwardly showing confidence, Steve kept a sharp eye on the man as he explained how to get to the desired destination. The man left quietly.

"I was frightened," Steve told me. "I kept my hands loose and ready, without appearing to threaten the man, and I tried to show a lot of self-confidence. But something just didn't feel right. What could I have done differently?"

We had not covered the concept of personal defensible space

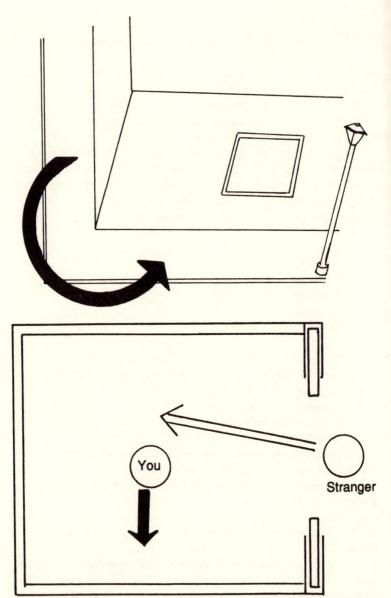

Figure 4.3. More about PDS. When rounding a street corner (above), allow extra space to foil an attacker who jumps out at you. In an elevator (below), use the maximum space available, but don't corner yourself. Stay mentally alert and pay attention to how the other occupant behaves.

Figure 4.4. Mental alertness means paying attention. This man is taking a mental siesta, and his lack of vigilance offers him no personal defensible space whatsoever. By being totally focused on his telephone conversation, with his back to pedestrian traffic, his face down, and his wallet clearly outlined in his right, rear pocket, he might as well hang a sign on his belt loop saying "Mug me. I need it." Never stand with your back to potential adversaries. Adopt at least a 90-degree stance when using a public telephone—a stance that allows you to see what is going on around you.

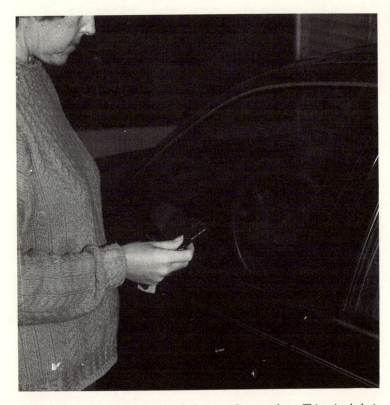

Figure 4.5. Mental alertness means being security conscious. This wise lady is mentally alert. She has her keys in her hand as she approaches her automobile, and her purse is held football-style under her arm and slightly to her front, using the vehicle as additional protection. Fumbling around in the dark as you rummage through your purse or your wallet in search of your car keys is an open invitation to an assailant.

in our classes yet, so I took a few minutes to explain to Steve that when he allowed the stranger to get so close to him, he had severely compromised his safety. By simply taking an innocent step backward he could have created enough personal space to inhibit a potential attacker. No, the man did not attack him, but he certainly could have. At close range you simply do not have enough time to react. You need not stand within reach of a stranger to give him directions. Do not allow strangers to violate your personal space. Move and create enough defensible space to respond if the situation turns sour.

APPEARANCES COUNT

Avoid the overt appearance of affluence. That is certainly easy enough for most of us—just making ends meet is hard enough. But whether you are wealthy or not, if you have something a criminal wants and you openly flaunt it, you are asking to have it taken away. When crooks see large bills floating around, they get interested quickly. Paying for a two-dollar item with a hundred-dollar bill in a crowded convenience store is not very smart. Would-be robbers watch to see who has the big bucks. Waving them around openly tells a hoodlum that you are a lucrative target.

People like to dress well and proudly display the results of their hard work and success. If you sacrifice to have nice things, then you should not be afraid to wear them or use them. But common sense must prevail if you want to *keep* them. If you own an elegant, expensive, gold necklace, you must choose carefully where you will wear it. Wearing it to dinner, to the theater, or at the fine arts center seems logical, and you can reasonably expect to still be wearing it when you return home. But if you allow it to dangle precariously as you stop to buy gas at a self-service station in a high-crime area of town, you may well have it jerked off your neck.

The whole idea of how lucrative you appear as a target and

how able you are to resist attack combines to create the image an attacker has of you (vincibility, Chapter Three). You will be chosen or not chosen as a victim based upon that image.

> "Leave your gold necklaces, diamond earrings, and Rolex watches at home," says armed robber Frank Hill. "Don't wear anything that attracts attention." . . . "You've accessorized correctly," says armed robber Ray Edwards, "if a crook looks at you and can't see anything worth stealing" (Wheeler 65).

LIFESTYLE

Whether you like it or not, the risk of crime is a function of your lifestyle. The jury is in. Certain preferences for behavior are more likely to get you into trouble than others. We already know that if you are single, you have a victimization risk that is twice as high as that of a married person. The reasons for this involve where and how you spend your time, and who you spend it with. For example, married women have a much lower crime risk because they have a daily routine that generally keeps them in public places, with people they know, and involves them in family-oriented leisure activities. Single males, on the other hand, can often be found out late at night, possibly in a drinking establishment, and usually alone. The more closely you associate (both physically and socially) with the people who are most likely to commit street crime, the greater your chances of becoming a victim.

Single people, like anyone else, should frequent their favorite entertainment spots, but everyone should be aware of the risks. If you know there is a nightclub in town where a fight breaks out every weekend, and you go there anyway, do not be surprised if you end up in the middle of a brawl. When people stop frequenting establishments that encourage or allow such behavior, then club owners will soon exert more effort to stop such activities just to get their business back. If decent, law-abiding people stop going to such places, then perhaps the criminals will get tired of beating each other up every week and we can all return to enjoy ourselves.

In any kind of drinking establishment, be it nightclub, tavern, or bar, keeping in mind a few general rules can improve your chances of surviving a fracas. Always locate the exit nearest your seat. This is not just a safety suggestion in case of fire, but should an altercation begin, it's a good idea to slip out of the building before someone decides to involve you. If you have the option, do not take a seat with your back against the wall, or in a position from which you cannot stand and move out quickly. Try to sit so that you have a good view of the rest of the room without making it easy for someone to corner you. And while it may seem extreme, a close friend of mine always backs into the parking slot at any kind of night spot.

"Hey," he says, "You never know when you might have to leave some place in a hurry!"

It may sound as if my friend is frequenting some rather shady locations, but at least he is taking a realistic look at his own risk. If you are serious about reducing your chances of being victimized by criminals, then some close introspection of your lifestyle is in order. Radical change may not be required, but certain alterations may be a good idea. Some people will virtually froth with righteous indignation at the very suggestion that they might curb their appetite for the pleasures of this world. Benjamin Franklin once wrote, "They that give up essential liberty to obtain a little temporary safety deserve neither liberty nor safety" (Marx 508). But then, was the honorable Mr. Franklin ever robbed of the contents of his coin purse? Take a look at where you are spending your time and who you are spending it with. Using alcohol and other drugs increases your vulnerability to crime. For example, Robin Room, in "Behavioral Aspects of Alcohol and Crime," tells us, "Homicides involving alcohol are more likely to take place in the evening and on weekends than at other times" (39), because those are the times when the general population drinks the most. You cannot be mentally alert if your brain is asleep. Most people would agree that if you are drunk, not only can you fail to recognize trouble before it comes, but neither can you deal with it once it arrives. What many are unable to realize is that you do not have to be drunk to be impaired. With a Blood-alcohol Content (BAC) of only 0.05%, your balance, coordination, timing, vision, and judgment are all impaired (Brewer 42). In avoiding a confrontation with a criminal, it is the latter quality, judgment, that is most important. Your tendency to take chances increases with alcohol impairment, so you find yourself going places, doing things, and saying things that you might not normally consider safe or reasonable. Criminals love to find victims who are impaired. It makes their job that much easier. Citizens under the influence of alcohol or other drugs are easy prey (Figure 4.6).

If two people have a disagreement, such as two fans at a sporting event, and both are sober, a confrontation is less likely to occur. If one is sober and the other is impaired, the chances for trouble increase. If both are impaired, look out! According to Robin Room, American studies on the relationship between alcohol and crime

> show that the offender is more likely to have been drinking if the victim has been drinking, and vice versa. This association is particularly strong for homicide and for rapes involving acquaintances and friends (39).

Be smart. Be the one with the clear mind who makes reasonable, responsible choices. Remember also that once alcohol or other drugs are used in excess, it gets easier to cross the legal and moral line from victim to offender.

KEEP IN MIND!

In review, here are the behaviors and tips for survival that help us stay away from trouble.

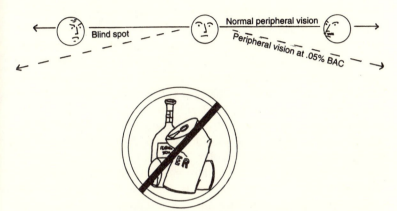

Figure 4.6. Alcohol, peripheral vision, and PDS. One of the key tenets of self-protection is being able to see an attack before it begins, or to intercept it as it takes place. Alcohol puts the brain to sleep, and the brain, recoiling from the assault of the drug, begins to shut down bodily operations just to survive. A study by the British Medical Council indicates that at a blood alcohol concentration of 0.05%, *peripheral vision is reduced by 30%*. Let us view this phenomenon in real terms. If you are a 180-pound male who ate a light dinner at 6:00 P.M. and arrived at a bar at 9:00 P.M., and you proceed over the next four hours to enjoy four beers with your friends, you blood alcohol level (BAC) when you leave the club at 11:00 P.M. will be approximately 0.05%. Not only is your judgment impaired, but, quite literally, you can't even see straight, though you may not be aware of it.

Confrontation Avoidance = Mental Alertness

Mental alertness involves:

1. *Being aware of where it is unsafe to be and when it is unsafe to be there*. In unfamiliar circumstances or high-crime areas, do not let strangers stop you to quiz you for directions, ask you the time, or borrow a match. There are plenty of community service people who are paid to answer those questions. If a car is parked alongside a deserted street, motor running, keep your distance. Avoid deserted laundromats or apartment laundry rooms late at night.

2. *Traveling in the company of others whenever possible.* Guardianship—the presence of onlookers—discourages criminal activity.

3. *Creating the impression of confidence and self-control.* Remember that how you walk and the overall image that criminals get will help them determine their target. A simple thing like having your car keys ready when you reach your vehicle saves time and creates the impression of a mentally alert individual.

4. *Staying in well-lighted, public places.* Criminals do not like lights. Lights make it too easy for you to recognize them or for some passer-by to see what they are up to.

5. *Trusting your instincts.* Humans have a sixth-sense about danger just as surely as do animals. Learn to listen to your inner voice. Trust your gut feeling about a situation.

6. *Maintaining personal space.* There is a time and place to be what the television networks call up-close-and-personal. Bring strangers inside the circle of your personal, defensible space only when you have gotten to know them.

7. *Avoiding the overt display of wealth.* Following the axiom of "If you've got it, flaunt it," will get you into serious trouble in a high-crime area. Keep valuables out of the sight of strangers.

8. *Knowing the risk of your lifestyle.* If you run with a crowd that looks for trouble, or if you hang out with people who get beat up, you will eventually be victimized.

9. *Controlling alcohol and other drugs.* All the research over the past two decades points to this as the number one factor you can control in limiting your own risk to assault.

Between the blissful naiveté that leads to becoming an easy target, and the paranoid fear that regards everyone as a potential enemy, there is a middle ground of confident awareness. The confidence that overcomes fear is based upon a combination of understanding and ability. The goal is clear: to be able to recognize trouble before it arrives, avoid it if it arrives, deal with it if you are forced to, and accomplish all of this without your fear destroying you. I said the goal was clear. I never said it was easy.

Chapter Five

FIGHTING BACK
VERSUS SUBMISSION

Sometimes, in spite of your best efforts to avoid it, trouble has an uncanny ability to find you anyway. Avoiding high-crime areas and learning to handle yourself confidently will only go so far to protect you. The police blotters are replete with entries about people who did all the so-called right things, but still became victims of crime. Hopefully, your mental alertness and forethought will permit you to dodge the average criminal and keep you out of the crime statistics. But what if it doesn't? What if, in spite of your consistent application of the techniques of confrontation avoidance, you are confronted with robbery, rape, or assault? Should you submit? Should you fight back? You *can* even the odds. You can take steps for self-protection, but it is important that you understand all the options and their consequences.

Our behavior in the face of assault is a product of both heredity and environment. When human life first appeared on this planet, existence was a struggle. One of the most important of the early human skills was self-protection, as people fought against wild animals and each other to survive. As civilizations became more ordered, the need to fight grew more specialized.

Fighting skills were concentrated more among the warriors and less in the average person. Thousands of years of history have brought us to a point today where most people never require the fighting skills of their ancestors. The use-it-or-lose-it concept applies to self-defense skills. Since our society is supposedly more civilized, we do not normally have to fight for food or self-protection, so our inherent abilities go unused. The physiological and psychological capability for self-defense is still present; only, it is dormant.

Some victims of assault have told me that at the moment of attack they felt this uncontrolled sense of rage and experienced a sudden burst of energy (adrenalin flow) as they fought savagely against their assailant. Those dormant, natural instincts took over and made the person viciously resist the aggressor. Sometimes this response is effective in thwarting an attack. Unfortunately, viciousness does not always equal effectiveness. The list is long of people who fought viciously, to their injury or death. It is not always enough to know that you should attack, you have to have some idea of when and how to attack.

Besides the physiological response to attack, there are responses that are conditioned by society. Our culture has given us certain roles to play. Men are supposed to be tough, physically capable, and ever-eager to respond to physical or verbal threat. The male ego (partly a product of the pressure of society) is not only supposed to be intolerant of personal insult or assault, but it also acts as the culturally appointed guardian of the opposite sex. Many men feel socially and culturally obligated to intervene when they perceive a woman is being threatened or even insulted. The notion of "that's no way to treat a lady" has led many men into physical altercations in the name of honor. But while men often are conditioned to fight with little provocation, many women cringe at the thought of physically striking another person. Women are expected to be dainty, delicate, feminine, and certainly not prone to wrestling around in the dirt in personal combat.

> In childhood, "popular" girls giggle and blush when
> being teased—rarely do they lash out. If a girl makes a boy

eat her dust in the 100-yard dash, she might win his admira-
tion, but probably not his heart. In short, helplessness in girls
is often rewarded on the playground (Kaylin 12).

These stereotypes have rendered tremendous disservice to females while placing an undue burden upon males. Both attitudes
are dangerous and must be overcome, lest you find yourself
coming out on the short end of an altercation.

So do I fight or not?

Let us examine the concept of "fight back when you should,"
and the factors that impact upon this decision. Resisting an
assailant is an individual decision. There are no easy answers,
convenient axioms, or comforting platitudes to guarantee that you
make the right choice. There is, however, a growing body of
statistical data on the subject of assault, which can help you make
an informed decision based upon fact. Combined with some
commonsense approaches to handling confrontation, it gives you
a good chance of making the best of a given situation.

Verbal insults do not constitute assault and are not legal
grounds for retaliation. If someone calls you a sonofabitch, or
some equally offensive name, no state in the Union will grant you
legal authorization to respond with violence. If you do, *you're* the
criminal. Even if someone threatens to physically harm you, you
can only respond with violence if: (a) you have no alternative, (b)
you have no route of escape, and (c) if the person threatening you
has the potential to immediately and seriously carry out the threat
of harm. For example, if an assailant with a crowbar steps out of a
darkened subway passage and says to a middle-aged commuter,
"I'm going to smash your head," and both (a) and (b) of the above
criteria are met, then a reasonable person could deduce that
criterion (c) is also met. In other words, the assailant has the
capability and intent to do the harm. However, if an 80-year-old
man threatens to chase down that same commuter, jump on him,
and beat him up with his bare hands, the chances are good that
the commuter could outrun the assailant (criterion b), and the
assailant's capability to carry out the threat (criterion c) is highly
doubtful. The commuter would risk committing a criminal act

himself if he responded with violence. We will look more closely at how to make a proper response to a physical threat later in this chapter.

Nobody likes being verbally abused, and being threatened or intimidated—even if the threat is unlikely to be carried out—is at once both frightening and insulting. When an incident happens in public, such as a verbal insult or an argument at a softball game, pride gets involved.

"I can't let this person talk this way to me," we reason to ourselves. Pride causes within us a near-compulsion to respond. If the confrontation escalates into a challenging shove, then our urge to respond has given way to physical retaliation. A fight develops. If you respond to verbal abuse with physical attack, you are no longer the victim, you are the offender. There are legal ways to deal with verbal abuse, such as slander and defamation of character laws, but coming to blows over words often results in the initiator suing you for assault.

We know from experience that verbal abuse is often just a prelude, an assault usually follows. Since each assault situation is different, there are no generic solutions that cover every contingency. But once a situation escalates to the threshold of assault, the statistics show that if you want to avoid injury, you had better figure out a way to diffuse the crisis short of physical violence.

FORCEFUL VERSUS NONFORCEFUL RESISTANCE

Forceful resistance is directly linked to victim injury in stranger-to-stranger assault. This category of assault does not involve robbery or rape, but does include barroom brawls, street confrontations, spectator struggles at sporting events, and gang altercations. Legally, they would be defined as either simple or aggravated assault. A National Crime Survey study of these types of assault victims from 1973 through 1979 indicates that 73% of the victims did something in their own defense (Barkas 221). The responses were divided into two categories: forceful and nonforceful. Forceful responses involved punching, kicking, scratching, and other forms of physical resistance. Nonforceful responses involved running away, screaming, reasoning with the attacker, and various methods of attracting the attention of passers-by. That pattern has continued as the 1989 figures show: 73.7% of assault victims acted in self-defense. Table 5.1 shows the percentages for all crimes of violence.

Since almost three out of four people do something in their defense when threatened with an attack, let us see how those actions relate to whether or not they are actually attacked or injured. Wesley Skogan and Richard Block found in their 1982 study on "Resistance and Injury in Non-Fatal Assaultive Violence," that:

TABLE 5.1. Does Taking Self-Protective Measures Help or Hurt?

	Helped situation (%)	Hurt situation (%)
Victim takes self-protective measures		
All crimes of violence	59.6	6.7
Rape	63.3	7.2
Assault	60.5	6.4
Others take protective measures on victim's behalf		
All crimes of violence	34.6	11.4
Rape	69.6	6.9
Assault	35.0	11.7

Note: Remember that self-protective measures do not necessarily involve fighting or physically resisting an attacker. These figures indicate that in the event of an assault, taking self-protective measures clearly improved the situation, even more than when someone else came to the aid of the victim. Percentages will not total 100% because of categories omitted, for instance, responses that both helped and hurt, or those that neither helped nor hurt the situation.
SOURCE: *Sourcebook—1990*.

TABLE 5.2. Self-Protective Measures Victims Use against Attackers
(1989 Figures)

Self-protective measure	Simple assault (%)	Aggravated assault (%)	Rape (%)
Attacked offender with a weapon	0.8	2.6	0.8
Attacked offender without a weapon	11.1	8.4	13.4
Threatened offender with a weapon	0.8	2.3	0.9
Threatened offender without a weapon	2.4	1.8	3.0
Resisted or captured offender	20.4	18.6	16.2
Scared or warned offender	8.7	8.2	10.6
Persuaded or appeased offender	16.5	13.3	14.2
Ran away or hid	15.5	20.8	11.2
Got help or gave alarm	10.6	11.6	9.7
Screamed from pain or fear	1.9	3.1	10.4
Used another method	11.4	9.4	9.5

SOURCE: *Sourcebook—1990* 268.

55% of the victims offered nonforceful resistance
25% of the victims offered forceful resistance
20% of the victims took combined actions

The results of their actions tell us something about which path to choose when confronting an assault situation. In situations where a threat of attack was made, and the victim responded non-violently, 34% of the victims were assaulted anyway. When victims responded violently to the threat of assault, 71% were assaulted anyway. The total is more than 100% because some people chose both responses (Skogan & Block 217). *Clearly, a violent response to the threat of attack increases the chance the attack will proceed.* And once the threatened attack actually takes place, the injury rate for those who forcefully resist does not look promising. Sixty percent of the victims who respond with force will be injured, while only 46% of the victims who respond nonforcefully will be injured (Skogan & Block 218).

So what does all this mean? Should we not fight back against an assailant? Should we be content to acquiesce? Since adopting a forceful method of resistance makes it more likely that the assault will actually take place, and once the assault begins, forcefully resisting your assailant makes it more likely that you will be injured, the wisest course seems to be:

When you have the option, offer nonforceful resistance to the *threat* of assault.

The key is in knowing when you have the option, and in recognizing the difference between the threat of assault and an assault itself.

REASONABLE RESPONSE IN KIND

Nonforceful resistance is not the most glamorous method of surviving an attack, but it is usually the most successful. Generally, it should be your *initial* response to the threat, allowing yourself to escalate to violent response only if you have no other choice. Keep in mind that within the laws governing self-defense is an interesting and hotly debated notion of the "duty to retreat."

> Should one faced with attack have a duty, subject to certain exceptions, to exercise any such opportunity as exists to retreat in safety before using deadly force? (Kadish 948).

Grounded in the belief that all human life, including that of an assailant, is more sacred than pride or "standing one's ground," the retreat rule can be difficult to accept. Does an attacker, by virtue of his willful, aggressive act, forfeit any respect he might have otherwise been afforded (Kadish 949)? Common sense would seem to support such a notion; yet should you respond in self-defense to an assault, the jury that hears your case will likely ". . . consider any failure to make use of retreat opportunities in evaluating the reasonableness of responding to attack[s] with deadly force" (Kadish 949). Even if your response does not involve deadly force, you must make a reasonable, measured reply to the level of the threat.

Establishing Levels of Response

One of the most difficult aspects of self-defense to teach a beginner is how to determine an appropriate level of response to a given attack situation. Once students learn the tremendous power their body can generate to repel an attacker, the problem is keeping students from over-responding. If your personal toolbox for assault protection contains only a hammer, the whole world looks like a nail. Over the years I have developed what I call Four Levels of Response to attack; and while I remind you this is not a how-to-fight manual, I believe the moral and legal liability for over-response to a perceived attack is such that I should share the philosophy with you.

Level One.   Verbal insults are never legal grounds for physical retaliation. Being called a "bitch" by an offensive passer-by or having your ancestry questioned by an irate motorist is not legal justification for you to strike that person. As previously indicated, a threat that meets the legal criteria for physical response, with its accompanying fear for your personal safety, might be legal grounds to resist a near-simultaneous attack; but it is probably smarter to reason with your attacker before it comes to blows.

"A soft answer turneth away wrath: but grievous words stir up anger" (Proverbs 15:1). This often-quoted biblical injunctive attempts to resolve a threatened assault nonviolently, and the statistics we have seen heavily favor such a response. Attempt to reason with a potential attacker, or even apologize for some perceived offense. There have been many times that I have apologized for things I did not do, solely to avoid a violent resolution to a difficult situation. My apology kept me from getting hurt or having to hurt someone else. Most competent martial arts instructors agree with this philosophy and teach it to their students. If an experienced, trained fighter can turn away from violence, why can't you? There is nothing to be proved. This does not lessen you as a person; it shows your courage and strength of character. You reduce the chances of the assault being carried out.

If you are leaving the grocery store with your arms full of bags, and you accidentally allow the door to close on the hand of the individual behind you, that person may have something to say about it. His verbal abuse constitutes a Level One threat and should be met with an appropriate response.

"Sorry, I hope your hand is not hurt."

Level Two. Unfortunately, a soft answer doesn't always "turneth away wrath," and a threatened assault may become actual in spite of your nonforceful attempts to resolve the problem. *Remember*: Be very careful what you say during a confrontation with a stranger. It is not uncommon for tempers to flare and for people to become involved in a fight over relatively minor matters, particularly at a public gathering, or any place where large numbers of people are packed in a small area and expected to remain calm for a long time. I have frequently observed such instances where two people become agitated with one another and exchange words, making a Level One situation rapidly escalate to Level Two. The more thoughtless the words, the more heated the conversation becomes. If you should find yourself in such a predicament, and the stranger you are arguing with threatens to harm you, you have a critical decision to make. You must decide very carefully what you will say next. Leave statements like, "I'll knock your teeth out," or "I'm going to mop the floor with you," in the movies where they belong. Such bravado usually provides just the impetus to push the encounter into violent conflict.

Be cautious with what you tell people you are "going" to do to them. If you say you are going to do something to a stranger, you had better be fully prepared to do it and not be running a bluff, because there are a lot of people out there who will take you up on your offer just to see if you can back it up. So if your conversation consists of big talk, intense bravado, or idle threats, you may quickly find yourself in a situation you cannot handle. On the other hand, if you are reasonably certain that what you say will dispel violence before it erupts, and if you are able to carry out your threat, then you may occasionally be successful in backing down a potential adversary. But as a good friend of mine once told me, "Don't talk the talk, unless you can walk the walk."

A threat reaches Level Two when a stranger puts his or her hands on you. By grabbing or shoving you, an individual violates your personal space and is usually attempting to make the situation escalate. With a shove, the aggressor is looking for something: either fear and capitulation, or retaliation. Do not offer either. In the instant of being shoved, take a couple of steps back away from the stranger and continue to try and resolve the confrontation nonviolently. If the offender again closes the distance and places his or her hands on you, you have every legal and moral right to *control* that person. Notice the word control, not punch or kick or gas or shoot. Control may mean anything from leaving before the situation becomes worse, to physically restraining the individual from touching you. You have now met your legal duty to retreat; however, only when your personal safety is directly and immediately threatened are you justified in a physical self-defense response. Let's consider an example of a gradually escalating threat.

You are standing in line in a popular restaurant, waiting for a table to come free and your number to be called. A stranger steps in front of you and tries to get the hostess to seat him and his companion.

"Excuse me, but we're all waiting in line," you say politely, gesturing at the line of people behind you.

The stranger just looks at you blankly and turns back again to get the hostess's attention. When the hostess, unaware of the man's line-cutting, starts to seat him and his companion, you rightfully object.

"Ma'am, uh . . . we were next," you point out, "and the line goes back this way."

The hostess is somewhat confused, but eventually realizes what has occurred, and prepares to seat you.

"Hey, what's your problem, man?" the stranger says, turning to confront you.

As the hostess waits, menus in hand, you look at the stranger and his companion and say forcefully, yet graciously, "We were next."

The stranger proceeds to call you some profane name or suggests he will see you after dinner. Presently this constitutes only a Level One threat, so you wisely choose to ignore him and move on with your companion to your table. After dinner, you pay the bill and step into the parking lot only to see the stranger get out of his car and start walking toward you. He starts using his offensive language again.

"I really don't want any trouble," you inform him, continuing toward your car.

The stranger steps up to you and grabs your sleeve, thereby escalating the encounter to Level Two. You pull yourself free and attempt to gain some distance, still trying to resolve the confrontation verbally. Again he steps up to you and grabs your sleeve, this time pulling his fist back as if getting ready to strike you. The situation has now escalated to Level Three.

Level Three. When someone seeks to physically harm you, by either punching, kicking, or otherwise striking you, the law governing self-defense in every state of the Union guarantees you the right to defend yourself. Your response will vary depending upon your size, temperament, skill, and training; and it may include blocking the person's attack, using an arm or joint-locking technique, or pushing the assailant out of range and trying to escape, or striking the individual before he can strike you. It is at Level Three that self-defense training offers you greater options for responding.

Let's go back to our example and assume for a moment that you have had some limited training in how to thwart or control an attacker. Instead of punching your parking lot assailant in the face, thus likely escalating the situation into a full-scale fight (which you might very well lose), you grasp the man's wrist at the spot where he has grabbed your sleeve, and you twist his arm down and away from your body. This movement not only frees you from his grasp, but it also misdirects his punch and keeps you from getting hit. Maintaining control of his arm, you again remind him that you wish no trouble and would like to quietly leave. Your opponent now has the option of stopping the assault or continuing at the risk of serious injury. You have just executed what martial artists and police officers call a control technique—a technique that causes enough pain to get an assailant's attention without applying deadly force. The pain will do one of two things: make him reconsider the attack or make him angry enough to really come after you. Even if the latter holds true and the assailant is more determined to press the attack, what have you really lost? You were going to be hit anyway. At least you made an effort to diffuse the situation. Let us say your opponent pulls free, and, after a few more disparaging remarks, decides to leave. You have then warded off a Level Three assault and kept yourself injury free. You should feel relieved about that.

Level Four.   Now let us say that instead of leaving, your stranger picks up a bottle from the gutter and says, "I'm going to bash your brains out." Under the statutes of most states, you now have reason to immediately fear for your life, thus you are legally justified in using deadly force to stop your assailant. If you had pulled out a gun or a knife and used it on your assailant prior to this, *you* would have been charged with assault, or perhaps even attempted murder. It doesn't seem fair, does it?

"Why should I wait until I am practically killed before I act?" you may ask. "Why can't I just rip out the guy's throat as soon as he grabs my sleeve? Why wait and give him a better chance to do his evil deed?" Keep in mind that the law is designed to protect *all* human life, including the bad guy's, and American jurisprudence simply will not allow a person to use deadly force without clear justification. The measure of any civilization is the value it places on human life—all human life—so consider this as just the price we have to pay for the society in which we live.

Once you are faced with a Level Four threat, as illustrated by the assailant's final act in our example, you have met the generally accepted legal requirement to protect yourself with an appropriate amount of force—"force intended or likely to cause death or serious injury" (Kadish 947). In the traditional position, reflected by the Supreme Court of North Carolina in *State v. Clay*, 297 N.C. 555, 256 S.E. 2nd 176 (1979),

> deadly force may be used only if the defendant . . . reasona-
> bly perceive[s] that the imminent attack create[s] a threat to
> his life or of serious physical injury, [and] if the defendant
> reasonably perceive[s] nondeadly force as inadequate to pre-
> vent this danger—that is, that deadly force was necessary to
> prevent the threatened harm (Kadish 947).

In our hypothetical situation, those criteria appear to be satisfied; but *response in kind* is the critical factor in governing a self-defense act in any assault situation. If what you do to your attacker is appropriate to the degree of the threat, then what becomes assaultive conduct for you will be justifiable. That involves considering:

1. your size, strength, and age relative to the attackers;
2. the attacker's fierceness and persistence; and
3. whether or not the attacker is armed (Kadish 949).

The second set of statistics we saw dealt with injury rates for those who forcefully resisted their attackers. Yes, if you fight back, your chances of injury increase. But consider why that is true: Either (1) you wait too late to respond, or (2) you respond improperly. Note also that the people who fight back with success are less likely to report such activity to the police (for a variety of reasons); thus, the statistics are not completely reflective of the success or failure of resistance. Few of us are willing to stand by and allow someone to beat us senseless, without trying to protect ourselves.

That is just not human nature. Once we see that we cannot avoid the assailant, and once the assailant is after us, it is natural and reasonable to try and resist. The greatest reason victims fail in their resistance efforts is that they do not understand when or how to resist.

RESISTANCE AND SUCCESS

Recent studies that consider the consequences of victim resistance to robbery paint an interesting picture. There is a clear relationship between victim resistance to robbery and the victim's ability to hold on to his or her property. While robbery is not technically an aspect of stranger assault, it is a complicated matter that involves several of the same variables that assault victims must face; so the results of these studies are important in developing a personal strategy of protection and crime avoidance.

The National Crime Panel (NCP) statistics show that only about 50% of all attempted robberies were successfully completed (Ziegenhagen & Brosnan 680). In almost every case the failure of the criminal is related to some aspect of victim–criminal interaction, as opposed to the actions of either the police or by-standers. What that means is that what *you* do is the single most influential factor in whether or not a criminal is successful in robbing you. In the equation of self-protection, *you* are the most critical factor. Earlier studies (Block, 1977; Conklin, 1972; and Wolfgangs, 1982) have come across clearly in favor of the victim submitting to a robbery without resistance, in an effort to avoid injury. But when you consider the data that these studies used and some other factors, it is easy to see why they came to such conclusions:

1. These studies reflected only the crimes reported to police.
2. The crimes in which victims sustain injury are more likely to be reported to the police than those instances when no injury was incurred.

3. We also know that people who resist assailants are much less likely to report the incident to the police, particularly if the assailant was unsuccessful in his or her attack.

So the data that suggest capitulation at all costs is over-representative of victims who were injured and under-representative of victims who successfully thwarted their attacker. In other words, people who fought back and won are not accurately reflected in the statistics, while those who were injured get the spotlight. Based upon those statistics alone, it is easy to erroneously conclude that resistance to robbery equals both property loss and injury. Still, deciding to engage an attacker in combat means taking a big risk, and a thoughtful person will carefully count the costs.

A Dangerous Gamble

When Denver resident Stephen Bunce, 25, looked out of the second story window and saw burglars loading his parents' possessions in the back of a pick-up truck, he decided to act. Running downstairs, he chased after the criminals, who, upon seeing him, tried to drive away. He caught up with the truck and dove into the bed where he began to scuffle with one of the thieves. Although the driver made the vehicle swerve to throw Bunce out, and his accomplice attempted to push him onto the street, Bunce stubbornly held on. When two punches in the face didn't faze the thief, Bunce, a trained Judo player, eventually got a choke hold that subdued the man and caused him to pass out. A few moments later, one perpetrator was under his control on the ground; the other one sped away in the pickup, but was arrested a few days later. "Police lectured Bunce on the danger he had faced. But later, Bunce, who runs his own limousine service, received five awards for heroism" (Treen 39–40). Mr. Bunce was a brave and skilled guardian of his parents' property that night, and for that he was rightfully commended. But he was also a very *lucky* man—lucky that the criminal in the back of that truck didn't pull a .357 Magnum from his belt and blow the top of Mr. Bunce's head off. And it might easily have come out just that way.

Mr. Bunce had no reasonable certainty that the thieves were not armed. He could not know, given the speed at which the situation developed. In that instant he gambled and won. Still, I would have advised Mr. Bunce, and others who might find themselves in similar circumstances, to take the license number and a description of the truck and immediately call 911 or the police. Remember, a confrontation like Bunce's could easily have ended differently. What material possession could be in the back of that truck that would be worth his life? Let the police handle what they can. And please . . . no gun shots into the back of a truck. Even experienced law enforcement officers wouldn't have attempted such a shot. How do you know where those rounds are going to end up? The National Rifle Association Hunter Safety Course teaches children as young as age ten to be "sure of your target *and beyond*." And from the legal criteria we have just reviewed, taking a shot at a fleeing robbery suspect does not constitute justifiable deadly force. In that instance, you had better pray your aim is off, because if you did hit the fleeing robber, it would most likely be *your* fingerprints they would be taking downtown.

A Trade-off at Best

Depending upon whether or not the offender uses a weapon, and the type of weapon (a topic to be addressed later), it seems that resisting a robbery attempt is a trade-off between maybe keeping your property and possibly getting injured doing it. How much is your purse or wallet worth to you in terms of physical pain, potential impairment, or time lost on your job? That is a situational call that you must make for yourself.

The question of response against an assailant with a deadly weapon (aggravated assault) is considerably more concrete than the case of simple assault. Clearly, the fear of being wounded or killed, coupled with the lack of confidence in one's ability to prevail, deters people from fighting back against an opponent armed with a gun. That is a wise choice. Only about 9% of the victims confronted with a gun attempt to forcibly respond to their attacker, and that corresponds with the relatively low injury rate among such victims. The property, they reason, is just not worth the trade-off. Self-defense students learn that weapon disarms are intricate, difficult maneuvers that should only be attempted if one is convinced that he or she is about to be seriously injured or killed. The average citizen has no business trying to be a movie-style karate expert.

But while guns demand a healthy respect, knives seem to encourage bravado. About 30% of those confronted with a knife respond forcefully and they have the injury rate to show for it. In case you haven't noticed, knives can be lethal. Forcefully opposing a knife-wielding robber is madness, unless you have no other choice. Those of us in the self-defense community have practiced thousands of knife disarms for a number of years, but fortunately many of us have had to do only one or two real ones. Only attempt a knife disarm *if your life depends on it*. Let them have the $20 in your wallet. It's just not worth the risk. Take your chances on outrunning him, an option that almost everyone, except the aged or handicapped, can use. You will be amazed at how fast you can run and how loud you can yell when you are terrified.

In summary, there are forceful and nonforceful responses to threatened and actual assault or robbery. My rule of thumb is this:

1. Talk them out of it if you can.
2. Apologize if you must.
3. Attract the attention of passers-by.
4. Scream, yell, and run like a jackrabbit.
5. If cornered by an assailant, fight only if there is an actual attack.
6. If a robbery is attempted with a deadly weapon, give up the goods.

7. If at anytime you feel that you will be seriously injured or killed *regardless* of your response, ATTACK IMMEDIATELY.

A CASE IN POINT

In 1981 a woman in her midtwenties was attacked while walking her dog along the street of a major eastern city. As she stood near an empty lot, a man came walking down the street and stopped briefly to ask her the time. He continued down the street but she noticed that he stopped about a block away and started back in her direction. As he closed the distance between them she saw that he had a knife. The assailant grabbed her, placed his arm around her, and pinned her arm behind her. Suddenly, she felt a burning sensation as he thrust the knife into the back of her shoulder.

"This guy is going to kill me," she told herself.

"From that moment on," she said, "I couldn't feel a thing. I had learned in my kung fu training to make decisions and not to panic" (Mason 37).

The attacker, who outweighed her by almost 90 pounds, continued to pull her down the street, stabbing her as he did. She resisted with all her might.

"I said to myself 'I'm not going into that parking lot.' I thought I was going to die anyway, so I decided I'd rather die on the sidewalk."

Eventually the woman was able to smash her knee into the groin of the assailant, forcing him to flee the scene. She spent a month in the hospital recovering from multiple stab wounds, but she is alive. Some people will argue that the woman should have cooperated with the assailant, and that by resisting, she just exposed herself to needless injury. Struggling with a knife-wielding assailant who is out to rob you may be unwise, but in this case, the attacker had no apparent motive other than to kill or injure the woman, and he had already begun to stab her. Once that intention was clear (and cold steel in your back is a rather vivid indication of intention), she had little choice. When the circumstances narrow down our choice to resisting or dying, most of us are going to give it our best shot.

LOCATION MAY DICTATE REACTION

The actions of the attacker, coupled with the environment of the attack, can cause us to make choices that we might not ordinarily make. It is one thing to be insulted or threatened by someone when the two of you are alone. Then it may be relatively easy to laugh off a remark or overlook the bravado and calmly walk away. It is easy to be "above it all" when nothing is at stake. But face the same individual in different circumstances and you may find that backing off is not so simple.

A man and his wife were inching their way along in the traffic on a downtown street one summer evening. They were on the way home from the wife's place of employment and they had made the mistake of using the city's favorite cruise way, where many high school and college students spend every Friday night just driving up and down the street and hanging out on the corner. It was bumper-to-bumper and they were making only about 50 yards per minute when they passed a street corner heavily populated with college-age boys. One or two of the boys yelled some rather crude remarks at the woman. She turned her head away from them.

"What did they say?" the husband asked. His wife just shook her head, trying to ignore the remarks. The young men then followed with a crude, insulting gesture. That did it. The husband was not about to stand for any more of that. He pulled over as far out of the line of traffic as he could get and opened the door.

"Don't go out there," his wife said. "It's just going to cause trouble."

"I'm not causing trouble," the husband replied, "*they* are! But I'll put a stop to it."

The husband confronted the young man who made the offensive gesture and an argument ensued, followed closely (as it usually is) by a brief shoving match. Eventually the husband found himself fighting the perpetrator, plus three or four of his friends. The husband suffered severe bruises, a laceration over one eye, a sprained wrist, and some skinned knuckles. The young men fled before the police could make their way through the traffic, and the husband went to the emergency room for stitches. When the encounter was over, the bad guys got away, the police were unable to reach the scene in time, and the woman was still insulted—only now she had an injured husband and a hospital bill to boot.

This man would probably never have attempted to fight multiple opponents under other circumstances. Had he been alone, he would have likely kept on driving and passed off the offenders as immature, with nothing better to do with their time. But because of the circumstances, that is, his wife's presence in the car, he *perceived* injury being done to her, and he was determined to rectify the situation. The anger he felt at his wife being insulted overcame his judgment and caused him to place himself in a no-win situation.

Of course he was angry. Almost anyone would be angered if someone insulted his or her spouse. But even if we are justifiably enraged, we still must evaluate the situation to determine the best course of action. Simply having the right to be mad does not guarantee you will win. The husband's zealous effort to punish the verbal assailants only ended up with him being hurt instead.

What did those streetcorner enthusiasts actually do? Did they verbally embarrass the wife? Yes. Did they offend the husband? Yes. Did they have the right to say whatever they pleased in public? No. Was either the woman or the man physically harmed, or even physically threatened by the remarks or gestures? No. Were the obscene remarks sufficient legal grounds for the husband to engage the offenders in a physical struggle? No. In fact, they could later have him charged with assault.

Did the actions of the young men threaten the ego of the husband? Yes. Is a husband not supposed to protect his wife?

After all, if you let people talk to your wife this way, what kind of a husband are you? Are you a real man? What will people think of you if you sit there and let others insult your wife?

All of these questions will arise in a situation like the one just described. In this case, the husband's thoughts and actions were greatly influenced by who was around him at the time of the offense. Under other conditions he might have behaved differently. But you cannot separate the offense from its environment. If you do, it is no longer the same offense. Change the environment by removing the wife, and you probably have a man who keeps on driving and does not respond to the insults. Of course, the nature of the insults would also change if the woman were not present. Because environment can radically alter our response to an offense, and because the circumstances surrounding an altercation can send us into all manner of psychological ruminations, we must learn to recognize the pitfalls and traps inherent in some situations, so that we can avoid unnecessary suffering.

Some people might say that it took tremendous courage for the husband to stop his car and confront those insulting young men. On the contrary, it showed extremely poor judgment on the part of the husband and was in no way a measure of courage. Since he and his wife were not in immediate danger, and since he was clearly outnumbered and in a location where he could not expect to receive any help, getting out of the car was foolish. It exposed him to unnecessary risk, and once he was incapacitated, the young men could have done whatever they wished to his wife.

If you take a few moments to evaluate the environment of an impending confrontation, you may realize that your courses of action are limited. Learn to confront only when you must, and try not to sweat the small stuff. Sure, those streetcorner loiterers were crude, rude, and socially unacceptable. But one man alone is not going to shut them up. Even if the husband had dispatched one of them and the others had not joined in to help, they would still be out there the next Friday night insulting other women and beating up other well-intentioned men. Could it be that this is just what they were looking for? The police department and the sanitation department have one thing in common: They are both tasked with keeping the garbage off the streets. They cannot get it all, but if citizens will tell them where it is, they will make an effort to collect it. By keeping cool and waiting the few minutes it would have taken to get to a pay phone, the husband might have called the police and reported the incident to them. No, the police would probably not have arrested any of the bad guys unless they happened to be up to their antics as they arrived, and even the bad guys are not that stupid. But the officers might have broken up the group for a little while, and at the very least, once alerted to the problem, the police could keep a close eye upon the situation.

By recognizing these ego-threat circumstances, or by watching for the no-win situations before they can escalate, it is possible to avoid many conflicts that put you at a disadvantage. Your emotional commitment to a confrontation will impact upon how level-headed your response. The key is remaining calm enough, long enough, to recognize what is worth fighting for and what is not.

WHEN YOU CAN'T WALK AWAY

Sometimes the circumstances surrounding a confrontation will make it impossible for you to walk away in good conscience. Decency and character will often demand that you intercede in situations where you would normally avoid trouble. The following story, related to me in 1987, is a good example of just such a situation.

Melvin Waller and Riley Montgomery were sitting in Melvin's living room one evening in late May. They were watching television and enjoying each other's company. Melvin was a thin, wiry, old gentleman in his late 70s and Riley was his 25-year-old grandson. It was getting dark outside and the two were so riveted by the "shoot'em up" western on television that they did not notice the front door was unlocked. Riley visited his grandfather at his home in the country about once a month. The nearest neighbors were a half-mile away, and Riley was fond of checking in on Melvin to see how he was doing.

Riley got up from the couch to get another soft drink when he heard a thumping sound on the front porch.

"You expecting anybody, Grandad?"

"Not that I know of," Melvin answered.

Riley walked over to the window and pulled back the drapes. "I think somebody's out there."

Melvin shook his head. "I ain't expecting nobody."

Before Melvin could finish speaking, the front door was pushed open and in stepped two men and a woman.

"What do you want here?" Melvin asked, getting up from his chair.

Riley just stood there and looked at the intruders.

"We want some money," the woman said. "We're trying to get to Florida, and we need some cash."

"I've got no money to give you," Melvin replied. He noticed a tall man holding what looked like a piece of lead pipe, and thought he had better come up with another answer. "I can give you a few dollars, that's all I've got here in my wallet."

The man with the pipe stepped over to Melvin and grabbed him by his arm. Riley moved toward them but stopped suddenly when the woman, bearing a kitchen knife, stepped in front of him.

"I know you've got more money than that," said the man with the pipe.

"No, no, that's all there is," Melvin repeated.

The tall man shoved Melvin over the arm of the chair and sent him crashing to the floor. He stood over him with the pipe. The woman was still looking at Riley, but now was talking to Melvin.

"You'd better give us some money," she said, "or he's (pointing to the tall man) going to beat it out of you."

Again Melvin tried to tell them that his wallet contained all the money he had, but the more he talked the more impatient they became. The tall intruder began to poke and hit Melvin in the ribs with the pipe. He had struck him twice, very hard, in the ribs before Riley decided he must do something. The third person had been acting as a guard, watching out the door the whole time. Riley decided to worry about him last. He had to stop them from beating Melvin. He saw no gun, but he was still very much afraid. He knew that he could get stabbed or even beaten if he tried to help, but he also knew that if he didn't do *something* they might very well beat his grandfather to death. Riley was a healthy young man, and although he was no trained fighter, he had spent a couple of years on the high school wrestling team. He knew he must act, and he thought about running for help, but even if he got away, he figured they would probably continue to beat his grandfather. He knew it was up to *him* and he knew he had to *physically* attempt to stop them. Riley had always been raised to believe it was wrong to hit a woman, but he delivered a crushing right fist to the side of the woman's face, sending her sprawling to the floor. The man with the pipe saw his partner fall, stopped beating on Melvin and turned to face Riley. Riley was beyond pain and anger at this point. He was all business, and all he could think about was "getting those guys."

Riley lowered his head and executed a better take-down than he ever dreamed of in high school, and although the assailant struck him in the back as Riley drove him into the wall, Riley never felt the blow. The sentry who had been watching the door started to intervene, but upon seeing the woman semiconscious on the floor, and his other associate having his head rammed repeatedly into the wall, he thought better of it. Instead, he picked up the woman and the two ran from the house, leaving the pipe-wielder to fend for himself. Riley struggled with the man for several more seconds until the criminal broke free of his grip and dashed out the door in hot pursuit of the others.

The county sheriff took a description of the three offenders and searched the area for them, but they managed to get away. Melvin suffered two broken ribs from the beating he received, but there is no doubt that he would have fared far worse had Riley not acted when he did. Riley suffered some scratches and some bruises, but overall, he came out of the affair reasonably well. The criminals got away, but I do not think they will try to rob Melvin Waller again, at least not while his grandson, Riley, is around.

Riley's situation is a classic example of a situation in which decency and character demand action. In this case, giving up the money was not effective in dismissing the criminals, and cooperation was getting them nowhere. Riley assessed the situation and quickly saw that the environment of the robbery/assault made the usual responses ineffective. He made the only reasonable choice under the circumstances. Although some might claim that Riley acted without regard to personal safety, he did, in fact, act in the interest of his own personal safety and in the best interest of all parties concerned. It was not unreasonable to assume that as soon as the offenders finished beating Melvin, he would be next.

In situations where you must protect others as well as yourself, such as a mother and child being accosted by a street thug, or in the instance of two friends when one is disabled, you must quickly assess the threat and consider all of the options for survival. You may be forced to engage in actions that might otherwise be unnecessary, or even dangerous. If your response would be dangerous by yourself, it will probably be just as dangerous in a group, but the difference is found in the necessity of the situation. Where a response was once optional, now it is mandatory.

If you are traveling with a business associate who is on crutches and the two of you are threatened with assault outside your motel room, you have the option of running away, but your associate does not. What are you going to do, leave him there to fend for himself? If you were alone, you might wisely decide to flee the scene, but now you must consider what will happen to your companion if you run to get help. Maybe you will find help in time to save him, and maybe you won't. The circumstance may force you to engage in self-protection and the protection of the disabled associate. Your attitude toward dealing with a criminal threat must be flexible enough to handle a variety of complicated situations, and only a clear mind, an anticipatory stance, and mental alertness can help you decide your response on a case-by-case basis. Mental alertness can help you differentiate between a true assault situation—one in which you must intervene—and, let's say, a couple of buddies wrestling around with a female companion in good-natured fun. Coming to the aid of someone else whom you perceive to be in physical danger is always ripe with risk, both in terms of the physical threat to you and in the possibility that you might be mistaken. If you get the urge to be Mighty Mouse and determine that where there is a wrong to right, you will join the fight, keep this in mind. Knock out one of those men play-wrestling with a female companion and you will probably be charged with assault. That is why the law demands that your actions be "pursuant to good faith and in reasonable belief that [your] conduct is necessary to protect [another] person from imminently threatened harm" (Kadish 952). Yet while there are clear and present dangers of intervening on behalf of someone else, the greater danger in our society exists when people refuse to go to the aid of others. Ignoring the pleas of assault victims is a far more pervasive problem than "the mistaken apprehension that the person aided has the right of self-defense" (Kadish 952). As a rule of thumb, you can and should go to the aid of others when you reasonably perceive the persons aided as having the right to act in their own self-defense if they could.

Fortunately for a seven-year-old girl in Bangor, Maine, Jeffrey and Lisa Mishou were mentally alert. One summer afternoon the couple was sitting in the shade and looking through their binoculars to watch boats in the harbor, when they observed a man emerge from the brush and entice a passing little girl from her bicycle.

"I can't believe it," Lisa told her husband. "She's going into the woods" (Treen 43).

The two watched aghast as the man grabbed the young child by the back of her head, struck her across the face, and pulled her into the brush. As her husband left to call 911 (good move), Lisa drove her car to the vicinity in hope, perhaps, of creating some attention without leaving the safety of her car (43). But when she heard the young child crying out, Lisa found herself in one of those environmentally dictated situations—she had no time to wait for a safer option. Leaving her vehicle, Lisa found the man lying on top of the child, and immediately she began to struggle with him, eventually succeeding in pulling him off the frightened youngster. As the assailant was running away, Jeffrey Mishou arrived from his 911 call and captured the man, threatening to "snap [his] neck like a twig." In this case, Jeffrey was big enough to back up his threat, so the man surrendered (43). Lisa would have been safer had she not left her car; however, when a human being is suffering, particularly a child, and you know that any hesitation on your part will cost greater suffering, or perhaps death, there really is no option for the civilized person—you must act.

VEHICLE SECURITY

In 1992 the U.S. had at least 21,000 carjackings—the number is probably higher since the FBI still includes this crime under the category of auto theft. Since carjacking involves a personal confrontation with an assailant, it is worthy of note as we seek to avoid assault situations. It is specifically disturbing because of its potential for physical violence (as opposed to the theft of an abandoned car while the owner is away).

One of the more prominent victims of carjacking was the 34-year-old Washington, D.C., mother who was pulled from her car and dragged to her death when her arm was caught in the seatbelt. The press made much of the story, particularly since the perpetrators tossed the woman's 22-month-old baby from the vehicle as they sped away. The woman died. The baby lived (Poyer 11).

What can drivers do to protect themselves?

Joe Poyer, in an article for *Home & Auto Security*, a new magazine targeted at average citizens who want to manage their risk of victimization, offers the following advice to vehicle operators:

- Be aware at all times of where you are driving.
- Lock all doors and keep windows rolled up.
- Memorize your license plate and driver's license number.
- Know your route and destination.
- Know where area police and fire stations are located.
- Tell someone you trust where you are going.
- Be alert at traffic signals.
- Use the lane farthest from the curb when possible.
- Keep the car in "drive" or in gear at stoplights.
- Keep valuables out of sight.
- Routinely check mirrors for activity around your vehicle.
- Park in garages as close to an exit as possible.
- Have your keys in hand and ready as you approach your car.
- Check out your vehicle as you move toward it.
- Keep the volume on stereos and radios low enough to hear outside noises.
- Pay more attention to your surroundings than to which radio station you're selecting.
- If you are rear-ended, or in some other accident, stay in the car unless other people are nearby. Have someone call the police, and if the other party gets belligerent or threatening, sound your horn or drive away.
- If a carjacker points a gun at you, get out of the car and move away quickly (Poyer 16–17).

Chapter Six

FEAR, SELF-DEFENSE, AND WEAPONS

The first time I parachuted from an airplane, my instructor told me that it was perfectly normal to be afraid. He suggested that if I were not afraid there might be something wrong with me. Fear is a normal human emotion in the face of the unknown. When people are unfamiliar with a situation, when they are uncertain about their ability to deal with a situation, or if they feel somehow out of control, fear is the natural result. Stranger violence is one of these situations.

The fear of crime is a fear of strangers, but it also consists of uncertainty about how to control the situation. We feel more at ease in familiar surroundings, and when dealing with repetitive actions in situations we can control. Controlling one's environment is another basic psychological need, and the fundamental underpinning of a sense of personal security. The idea that an unknown person will commit an unpredictable attack against a vulnerable citizen, who is attending to his or her normal, daily activities, is a frightening thought. If you believe that the attacker chooses a victim indiscriminately, and that the victim has little chance of avoiding the attack or protecting himself or herself, then you will

113

live in constant fear. But we have already seen that this is just not true. The criminal is predictable in choosing a victim, and you are not powerless in avoiding or repelling an attacker. Still, your fear must be addressed.

An article entitled "Criminal Violence," appearing in a 1978 issue of *Criminal Justice*, illustrates an interesting paradox. We fear strangers more than anything else, and yet we live our lives among strangers (Silberman 11). Every time we take a walk, ride the subway or bus, shop in the supermarket or department store, enter an office building lobby or an elevator, work in a factory or large office, or attend a ball game or the movies, we are surrounded by strangers. The potential for fear is as immense as it is unavoidable.

While the potential for fear is unavoidable, the level of fear is manageable. If fear is not controlled, there are dangerous consequences for both the person and society. Remaining locked behind your doors, avoiding public transportation and denying yourself contact with strangers is an unacceptable lifestyle for most people. For if we allow our fear of criminals to prevent us from being a functional part of our community, we must ask ourselves the question, "Are we really living?" A society that radically alters its lifestyle due to the fear of crime is said to be paying "opportunity costs." The quality of life in any culture is diminished when that culture loses its sense of trust, the basis for personal interaction (Riedel 224).

In 1985 the Citizen-Oriented Police Enforcement Unit (COPE) of Baltimore, Maryland, interviewed hundreds of people to find out specifically what they feared in relation to crime. They identified these major fears as:

- fear of going out at night
- fear of opening the door when someone knocks
- fear of walking past a stranger
- fear of coming out of the bank
- fear in the grocery store parking lot
- fear of leaving their curtains open

- fear of calling the police or signing a complaint if they saw a crime or had a specific problem (Behan 13)

While some of these fears may appear unusual or foreign to us, others we will recognize only too well. In addition to its impact upon the quality of an individual life, the fear of crime inhibits the way the community behaves. The fear of crime may itself lead to an increase in crime (Goodstein 133). Criminologists refer to the Fear of Crime (FOC) Model (Figure 6.1) to explain that as people become more and more frightened about the potential for crime, their behavior alters radically enough to reduce the available inhibitors against crime (observers, guardians), which causes

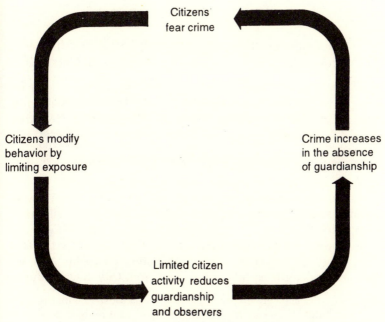

Figure 6.1. The Fear of Crime Model.

crime to increase. As more information becomes available about the increase of crime, fear increases, behaviors change even more, resulting in still fewer bystanders and less surveillance of the criminal. This causes more crime (Goodstein 134).

So the collective impact of individual responses to the fear of crime can directly influence the level of crime. When citizens impose a type of "house arrest" upon themselves and their families, it becomes easier for the bad guys to roam the streets. It makes common sense to try and place some distance between yourself, the criminal, and high-crime locations. But when persons allow fear to completely control their lives, and a community collectively alters its lifestyle because of the threat of crime, the situation will deteriorate.

THE PHYSICAL EFFECT OF FEAR

Laura Goodin, the Maryland-based, part-time self-defense instructor mentioned in Chapter One, says her students' fear of crime

> [used to be] a vague, nameless dread. Now it's a specific dread. Now I'm hearing, "There have been so many shootings in my block," or "Well, I used to think my neighborhood was safe." Some women are openly angry [that] it's they who have to change their lifestyle instead of the assailants (Miller 12).

"I'm tired of feeling as though evil is lurking around every corner, stalking me like a psycho killer," says Lucy Kaylin in an article for *Mademoiselle*. She recognizes fear as "enervating," and wisely seeks balance between a healthy awareness of the threat to her safety, and what she calls debilitating paranoia. A career woman making it on her own in New York City, Kaylin admits,

> I'm allowing myself to feel somewhat satisfied with the fact that, if I fortify myself and my apartment to the best of my ability and don't let my guard down, the odds are pretty

> good that I'll live to tell this glamorous (ha ha) big-city
> chapter of my life. The key is to be careful without being
> crazy (113).

Being "careful without being crazy" is a good description of a
person dealing with the threat of stranger assault. Still, there are
times when fear cannot be dismissed. If a 200-pound, crazed felon
approaches you wielding a knife, it would be foolish not to be
afraid. Your fear will cause one of two consequences: Either it will
paralyze you and render you incapable of a response, or it will
invigorate you and improve your ability to respond. Which of
these situations will occur is largely dependent on your will.
Although some fear response is automatic, much of how fear
affects your body can be controlled.

> The mind and body work together when confronted with
> a potentially harmful situation. The mind first recognizes the
> possibility of injury and signals the body to get ready to
> prevent injury. The body then starts to shut down all unnec-
> essary functions and fuels up for action. One of the fuels is
> adrenaline, a chemical product in the body which feeds the
> muscle groups. Up to a point, the more fear the more adren-
> aline produced. The adrenaline makes the muscles capable of
> stronger and faster movements. It also makes the body less
> sensitive to pain (McKee 13).

The key to dealing with fear during assault is understanding
the nature of that fear and effectively managing it to your benefit.

Courage is not the absence of fear—it is the *control of fear*.
Some of the most courageous people in history were frightened.
Their heroism or bravery was accomplished not in an absence of
fear but in spite of it. What separates victims from victors in an
assault is how the former handle their natural fear. The lack of
confidence in your ability to control the outcome of an assault, or
an impending assault, is one of the primary causes of fear. When
you feel powerless, you usually are. Without self-confidence you
are a target of opportunity for the criminal. You are easy prey.
Since you believe yourself incapable of stopping an attacker, your

fear increases and you are eventually frozen, so to speak, with terror.

Fear of the unknown contributes to our inability to handle assault. For most, being the victim of an assault is an unknown experience. Many people are lucky enough to never experience a physical confrontation with another person. So when an encounter occurs they simply do not know what to expect. In an article entitled, "Fear: Your Best Friend and Worst Enemy," Robert McKee describes the sensations of facing an assailant:

> Your mind will have weighed the options: Can you get out of this situation without fighting? Can you talk your way out? Can you turn and walk away? Can you run? Is this a matter worth fighting over? How serious a fight is this going to be, life or death? Are you capable of fighting? What is your emotional commitment to the situation? All of the mental processes and the physiological reactions take place in just seconds. I know it feels like forever, but it's not. It's just a few seconds (74).

The mere shock of the situation and the uncertainty of what an attacker may do is enough to frighten the average citizen, regardless of previous experience in dealing with people on a physical level. A contact sport you played in high school or college is not an adequate criterion on which to judge your ability to handle a street assault. Sports are played by rules, with referees, penalties, and a prize for the winner. Out on the street there are no rules. No umpire will step in, and the only prize is survival itself. It is no wonder that even athletes and other physically well-conditioned people are often victims of assault, immobilized by their own fear. Predicting how someone will react to an assault is difficult, for as Carole Mulhern, director of a victim/witness assistance program says, "People you think will be absolute and total pillars are often the ones who will fall apart" (Mills 1A).

The key to being able to control natural fear in the face of an impending assault is familiarity with the nature of assault (knowing what to expect) and confidence in your ability to handle the threat. By applying the principles of confrontation avoidance, you can have peace of mind from knowing that you are making a calculated, measured response to the situation. You have a good picture of what criminals look for in a victim, where and how they are likely to strike, and what you can do to avoid them. This knowledge about the nature of assault reduces uncertainty and helps you to control your fear. And action itself can help to dispel fear. This is the principle of focusing fear into action, thereby gaining control of the situation instead of being controlled by it.

Some individuals handle the fear of assault through the belief, be it religious or humanistic, that people are basically good. They maintain that people can be reasoned with, and by not appearing as a threat to a potential attacker, they can avoid injury. This modified pacifist approach gambles personal safety on the goodness of humankind. Such a technique may possibly alleviate fear at the moment of confrontation, but it offers little to ease the physical suffering that results if you are wrong about your belief in people's basic kindness. The morgue is full of people who hoped for the best from their attackers and were dead wrong. It usually only takes one mugging, one beating, or one robbery to demonstrate that such an attitude is not realistic. The security that comes from knowing how to protect yourself cannot be equaled. There is no substitute for the confidence and self-control that is a by-product of training in self-defense and conflict avoidance. Yet there is an inherent danger in self-defense training. It is easy to develop a false sense of confidence in your ability, which can lead to carelessness. In some instances, poor or improper self-defense training can actually contribute to injury.

BAD TO THE BONE—BUT NOT BAD ENOUGH

Consider the story of Mike, a young factory worker who lives in New England. He decided in the late seventies that he wanted to learn self-defense. Choosing a karate school near his home, Mike enrolled and paid his tuition for six months. During that training period he was introduced to the basics of karate. When his enrollment ended Mike was feeling good about his ability to protect himself. He decided that he had learned enough. He quit the school to save his money, and planned to practice on his own. Mike saved the tuition all right, but as people often do, he failed to continue his training. He became complacent. Mike paid no heed to his *sensei's* (teacher's) warning that he had only received basic instruction, and that he was not advanced enough to successfully handle many threatening situations. Mike allowed himself to become a six-month wonder. He developed a false sense of confidence in himself and he was sadly disappointed when his skills failed him one year later during an assault. For months after his victimization Mike openly ridiculed karate and all other forms of self-defense, saying they were ineffective and just a bunch of hype.

Improper or misdirected self-defense training can be worse than no training at all. If you are going to forcefully resist an assailant, you had better have some skills, or you are likely to get yourself in a worse situation than had you capitulated. A weak, fearful victim attempting some ineffective counter to an assault will likely succeed in just antagonizing the attacker and making the situation more dangerous.

Through proper self-defense training that emphasizes simple, direct response to attack, the average citizen can gain enough basic knowledge to handle many potentially dangerous situations. As we have learned, given a choice, no one should fight if he or she can avoid it. But often there is no choice. It is then that the confidence derived from solid self-defense instruction can channel your fear into action. The extra energy precipitated by your fear-driven adrenaline flow can be successfully directed against the assailant. But without self-defense knowledge you may not act effectively.

The past 23 years of my life have been spent involved in self-defense instruction. I have had the opportunity to be associated with hundreds of dedicated self-defense students, and I have watched them grow both physically and emotionally. Still, my experience tells me that self-defense training is not for everyone. Some people, due to their personality or religious preference, do not enjoy or progress in self-defense training. They are worthy individuals who have a different direction and focus in their life. It is just not for them. But for the hundreds I have worked with, self-defense training has become another weapon in the arsenal against violent crime, saving many people from certain injury, and producing many byproducts for mental and physical health.

Remember that self-defense, in its legal sense, is conduct that is reasonably regarded by the victim as necessary to defend against what he or she reasonably perceives to be an unlawful and imminent attack upon his or her person (Kadish 947). As seen in the last chapter, a self-defense response not only from a trained martial artist, but also from the average citizen, must be proportionate to the level of threat. I have made it plain that I do not believe in violence as the answer to most instances of stranger assault; indeed, it should be the very last alternative to resolving an encounter with a criminal. Violently executing a physical self-defense technique means that all other options have been unsuccessful, and that there is no choice outside of capitulation that would not result in serious injury or even death. While violence is certainly not the best response to stranger assault, it is definitely an option. Confidence in your ability to execute this option is critical to personal security and overcoming fear. We saw in the last chapter that the kind of fear that citizens express in relation to crime is most often the fear of being injured or killed. We noted that much of that fear is due to lack of knowledge as to what to do when facing an assailant. Building a solid sense of physical security involves learning the concepts of confrontation avoidance. But the job is not complete until you acquire basic skills in self-defense, and you cannot learn that from a book.

Basic skill in self-defense does not mean that everyone should reach black belt proficiency in karate or some other martial art. It does not mean that you have to be 22 years old, six-feet tall, and as strong as a bodybuilder. It means learning when and how to strike opponents to disable or distract them long enough to escape. It means learning how to get away when someone grabs you by the arm or from behind. All of these techniques can be acquired by the average citizen, regardless of age or physical stature (Figures 6.2 and 6.3).

When you face a stranger in an assault situation, your primary goal is to escape unharmed, not to subdue the attacker until the police arrive. The latter idea is the Lone Ranger syndrome.

Figure 6.2. Self-defense training: A supplement to confrontation avoidance. For young and old alike, training in self-defense is a natural step to enhance the ability to survive. Not only does effective self-defense instruction offer quiet self-confidence when facing a potential attacker; it also can provide cardiovascular conditioning and endurance that can spell the difference between living and dying. Judo, karate, taekwondo, and kung-fu are some of the traditional styles of self-defense; but many local police agencies and YMCAs offer a generic course in self-defense that, over a shorter period of time, blends many of the best techniques found in systems that normally take much longer to master.

Figure 6.3. Specific systems meet specific needs. Grappling arts, such as judo (above) or Wing Chun kung-fu (an ancient system maximizing efficiency of motion, designed by a female), emphasize handling an opponent in close. They complement other systems like karate or American boxing, which emphasizes dispatching an opponent at maximum range. Choosing a self-defense system should be based on one's size, strength, and personality, as well as the amount of time available for study.

Many of us grew up watching the Masked Man and his Indian Friend foil the bad guys every week. Clayton Moore single-handedly beat up villains, and the worst punishment he ever received was the momentary loss of his hat. The Lone Ranger syndrome is reflected in many action films today. It is exciting to watch Chuck Norris or Steven Seagal beat up 20 attackers. But remember what it is—entertainment, not self-defense. When Chuck Norris knocks an assailant down, that bad guy receives a healthy paycheck to stay down. The audience expects and enjoys that. No matter how many times the assailant comes after him, the Hollywood hero will ultimately prevail. However, in a real stranger assault, if you knock your assailant to the ground, you had better not be there when he or she gets up. It is foolish to consider waiting around just to have some Hollywood fight-to-the-finish, in which you heroically defeat the offender just as the police roll up with sirens screaming. That is not what self-defense is all about. Self-defense is stopping or inhibiting an offender just long enough to escape the intended crime.

It is the desire to dominate another person that leads many criminals to commit assault, robbery, or rape. But when the assailant fails, or when the attempt is foiled by the intended victim, the balance of power quickly shifts. Bruce, a self-defense student from South Carolina, came upon a prowler in his garage one evening just after dark. He heard a noise he thought was probably the cat, but when he opened the side door to the garage, he saw a shadowy figure duck behind his car.

"Who's there?" he called, but before he could get a response, a stranger emerged from behind his vehicle and came toward him. The streetlight cast enough illumination into the garage for Bruce to see the man swing what turned out to be his son's Little League baseball bat. Pulling himself outside the door, Bruce felt the breeze as the bat crashed into the door facing, splintering wood. Somehow, in his attempt to get out, the prowler tripped and fell—half-in and half-out the door. More importantly, he dropped the bat in the process and Bruce picked it up.

"I felt this sudden sense of power," Bruce told me. "I had the bat and I was between him and escape. He was mine."

Bruce shouted for his wife to call the police and told the man if he moved he'd "bust his head." He must have made a believer of the man, for the prowler didn't challenge Bruce, and, in fact, he seemed glad when the police arrived.

"I was tempted to bust him up a little," Bruce said. "You know, just to teach him a lesson." Bruce wisely chose to use deterrence rather than force (remember the rule of imminent danger and justifiable force), and resisted a Hollywood-style fight to the finish. It is hard to resist using that kind of power in a sense of righteous indignation, but by engaging in an unnecessary battle, Bruce would have run the risk of losing his bat to his opponent, who might not have been so restrained.

Confrontation avoidance is just as surely a form of self-defense as a solid left hook or an eye gouge. You do not have to attack another person to be executing the principles of self-defense; in fact, effective self-protection is 75% mental and only 25% physical.

In the physical aspect of self-defense, there is one basic concept:

Self-defense is making the price someone pays for harming you greater than the reward they receive from doing it.

If attackers discover early in the sequence of events that they are going to get hurt, they may change their minds. It does not always work, but it works quite often. You try to make it cost your assailant more than what the attack is worth.

SELF-DEFENSE IN ACTION

Earl, a Denver truck driver in his late twenties, and one of my self-defense students, related this story to me in 1987. He was driving to a warehouse to make a delivery, when in his rearview mirror he noticed an erratic driver darting in and out of the traffic behind him. The man got behind Earl just before the exit ramp and stayed on his tail as he moved off the expressway and on to a two-way street. The driver kept looking for an opportunity to pass but the oncoming traffic would not allow it. Earl could see the man's face in his mirror and could tell that he was getting rather agitated. When the road widened to four lanes again, Earl started moving over to the right lane to let the man pass. Unfortunately, the driver had already moved into the right lane to pass Earl, and the two narrowly missed a collision. The driver followed Earl a mile or more until he reached the warehouse parking lot, and before Earl was fully out of the van, the driver was on his way toward him, shouting obscenities and threatening him. The conversation went something like this.

"You cut me off, you _____," he screamed. "I ought to knock the _____ out of you, you stupid _____!" (You get the picture.)

Earl took a couple of steps back and tried to apologize, but the man was not listening. He was still yelling and threatening, and it looked like only a matter of seconds before he would attack. Earl's efforts to diffuse the situation were fruitless. Trouble was coming and he did not see how he could avoid it. As the man continued to tell Earl what he was going to do to him, Earl spoke calmly.

"I'm sorry if I almost hit you, but I didn't expect you to be coming around the right side. Now you're a big man, and you can probably hurt me pretty bad. But I promise you it will cost you something. I may not win, but you'll have something to remember me by." As the man kept ranting, Earl took another step back. "It may be an eye, it may be your knee, I don't know. But I'll get something before I go down." The man hesitated momentarily. "It's not worth it, man," Earl said.

The driver looked at Earl and, in an effort to save his ego, said, "You'd just better watch where you're going." He walked back to his car and screeched away.

Earl took a chance in this confrontation. He assessed the situation and when he saw that he was unable to avoid trouble, he quietly and deliberately faced his opponent with the facts. He was able to do this because he felt capable of carrying out his threat against the stranger, and he made sure the stranger knew it. Although Earl never came to blows with the driver, he successfully defended himself. Earl had nothing to prove to anyone, and he had learned through his training that it is foolish and dangerous to feed your ego by means of a fist-fight. He successfully convinced his potential attacker that fighting him was not worth the risk. Being a peaceful person, Earl did not want to get involved in violence; yet if the situation had escalated, he would have responded according to this philosophy:

- AVOID rather than check
- CHECK rather than hurt
- HURT rather than maim
- MAIM rather than kill
- KILL rather than be killed

It does not always work out this well. Sometimes the bad guys are determined to attack you and will not respect your ability to hurt them. They occasionally mistake kindness for weakness. Just remember that you must be able to carry out your promises to an offender, because eventually someone will test your sincerity.

Quality instruction in the physical skills of self-defense is available from numerous sources. Some cities offer self-defense instruction through their adult education programs. The YMCA and other community organizations frequently offer seminars and classes in many locations. Law enforcement agencies provide self-defense training in some cities. Many martial arts schools offer abbreviated courses in the *basics* of self-protection. I emphasize the word basics because the process of learning a martial art to proficiency involves more time and commitment than a short course in self-defense. A good example of the kind of self-defense instruction available to the general public is that offered by Matthew Bayley of Colorado Springs, Colorado. Bayley is a respected security and human resource consultant with years of experience as a martial arts instructor. He teaches his *Citizen-Safe*, a short, intensive self-defense and awareness course, to various community organizations. Bayley and others like him have tailored their instruction for particular high-risk groups, or to address specific threats, such as, self-defense for senior citizens or kidnap/ abduction prevention for children.

Look for instruction in your community that emphasizes both the mental and physical aspects of self-protection, stressing conflict avoidance procedures. Stay away from fly-by-night operations that promise to turn your hands into deadly weapons within a couple of weeks.

If you decide you are interested in pursuing mental and physical discipline through the study of taekwondo, karate, or some other martial art, be prepared to invest in at least one year of steady training to achieve basic proficiency. The expenditure of time and money is greater than that of a short course in self-defense, but then the rewards and the quality of your skill will be greater as well. I am always amazed at how much money people will spend to insure their homes, their cars, their coin collections, or their lives, yet how little time and money they are willing to invest in insuring their safety through basic self-defense training. Skill in self-defense is like a shot of morphine. You may get through your entire life and never need it. But if you ever do need it, you need it immediately, and you need it badly, and nothing else will do.

ARMED AND DANGEROUS

Once reserved for the back pages of detective magazines, items like Mace, tear gas, electric stunners, and handguns are appearing more frequently in advertisements around the country. *Home & Auto Security* magazine not only runs articles on handgun safety and handling, but also advertises Paxton Quigley's book *Armed and Female*, and advertises a number of personal alarms, chemical sprays, and defense systems. An article, "The Body-Guard 3: Personal Security in the Palm of Your Hand," is basically a product-test piece designed to help readers choose a mode of self-protection (May–June, 1993, p. 48). Not only are these weapons appearing in ads, but they are selling briskly to a wide demographic group of frightened citizens, bent on finding some way to balance the scale in a confrontation with an assailant.

> Purveyors of Mace and other chemical weapons are responding [to the public's fear] by moving their wares into the mass market. Hardware-store blister packs of Mace are impulse items next to cash registers. Shoppers can browse among spray cans of tear gas or hot pepper extract, foams that dye an attacker for police identification and—shades of Captain Kirk's phaser weapon—electric stun devices that deliver a knockdown shock (Sussman 82).

Merchants in Virginia and Maryland struggle to keep pepper repellant sprays in stock, and the owner of one gun store there was selling 100 canisters a week in 1992 (Miller 12). Once you have been threatened, you will be more likely to agree with those who say having a weapon will give you peace of mind; but it is equally important to understand the advantages and disadvantages of being armed and dangerous—and preferably more dangerous to the criminal than to yourself.

Citizens are turning to various weapons, not only because they are afraid, but also because these weapons are more readily available in recent years and relatively easy to use. When Sheri Lawless aimed and fired a can of tear gas at an attacker outside her East Orlando apartment building three years ago, she took an active role in self-defense with the help of a popular incapacitating agent. An accurate shot of her Defender Plus stopped a convicted rapist out on parole—a man no doubt planning to make her his next victim (Sussman 82). Like Sheri, many Americans have successfully fought off assailants with the help of gases and sprays; and these people seem pleased to find an alternative short of using a gun. An incapacitating agent generally stops a criminal quickly, but wears off in a few hours with no lasting effects. Since these products are legal in most states, citizens do not have to be law-breakers to feel protected. And feeling safer is a significant goal, particularly in high-crime neighborhoods. Little training is required to use chemical sprays or stun guns, and as long as one is prepared with the device, it can be brought into action immediately. As the owner of a Maine hardware store that sells self-defense sprays said, "Most women don't really want to hurt or kill anyone. They just want to be left alone" (Hoose C11).

But with any weapon, there are dangers. As Detective Sergeant Steve Rutzebeck, former commander of the Maryland State Police Crime Prevention Unit, points out in a *U.S. News & World Report* article,

> Under stress, using *any* weapon is difficult, and *no* weapon offers 100 percent protection. The wind can blow a chemical spray back in your face; a drug-crazed assailant might use your weapon against you. Even experienced police officers often freeze when confronted by an attacker. Of the police officers shot on duty, more than 20 percent are assaulted with their own guns (Sussman 82).

Craig Silverman, a chief deputy district attorney in Colorado, warns, "If you have a fight between somebody with a can of Mace and the other person has a gun, I'll bet on the person with the gun. [A defense spray has] the potential of prompting him to kill you" (Seipei C9). Why is there always a downside? Just when you thought a can of chemical spray might be the right choice, you go and read something like that. But do not give up on weapons just yet. Let us examine the different types of nonlethal weapons and weigh their advantages and disadvantages.

Chemical Sprays

Tear Gas and Pepper Sprays.   Tear gas or Mace (a trademark of Manufacturer of Security Items [MSI]) causes an assailant to choke, amid watering eyes and a burning sensation on the face, provided *you hit the face*. Miss with this stuff and you have an even angrier assailant determined to finish you off. Hitting the bad guy on the arms will certainly sting him, but it may not stop him. Still, tear gas is effective up to five yards—well outside your personal defensive space—and can serve as an effective equalizer. Pepper spray (made from hot pepper extract) absolutely must be delivered into the attacker's face, and it will often stop a drunken or mentally deranged assailant where tear gas will fail. The bad news is that pepper spray usually doesn't have the range of tear gas spray; thus you must be closer to the assailant for the spray to be effective. Solution? Look for a spray that combines the two chemicals. Remember that tear gas and pepper sprays are illegal in New York, Wisconsin, and Washington, D.C. If you live in California, you must pass a state-certifying course to carry Mace. One other type of spray is called DYEWitness, a green foam that stains the skin and obscures vision. The theory behind this weapon is that the assailant, once aware he is marked with a semipermanent dye, will reconsider his intended action and stop the assault (Sussman 88). More than 75% of all self-defense sprays are purchased by women, and a canister usually sells for between 10 and 15 dollars (Hoose C11). According to Al Stutman, an ex-police officer and owner of a law enforcement supply company in Aurora, Colorado, "chemical sprays can't kill attackers but it kind of puts their mind somewhere else . . . If a male has certain ideas of doing something to female, and they're hit with this, they'll be concentrating on breathing instead" (Seipei C9).

Electric Stunners. Pressing the button on an electric stun gun creates a crackling, blue-light static arc that might just frighten a criminal away without your having to actually physically apply the high-voltage weapon. At the very least, it immediately informs your assailant that you may be a harder target than he or she originally planned on. If the bad guy is still not dissuaded, a quick zap with the stun gun can cause enough pain to compel a hasty withdrawal. A jolt of three to five seconds can drop an attacker like a hot rock, provided you get close enough to use it and are willing to maintain contact for that long. Five seconds can seem like an eternity in the grasp of a criminal bent on assault or rape; and it is precisely this proximity to the attacker that is the biggest disadvantage of a stunner. Usually the first application of voltage will stun and incapacitate, but if it takes another shot, can you keep your opponent from taking the stunner away from you? Although some would argue that having to cause pain to another person is also a deterrent to using a stun gun, I have found that once a person's life or health is seriously threatened, the humanitarian concern for the criminal's well-being fades in the blink of an eye.

Personal Alarms. As a supplemental device, or perhaps for that rare person who cannot do harm to another human being, regardless of the attacker's intent, there is another option—the hand-held personal alarm. Nonviolent in its application, it requires no physical contact with the assailant, and its ear-piercing shriek (up to 120 decibels) can draw the attention of others and compel a nervous bad guy to retreat from the scene. Detective Carrolyn Priest of Denver, Colorado recommends these alarm devices. "Most police will tell you criminals don't like noise or bright lights," Priest says (Seipei C10). The good news is that this weapon cannot be used against you; and one of these siren-driven alarms can be carried—finger on the switch—to and from your car or while you are walking a particularly threatening stretch of city street. The bad news? When was the last time you got excited about an auto alarm going off in a crowded city?

Keep in mind that you can carry all the sprays, stunners, and alarms you can fit into your purse or pockets, and you will still be vulnerable to assault if you are not paying attention to what is going on around you. Never depend solely on a weapon to protect yourself; have some other strategies in mind as well.

GUNS—THE PROS AND CONS

It inevitably comes up in a discussion about street crime. One person bemoans the terrible state of our society and the fact that you cannot walk down the street without fearing for your life, then another points out that if we all carried guns, we could put a stop to crime. We could feel safer. Criminals would know we are all armed and they would reconsider their chances of successfully assaulting us. Guns are a deterrent, he says, and carrying one gives you a feeling of power and security that nothing else can match. Everybody should have a gun, as big a gun as they want, and they should be allowed to carry it anywhere. But still another citizen has heard enough. She can't stand anymore of this crazy talk, so she rattles off a couple of horror stories about children who have been killed by loaded guns left lying around the house, and tops it off with a quick anecdote about how a woman accidently shot her husband, thinking he was a burglar.

Such is the rhetoric surrounding gun ownership, and unfortunately it is usually characterized by heated, slanted, extremist posturing, with little regard for dealing with the facts and realities of self-defense. Pro-gun and anti-gun lobbyists spend millions of dollars each year trying to convince the government to legislate their particular versions of what is best for the rest of us. Rather than fuel that debate, let us consider the advantages and disadvantages of using a gun for self-defense.

People who would promote throughout a wide spectrum of our society the possession of handguns, rifles, and even assault weapons, with little or no regulation, would have you believe they are working in your best interests. By opposing any legislation restricting ownership of handguns, they want you to believe they are preserving the essence of your constitutional right to bear arms. They try to convince you that the number and type of handguns available, for instance, the "Saturday Night Special," has nothing to do with the amount of crime in our society; and that "guns don't kill people, people kill people."

Citizen beware!

Common sense tells you that the availability of guns *must* be a factor in the crime rate and that a gun in the hands of a criminal makes it easier and quicker to take a life than a sharpened avocado in the same hands. No, guns don't kill people, but people do kill

people *with guns*. Responsible gun legislation is not only appropriate, it is a must if we are to get our streets under control. As a
soldier I have seen what a bullet can do to a human being, and the
thought of an innocent bystander, or even an unsupervised child,
being shot with a hollow-point round is enough to make me sick.
Far too many children and adults die in this country every year
because of gun accidents. The *New England Journal of Medicine*'s
1986 study found that "for every case of self-protection homicide
involving a gun kept in the home, there were 1.3 accidental deaths"
(Rossi 68). Think back to the notion of everyone carrying a gun. Stop
right now and think about the three dumbest, most irresponsible
people you know. Name them aloud to yourself. Now I ask you,
would you really feel safer if you knew they were carrying a gun?

On the other hand, guns do offer a sense of security to many
citizens who would otherwise be too terrified to live a normal life.
A 27-year-old marketing director living in Fairfax, Virginia, isn't
advertising the fact that she has purchased a handgun and is
learning to handle it safely at the Gilbert Small Arms Range in
Newington.

> The first time she fired the .357 Magnum, the woman
> fought back tears. In class, however, she was collected. After
> lots of thought, she said, she decided she could shoot to kill.
> "I would never want to have to use it," she said. "I would
> probably not have an easy time afterward . . . It really upsets
> me that I have to get to this point (Miller).

Over 70 million Americans own handguns, and "the Federal
government estimates that half of all homes in the United States
contain one or more firearms" (Paige 33). The Maryland State
Police, for example, processed some 29,000 applications for firearms licenses for a period in 1992—a period that saw only 4,000
such applications the previous year (Miller). During the Los Angeles riots, the television screen was replete with images of grocery store owners clutching weapons as they stood in defense of
their lives and property, and many will tell you unashamedly that
they and their guns were the *only* deterrents to looters and

criminals run amok over an overwhelmed police department. Many responsible Americans own guns, safeguard their guns, and have gone to the trouble to learn how to use them safely. But Hollywood would have us believe otherwise. From this medium we see a determined agenda—an agenda to declare anyone who could even consider guns as a viable alternative for self-protection as some kind of unbalanced throwback to a more primitive society. Can you recall a TV drama or miniseries that has not portrayed private-citizen gun owners as shallow, irresponsible, vindictive, impetuous, short-tempered characters? Gun owners, like deeply religious people portrayed on television, are frequently made out to be buffoons, unable to intelligently articulate their views. From sitcoms, to detective shows, to made-for-TV-movies, there is a recurrent message—leave the guns to the police and keep them away from these foolish citizens. Inevitably in these television shows, the wise anti-gun spokesman must condescend to the narrow-minded gun owner and bring him or her to the politically correct realization that the gun poses an undue threat to himself or herself, his or her family, and society. Yet it was amazing how quickly the politically correct residents of the Hollywood Hills started blocking off their streets and walking guard with semi-automatic rifles as the Los Angeles riots grew more intense. Television and movie scriptwriters and producers acting as self-appointed guardians of us all are leading us to a warped, mis-guided picture of the value of guns in self-protection, and must be balanced with a little healthy reality.

Yes, guns are dangerous; and unless you learn how to use one correctly and safeguard its whereabouts, it will probably be more dangerous to you than to anyone else. But with proper training, a cautious attitude, and a healthy respect for the potential of such a weapon, it is possible to own a gun and use it responsibly for self-protection. Everyone who owns a gun is not a paramilitary kook, ready to squeeze the trigger at the slightest provocation. Most of the gun owners I know are quiet, responsible, thoughtful individuals who hope they will never have to fire a round in anger. But they have trained themselves in the art of shooting, and they are

confident that if the situation demands they must protect themselves or their family, and they have no other alternative, they can
effectively and safely handle the weapon.

"The last thing I would want to do is shoot somebody," Phillip
Anderson, a night clerk at a major motel chain, once told me. "But
I've been going to the range, and if I have to, at 50 feet I can put
four out of six rounds in a spot the size of an orange, and I've got
to admit, it feels pretty good to know that."

The National Rifle Association runs thousands of gun training classes every year, and local gun clubs in many cities will not
only teach citizens to shoot but also will explain the law governing
when and how an individual may carry a gun.

More and more women in our society are turning to guns as a
personal weapon of choice. Gun clubs—formerly the primary
domain of men—are seeing a tremendous growth in female
membership. Portland, Oregon's *The Place to Shoot*, which opened
in 1991, now says that 37% of its 17,000 members are women. Chris
Dolnack, a spokesman for Smith & Wesson firearms manufac-
turers, says that about one out of six adult females presently owns
a gun (Rossi 66), and the May 12, 1992, *Orlando Sentinel* cites a
Gallup survey that indicates 12.1 million American women own
handguns, 90% of them owning these guns for self-defense.
While there will surely be accidents among this demographic
group, all of these women are not misinformed and misguided
citizens in need of some anti-gun lobbyist's counsel. Many of
them are intelligent, competent women in search of some peace of
mind amid the growing threat of crime. Paxton Quigley has
written *Armed and Female*, a popular book among those women
who have turned to guns for security. A former dedicated gun
control lobbyist, who labored to found the National Committee for
Handgun Control, and a worker in the Robert Kennedy campaign,
Quigley changed her mind about guns when a close friend was
viciously raped. Now the instructor of an intensive, street-related
shooting course, Quigley says that one third of her students
signed up for her course after suffering an attack themselves or

"living through an experience with a friend" (Rossi 68). In *Armed and Female*, Quigley cites some frightening statistics, for instance, if you are a female over age 12 you will be criminally assaulted at least once in your life; if you are aged 30, you run a 50–50 risk of being raped. Her book makes interesting reading as it features a number of interviews and personal testimonials about the role and value of firearms for self-defense. Amid the barrage of anti-gun rhetoric, Quigley offers a much needed balance to the question of whether or not to own a firearm.

But as Sonny Jones, editor of *Women and Guns* magazine, warns,

> Some women buy a gun, have a gun dealer load it at the store, then drop it in their purse and forget about it. Some people think that a gun is a magic totem that will ward off all evil. That's a dangerous misconception (Rossi 70).

Jones and others like her would agree that, for men or women, learning to use a gun safely and effectively—not just owning a gun—is the key to self-defense.

When Robert Bizon got tired of burglars breaking into his garage, he decided to set a trap to catch them. When his alarm went off one night in 1991, he grabbed his .357 Magnum revolver and confronted the thieves outside. They took off running and Bizon ordered them to stop. When they didn't, he fired four rounds, one of which struck James Ashcroft, 17, in the hip. While the boy lay there bleeding from a severed artery, Bizon questioned him, refusing to allow the young man's accomplice to call for help until he had obtained his information. The boy eventually died of the wound and Bizon was charged with involuntary manslaughter (Treen 42).

The boy committed a crime by robbing Robert Bizon. Bizon had a right to protect his property, but it is just this kind of incident that lends credence to the Hollywood-induced paranoia about gun ownership. Bizon had threatened "to shoot anyone who came on his land," and was described by his own lawyer, Peter

Langrock, as "a kind of Rambo" (Treen 42). While a jury found Bizon not guilty of involuntary manslaughter, he still must face a wrongful-death suit brought by the boy's parents.

We must keep in mind a delicate balance here. People like Bizon are the exception, not the rule, when it comes to using a gun in self-defense. A young make-up artist in northern California, Julie, had logged numerous hours at a shooting range to ready herself should an incident require her to use her gun in self-defense. The test of her skill and judgment came when a man, having stalked her for several weeks, eventually confronted her. Her assailant had been peeping at her, appearing and disappearing outside her bedroom windows, for several months—always managing to escape before the police could arrive. Although she was frightened by his presence, and though she frequently had her .22 Magnum ready, she wisely opted not to shoot at her stalker while he was outside her home—even when he eventually tried to kick her door down. Wisely, she called 911 and waited. Had she fired upon her intruder while he was outside, she would have, in many states, been subject to prosecution. What is known in Colorado as the "Make My Day Law" (coined after the popular Clint Eastwood line in a *Dirty Harry* movie) demands that an assailant be physically within the walls of your home before you can apply deadly force. At any rate, the police arrived at Julie's home, but, alas, not in time to catch her stalker. They only frightened him away. Even with Julie possessing a gun and knowing how to use it, the trauma from the encounter was overwhelming (Rossi 70).

> Seven years later and several states away from her initial trauma, she still carries [her gun] with her late at night and stashes the loaded weapon beside her bed. "If anyone breaks in here," she says, "I'm going to shoot. And I'll keep shooting until they're dead" (Rossi 70).

If Julie's attitude may seem callous, consider what she has been through, and consider also that most gun instructors are adamant about the resolve to shoot. If you are not willing to pull the trigger in the critical instant of assault, a gun may be your worst enemy. The assailant may take it away from you and use it on you or your family. If you decide to own a gun, get training with it and be prepared to use it. Load it and keep it stored safely. An unloaded gun is potentially more dangerous than a loaded gun, particularly if you think you can display it before an attacker and frighten him or her away. Nothing infuriates a person more than having a gun pointed at him or her, and once your attacker discovers the weapon is unloaded, you have set yourself up for big trouble. As professional gun instructor Jo Anne Aune says,

> You have to have the mind-set that it's going to be them instead of you . . . You should be prepared to shoot to kill, and if you're not, you have no business owning a gun" (Rossi 70).

It would be arrogant and condescending for me to suggest, as have many writers, that possessing a gun is somehow contributing to the crime problems—that carrying a gun will not improve your chances of surviving an assault, and that your belief that you are somehow safer is a farce. Likening responsible gun owners to street gang members, that is, in the proliferation of firearms, is narrow-minded and bigoted. Still, it is important for every person to consider his or her own personality, a willingness to be trained, and a vulnerability to crime before deciding upon firearms in self-defense. But you can and should have the right to make that choice for yourself.

Chapter Seven

RAPE

The crime of rape has its own category within the FBI and Justice Department Crime Statistics. Because of its specific nature as a sex crime, rape is not characterized as an assault, and as such, it is not included in the figures on simple and aggravated assault. But of all the crimes against people, rape is one of the most humiliating, degrading, and psychologically damaging. It carries with it a sense of viciousness and callous disregard for individual rights. Stitches can close the gash that someone's fist makes above your eye, and a few extra hours of overtime will replace the money that a thief takes from your wallet; but the violation of the sanctity of the human body that a rape victim experiences remains long after the attacker has departed.

The fear of being raped is one of the most prominent concerns among women (Table 7.1), and is a major contributor to the National Victim Center's finding that 73% of women say they limit the places they go to by themselves (Peden 78). While there are cases of men being raped, the vast majority of rape victims are women. Researchers tell us that the threat of rape is a central and consuming concern among all women. Not only do women fear the violence of the act itself, and the accompanying physical pain,

TABLE 7.1. Most Prominent Fears among Women

1. Being hit by a drunk driver
2. Being raped
3. Discovering your child has been abducted
4. Finding out your child has been sexually abused[a]
5. Having the car break down while you are driving alone at night
6. Awakening to find an intruder in your home[a]
7. Being mugged at gunpoint
8. Finding out that a bomb may be aboard the plane you're on
9. Being poisoned by food or medication that has been illegally tampered with
10. Being the victim of a violent racial attack

[a]The response actually tied with the one immediately preceding it.
Note: Notice how many of these fears revolve around what a stranger might do to an unsuspecting victim. All the more reason to remain alert and prepared!
SOURCE: *McCall's,* May 1992, p. 78.

but they dread the emotional cost of violation. Many fear they will somehow be held responsible for the rape—for either causing it or for not preventing it (Keenan 2). A man cannot claim to fully understand the feelings of a woman who has been raped. He can only imagine the unique mental and physical trauma that such a woman experiences. Men can only hope to empathize with the woman, in a very narrow sense, for the physical results of the crime and for the fear that persists beyond the crime. Laura Kaufman, chair of the Chicago Sexual Assault Services Network, says,

> If, in fact, you happen to be born a woman, that means that for the rest of your life you have to make decisions that limit your actions, because you're worried you're going to experience violence (Keenan 2).

But just because males cannot fully comprehend what a woman experiences with rape, it does not mean they cannot appreciate the heartache, sorrow, and suffering. Men can certainly try to understand the problem, although they may not be able to completely identify with it.

Joseph Weinberg, past president of Men Stopping Rape and now the operator of a Wisconsin-based rape prevention/education program, says:

> Rape is rooted in a society that teaches people of both genders that women are objects whose purpose is sex and that it's men's role to get it. That message is echoed throughout the culture: in advice from fathers to sons ("Just don't get her pregnant") and from mothers to daughters ("All men want is sex") . . . (Read 7A).

Weinberg says that when men declare rape to be a woman's issue, they fail to realize how they, too, are hurt by the crime, for example, by worrying about a sister or other family member, or perhaps by marrying a woman who has been raped (Read 7A). But Mr. Weinberg, for all his cogent points about men and rape awareness, goes overboard when he suggests that "significant numbers of us [men], perhaps half, have done something that would qualify legally as rape" (Read 7A). Weinberg may speak for himself, and perhaps even for many he has interviewed, but I doubt he has insight into, or proxy to speak for, half the men in the United States.

Because rape is a growing threat in our society, and because of the increase in acquaintance rape as well as stranger rape, the subject is important enough to stray from the stated plan of dealing primarily with stranger assault, to address both the stranger and the nonstranger aspects of this heinous crime. Many women who study self-defense with me share their fear of someday being raped, and much of their motivation to learn self-defense and confrontation avoidance techniques is prompted by the desire to avoid the situation entirely, or at the very least, to be prepared to deal with it should it occur. They share with me their sense of outrage at the idea that an assailant, in a moment of rage or misdirected passion, could violate the sanctity of their body and disrupt their life. They do not want to be powerless to stop it. By paying close attention to what women say, studying the circumstances that combine to create a rape situation, examining the types of individuals who commit rape, and what behaviors help a potential victim to avoid a rape, women can prepare themselves for many possible confrontations. Tools of avoidance *may* work in some situations, but keep in mind that there is no advice that will apply in every circumstance.

There are really only two ways to avoid rape—either deny the assailant an opportunity to initiate his crime, or escape or disable an attacker once he has begun the assault. You will hear from me no mindless platitudes or magic formulas, since each situation is different. Do not listen to anyone, whether he or she is a law enforcement official, a self-defense instructor, or a mental health worker, who tries to tell you what you should *always* do in every rape situation. Advice like that is replete with danger. You, the potential victim, are the only person who can decide what response you will make in the event of a sexual assault, and since each woman has her own personal agenda and value system, there will be as many varied responses as there are people.

Some women say, "There is no way I'm going to let myself be raped," or, "Someone would have to kill me first!" They mean that statement with every fiber of their being, and as long as they are conscious and able to resist, they will attempt to resist their attacker. But what if they are not conscious? What if they have been knocked out or otherwise incapacitated, so that the rapist can continue his attack? You must be very careful making claims about what you will *never* allow to happen to you. Other women believe that their life is worth more to them than the sanctity of their body, and they would rather submit to a rapist than lose their life. Those who would submit are just as serious about their choice as the group claiming to never submit; but some of the people who make broad, sweeping declarations about how they will act find themselves doing just the opposite.

Linda, a dietician at a Chicago hospital, was a rape victim in 1986. She was 21 years old at the time of the attack. She tells how some of her friends became angry with her for not reacting to the rape in the manner *they* thought appropriate. "I would've scratched his eyes out," one friend told her. But that friend was not the person raped, and Linda speaks of the turmoil such remarks cause.

> I tell people the guy was threatening to kill me. If lying there would have kept me alive, then that's what I would have done. I know now their [the friends] reactions are their only defense mechanisms. They are so afraid, they convince themselves that somehow they could get out of the situation. Even if I didn't. I've learned that if people are not supportive, it's because they're terrified (Keenan 2).

And the rape prevention community has been peddling some myths about resistance that shall be shortly exposed—myths that have led many women to some false choices. Between the two extremes is a reasonable position that most women can live with. This viewpoint is based on an informed mind—a mind aware of the advantages, disadvantages, and risks of various courses of action. It is an attitude that bases avoidance techniques on the "Three P's": *Place*, *Personality* and *Perpetrator*. Self-defense instructors, like myself, lean toward active measures of rape prevention, but we are not so naive as to believe that Mom's standby advice to her daughters—a swift kick in the groin—will stop every rapist in every situation. Successful rape avoidance, and successful self-defense for that matter, involves a person maintaining an alert mind and controlling fear, while implementing a series of options to stop the attacker. Some of the techniques may be active and some passive, but when combined, they can be most effective. But before we closely examine those Three P's, let us consider some of the demographics of rape and its victims.

According to the 1991 Uniform Crime Reports published by the FBI, in the United States there is a woman raped every five minutes (4). That is a sad commentary on our society. Between 1983 and 1985 the incidence of reported rapes increased 3.7%. From 1989 to 1990 rape increased another 3% (*Sourcebook—1991* 252). Some of this increase can be attributed to better reporting of the crime, as attitudes about rape and rape victims began to be modified for the better. But rape is still on the increase. The familiar image of rape involving a lone woman accosted by a stranger in a dark alley has been betrayed, turning out to be the minority of cases, since the term rape has been expanded to encompass a wider range of forced sexual activity. We now know that date rape and spouse rape constitute the predominant rape experience, so let us focus first on nonstranger or acquaintance rape.

NONSTRANGER RAPE

Over the past two decades, most of the broad-based studies that analyzed rape avoidance, statistically recording the instances of rape, have concentrated on rape by strangers. A study by the Queens Bench Foundation (1976) found that 81% of rape victims were assaulted by a stranger. In P. B. Bart and P. H. O'Brien's 1981 study of rape avoidance, 78% of the victims were attacked by strangers. Block and Skogan's data indicate that 82% of rape victims were attacked by strangers. If left to consider these figures alone, you would conclude that most women are raped by strangers. That is not the case. As rape reporting procedures improve and the stigma of the crime is modified via public information, more and more victims are coming forward with their stories. Scholars and researchers are now arguing that non-stranger rape is the predominant form of the crime. Amir, in his book *Patterns in Forcible Rape* (1971), claimed that rape victims and offenders were acquainted in up to 50% of all rape cases; and when you consider instances of "hidden rape victims," or victims who did not report their experiences to authorities, up to 76% of the victims knew their attacker (Levine-MacCombie & Koss 312). The 1989 Bureau of Justice Statistics indicates only 34% of all rapes were by acquaintances, but that is likely to be a very conservative measurement (*Sourcebook—1990* 265).

Wade out of the ankle-deep statistics and what you find is that we as a nation have a much bigger problem with acquaintance or nonstranger rape than we believed in the past. As our understanding of the crime increases, we are better able to categorize the various rape situations, and this enables us to draw an emerging picture of a crime that is multifaceted and complicated. Our response to the crime can be no less multifaceted and flexible.

The following are some subcategories of rape:

Nonromantic rape is defined as a rape situation in which the two parties are acquainted but demonstrate no romantic (e.g., they are not dating) inclinations toward one another. This category is also seen by some as addressing a more anonymous type of sexual assault that precipitates from men and women meeting at a social function, such as the college social scene. One such victim described her encounter this way:

> My senior year in high school I visited a girlfriend who was a freshman at the time. I was at a party, got very drunk, got separated from my friend and ended up going back to a guy's apartment, and although I said "No" many times, he [had sex with] me. I was too young to know or say anything (Ward et al. 66).

Other researchers opt for a special category to describe these rape situations: party rape. Party rape does not involve an acquaintance in the traditional sense, but more closely resembles stranger rape, in that the two individuals are part of the same social community. S. K. Ward, Kathy Chapman, and a team of researchers say in their 1990 study on "Acquaintance Rape and the College Social Scene," that the *context* rather than the acquaintance separates stranger from nonstranger rape—two people may be relative strangers yet both be part of the same social scene (66). They may even have been introduced, and perhaps had a brief conversation, but they remain, in effect, strangers to one another. That which offers commonality is not a shared past or even a working knowledge of one another—it is their simultaneous presence at the same social gathering.

Casual date rape is an instance where two people may have been out on one or two dates before the rape occurs—more than a casual acquaintance, but less than a steady dating relationship.

Further, date rape is defined as "nonaggravated sexual assault, nonconsensual sex that does not involve physical injury, or the explicit threat of physical injury" (Pineau 217). Presently, the judicial system seems stacked against a woman who experiences date rape. Bringing a complaint of sexual assault against someone is an uphill battle, largely because of the present legal view of consent. A woman is generally considered to have offered consent unless she makes some "emphatic episodic sign of resistance" (Pineau 220), and that resistance can be verified. So unless you actively resist, and you can show that such resistance took place, you will have a tough time proving a case against your attacker.

Steady date rape is a rape situation where two people have been seeing each other over a period of time and have established a relationship beyond the casual.

Spouse or family rape involves violation of the family member in a forced sexual encounter.

Regardless of the label pinned on it, rape is a disgusting, degrading crime; but understanding the various shades of the offense can help you better forge the weapons you need to protect yourself.

The terms "sexual aggression" and "rape," while not synonymous, are closely related. The distance from forced kissing/fondling to forced intercourse requires neither a great mental nor a great physical leap. If a man convinces himself that a woman enters into some contractual obligation whenever she behaves in a seductive manner, he is liable to cross the line of sexual aggression. Men who view coquettish behavior as striking some kind of unspoken contract between a man and a woman are laboring under one of the major myths that contribute to rape. Promises do not make for a legitimate legal contract, much less a personal one; and even in a legal contract, one party is not allowed to use physical force to exact payment from the other. Both parties must agree to what they are engaging in and then only after sufficient time for reflection. If the woman subsequently changes her mind and informs her partner, and the man continues the act, he commits assault. Under common law, "a person cannot consent to aggravated assault"; thus, the notion of contractual agreement by consent of both parties is invalid. According to Lois Pineau, writing for *Law and Philosophy* (1989), even when a woman does agree to sex, that initial agreement does not give the man *carte blanche* to force any activity he chooses (229–230). Still, a woman is wise who carefully watches a sexual encounter as it is developing. Where uninvited and undesired sexual aggression is tolerated in its initial stages, it is usually only a matter of time until rape is attempted. That is not to say that a woman is "asking for it" when she engages in sexually provocative behavior, as such behavior does not generate a contract on which she must make good; but in all fairness, a woman cannot on the one hand claim to be an equal partner in a sexual encounter, having equal say in its outcome, and then claim no responsibility for creating conditions conducive to sexual aggression. As indicated in the book, *Coping with Date Rape and Acquaintance Rape* (1988), by Dr. Andrea Parrot, Clinical Assistant Professor of Psychiatry at the State University of New York (SUNY) Health Services Center in Syracuse, New York,

> when you have decided what you want sexually, you must communicate that clearly, giving the same message with your words and your body language. If you really don't want to have sex with him, don't tell him that you just want to be friends while you let him unbutton your blouse (91).

Dr. Parrot indicates that women have the responsibility of resisting societal conditioning to be shy and nonassertive, and of saying what they really mean—sending unmistakable signals to their partner.

> Don't tell him that you don't want to have sex because you don't have any means of birth control; he may have a condom (rubber) in his wallet. If you don't want to have sex, make that clear with time parameters, such as, "I don't go to bed on the first date," or "I want to wait until marriage." If you say, "I don't want to have sex right now," he may think that five minutes later will be all right (91).

The questions of "How far is too far?" and "When does aggressive sexual activity become a crime?" are not just questions that men must take a stab at and hope they are right. This is not a carnival shell game where someone is supposed to guess which shell the pea is under. Women have the responsibility—not as sexual gatekeepers, but as equal respondents in a mutually sought-after encounter—to help draw and enforce the ground rules.

When young men and women, each with differing culturally induced expectations for sexual role-playing, find themselves in private situations, you have the ingredients for miscommunication. Studies of sexual communication and perception, like those of A. Abbey in *Journal of Personality and Social Psychology* (1982), tell us that men are more likely to view the world in sexual terms and more likely to misinterpret sexual communication in their partner (Abbey 837). In one study, 72% of the women and 60% of the men reported being misperceived, usually at a party or with a casual friend (Ward et al. 70). While both sexes are guilty of clouding the line between platonic friendliness and sexually provocative behavior, men are more likely to interpret a gesture of cordiality as sexual attraction. According to Joseph Weinberg, the rape-prevention educator mentioned previously,

> To prove their masculinity men learn to lie about their sexual activity, to talk about sex in crude and violent language and to refer to it as something done *to* a woman rather than *with* her. They learn that it's the woman's job to say no if she doesn't want sex and that "real men don't ask" (Read 7A).

Not *all* men, Mr. Weinberg, but certainly many, do evidence this approach.

The ambiguity of these questions of "How far is too far?" resounds throughout high school and college campuses, and female students have the victimization rates to show for the uncertainty. Up to 83% of the university females in one survey had experienced offensive sexual advances by males (Amick & Calhoun, 153). Mary Koss, writing in the *Psychology of Women Quar-*

terly (1988), indicates that a 1984 sampling of 930 San Francisco victims showed that 88% of them knew their offenders (2).

According to Koss, one of the factors complicating acquaintance rape is that it often takes a woman longer to recognize when an encounter with an acquaintance is progressing toward rape. She has a "greater investment in not labeling that situation as rape" (Koss 2). Koss is not suggesting that a woman causes a rape or even allows it, but that facing the reality of the situation is more difficult with an acquaintance. Still, a note of caution is in order. For example, a 1985 survey done by *Ms* magazine, and financed by the National Institute of Mental Health, found that 73% of "women categorized as rape victims did not initially define their experience as rape; it was Mary Koss the psychologist conducting the study, who did" (Roiphe 28). As Katie Roiphe points out in a June 13, 1993, article in *The New York Times Magazine*, these survey questions define rape loosely, attributing fault to a man if he gave alcohol or other drugs to the woman. Roiphe sounds an alarm against the erosion of women's responsibility in social situations:

> If we assume that women are not all helpless and naive, then they should be held responsible for their choice to drink or take drugs. If a woman's "judgment is impaired" and she has sex, it isn't necessarily always the man's fault; it isn't necessarily always rape" (28).

If anyone misconstrues the developing nature of a rape situation it is probably the male. As Judith Bridges points out in "Attributions of Responsibility for Date and Stranger Rape," in *Sex Roles* (1991), males tend to attribute behaviors or draw inferences based on their understanding of social sex roles. When 62 college students read and responded to one of three rape scenarios—for instance, steady dating partners, acquaintances on the first date, and strangers—the men in the groups tended to see women as gatekeepers for sexual activity, and more often to perceive sexual intent in a social situation (304). They apply these expectations more widely to date rape than to stranger rape. As common sense would indicate, victims are more likely to call their rape encounter with an acquaintance a "miscommunication" than they are with a stranger; but equal numbers of both casual and steady date rape victims attribute the act to miscommunication. Both men and women tend to view the victim of a steady date rape as being less psychologically damaged than the victim of a stranger rape. This unrealistic view often translates into less sympathy and a greater difficulty in proving the crime (Bridges, 395).

Remember: Women have the right to dress as they please, to consent to sex and (before or during the act) to change their mind. They have the right to be treated with respect; but they have the responsibility to talk openly and honestly about their sexual expectations and intentions, to assert themselves and stand up for their rights, and to take a mutually active role in defining a relationship. Men must keep in mind that buying a woman dinner or taking her out for the evening does not give them the right to force her into sex—even if you have had sex with that individual before (*Date Rape* 8–9). Weinberg argues,

> When I assume that because [a woman] doesn't say "no," she means "yes," I'm taking a tremendous risk. I would rather hear "no" than hear later that she thinks I raped her . . . Do we want to be men who are dangerous and stupid, or do we want to be people? (Read 7A).

Meanwhile, Roiphe offers a much needed corrective to this difficult area of women's responsibility when she says,

> The idea that only an explicit yes means yes proposes that, like children, women have trouble communicating what they want. Beyond its dubious premise about the limits of female communication, the idea of active consent bolsters stereotypes of men just out to "get some" and women who don't really want any (30).

AVOIDANCE STRATEGIES AND VINCIBILITY

The rape avoidance strategies, which I discuss, will work in some instances and be ineffective in others. But I will offer you some criteria by which to evaluate various situations to determine the best option for avoiding rape.

A Case of Stranger Rape

The student newspaper of a major university reported the following incident in September of 1988.

> The incident occurred at 1:55 A.M. while the victim was walking home along west on Devine Street. The 18-year-old female freshman had just left the Five Points area bar, Pugs, and, according to the [city] police report, she then decided to walk up Devine Street rather than walk up Blossom Street, which has no sidewalk. [Devine street was also poorly lit.] She was passing the about 3-foot-high wall that is in front of . . . a home for senior citizens on Devine Street, when the attacker briskly came up to her from behind. She was then forced to climb over the wall into the nearby shrubbery on the western side of the building. The victim said her attacker told her he had a pistol and would kill her if she did not cooperate. She immediately went to a [h]ospital where she was examined and looked after by a rape crisis team. No bruises were found on the victim (*Gamecock*, September 1988).

This young woman came to the university to get an education and take advantage of her opportunities in life; instead, she was victimized by an individual with no respect for the dignity or human rights of others. You cannot blame a rape upon the victim. But while the victim is not responsible for the mad act of a felon, we know from the principles of confrontation avoidance and the factors of vincibility that certain actions enhance our chance of being assaulted (that is, the "lifestyles and routine activity theories" of criminal victimization). In this case the victim was single, female, and alone. Assuming she had consumed alcohol, her V-factor was at three the moment she left the bar. When you consider that she was walking on a poorly lighted street at 1:30 in the morning, her V-factor was actually four. Unfortunately, despite the warnings of security officials and the publicity surrounding this rape, a second female was raped two weeks later, within five blocks of the first location. Like the previous victim, this woman was also walking alone from a tavern at 1:30 A.M.

TYPES OF RESISTANCE

Just as conflict avoidance involves considering the factors of behavior, circumstance, attacker, and victim, so does the choice of whether or not to resist a rape. By understanding rape situations and your options as a defender, you can select a reasonable response that will have a good chance of successfully thwarting an assailant.

> Victim resistance makes rape completion more difficult, that is, it raises the cost of rape. It increases the effort required of the rapist to complete the act, and it can prolong the time required and thereby increase the risk of discovery by other parties and of capture by the police. Further, when resistance is forceful, it can raise the probability of the offender suffering injury and pain (Kleck & Sayles 149).

Reviewing the statistics of rape and studying how people have effectively avoided the crime demonstrates what works and what does not. But after all the books are read, all the television shows are watched, and all the seminars are attended, the response to a rape attempt comes down to one thing: your individual, informed choice based upon the facts.

When you compare people who successfully avoided rape with those who did not, several distinctions appear. Avoiders of both stranger and acquaintance rape:

1. were less likely to experience passive or internalizing emotions at the time of assault;
2. perceived the assault as less violent;
3. were more likely to have used active response strategies (Levine-Macombie & Koss 311);

4. knew how to cope with life as an adult, for instance, knew first aid, or how to put out a grease fire, and thus were more likely to know self-defense (Kotulak 1).

We already know that fear can render people helpless, incapacitating them at the very time they should be aggressive. By maintaining some sense of self-control and trying to keep a clear head during this terrorizing event, a victim may be able to perceive the attack in less violent terms. Feeling a knife at your throat or staring at the balled fist of a 240-pound assailant is certain to make you feel terribly vulnerable; yet allowing fear to convince you that you cannot affect the situation at all leads to paralysis. But when your mind remains clear, you need not turn into a quivering mass of gelatin.

Recent research has served to dispel some of the myths about resisting a rapist. For years, experts told women that if they dared to fight back against an assailant they were likely to be injured *and* raped despite their efforts. Pauline Bart of the University of Illinois explains one of these myths.

> The myth was that [rapists] were deprived guys and you should be nice to them and show that you understand them, and then they wouldn't do anything. But if you resisted, you were going to be in deep trouble (Kotulak 1).

Even some law enforcement officials suggested that women simply submit to their attackers and spend those horrible, life-altering moments memorizing their assailant's face, height, weight, accent, and any other identifying features. But P. B. Bart and Patricia O'Brien (also of the University of Illinois) began to challenge that notion. Their studies showed that the more techniques a woman used, the less likely she would be raped; and they also found that active resistance, such as, yelling and fighting, was the most effective combination. They further discovered that women who successfully foiled their rapists were operating from the gut-level notion, "Nobody's going to do this to me" (Kotulak 1)!

RESISTANCE AND INJURY

Rape resistance techniques are generally divided into two broad categories: active measures and passive measures. Later in this chapter we will examine these actions in more detail, but for now, just keep in mind that active measures include running away, screaming for help, fighting back, making noise, and using weapons. Passive measures include seeking to con the offender, reason with him, negotiate, or claim pregnancy or disease. Using a narrow range of research and some nonrepresentative police horror stories, some scholars and crime prevention specialists have adopted an antiresistance philosophy for confronting a rapist. They suggest that women who physically resist their assailants are more likely to be injured than those who do not. Often relying only upon rapes reported to police, as did Menachem Amir in his 1971 study, they falsely advise all women to engage in some elaborate (yet admittedly instantaneous) analysis of their attacker. By trying to reason with him, these theorists claim, a woman can avoid both rape and injury. But the facts simply do not support such advice; and often those who peddle it have an antiviolence agenda underpinning all their assessments.

> I refuse to advocate any method of rape prevention that could cause the bodily harm or death of *any* person using it. That's why I believe all antagonistic techniques . . . [physically fighting with your opponent, using weapons, screaming, fainting] are the wrong thing to do in the event of an assault (Storaska 31–32).

In all fairness to Frederic Storaska, who genuinely seems to have women's safety at heart, his book *How to Say No to a Rapist and Survive* offers some worthy examples of a victim's passive resistance options; but he is seriously in error in his views of active resistance. Gary Kleck and Susan Sayles, in a study on "Rape and Resistance" published in the May 1990 issue of *Social Problems*, clearly show that "victims who resist are much less likely to have the rape completed against them than non-resisting victims," and they further state that "most forms of resistance are not significantly associated with higher rates of victim injury" (149). Analyzing 378 incidents of stranger rape in the U.S. between 1979 and 1985, Kleck and Sayles included both reported incidents and those not reported to police. As was the case with assault reporting (Chapter Six), instances where a rape victim successfully fought off or otherwise deterred her attacker are the least likely to be reported to the police; thus, reported crimes are overrepresentative of injury and not truly reflective of actual resistance effectiveness.

Active measures of rape avoidance are clearly superior to passive measures in rape situations. Screaming and crying for help seem particularly effective (Table 7.2). Another study shows that 43% of the women used this tactic, allowing 72% of that group to escape without being raped (Levine-Macombie & Koss 312). But author Frederic Storaska advises against screaming, arguing—as do others who favor passive resistance—that not only will screaming be ineffective, it will only serve to antagonize an attacker. The only circumstance where a victim should scream according to Storaska is

> . . . if you can be a hundred percent sure that help is actually within hearing distance . . . a hundred percent sure help will

TABLE 7.2. Are Self-Protective Responses to Rape Effective?
(for the period 1973–1987)

	Rape	
	Attempted (%)	Completed (%)
All victims	66	34
Victims who took self-protective measures	71	29
Victims who took no self-protective measures	40	60

Note: While the statistics tell that most rapes attempted against women were not completed, those women who took self-protective measures clearly had a greater chance of avoiding the rape than those who chose not to protect themselves.
Source: *Sourcebook—1990*.

> respond, a hundred percent sure that the help will be ade-
> quate to meet the situation, and a hundred percent sure that
> the assaulter . . . won't do away with you before help ar-
> rives (34).

Again, this author makes an unrealistic suggestion. If you dealt in 100% degrees of awareness and certainty, the chances are you would not become a victim in the first place. Most experts say that when you are reasonably certain no weapon is involved (and I do not think you can ever be entirely sure there is no weapon), active resistance measures are highly successful in preventing rape. Stephanie Riger, associate professor of psychology at Lake Forest College, interviewed thousands of women in Chicago, Phila-delphia, and San Francisco. She suggests,

> You should resist early and resist [by] using multiple
> tactics, which may not necessarily mean physically fighting
> back unless you're physically competent and you choose to
> do that. But it can mean talking your way out, yelling,
> screaming, telling the guy somebody's about to meet you or
> that you have AIDS—lots of different tactics (Kotulak 1).

Of the 29% of women who fled from their rapist, some 76% managed to avoid the crime. Yet when the victims chose neither of these responses (fleeing or attracting attention), 80% of them were raped. Being aware of this information and knowing what your chances are is the first line of defense in dealing with the rapist. P. B. Bart and P. H. O'Brien, in their 1985 study *Stopping Rape: Successful Survival Strategies*, point out that although running or attempting to run was the most effective means of avoiding rape (81% avoided the crime), it was the method used *least*. Perhaps this is because victims allowed their fear to paralyze them. Apparently that fear abated enough to allow women to choose physical resistance as the next most often used defense—some 68% of the victims using physical resistance managed to avoid the rape. But as we move from active to passive measures we see a decline in effectiveness. Only 54% of the victims who chose verbal resistance, such as flattery or attempts to negotiate, were successful in avoiding rape. The least effective measure, allowing only 44% of the victims to avoid rape, was pleading with the assailant (Levine-Macombie & Koss 312). Some evidence even suggests that threatening, arguing, or reasoning with an attacker may increase the victim's chance of injury (Kleck & Sayles 155). Certainly in some cases you can talk a rapist out of his act—there are documented examples of women doing this—but it is usually ineffective. Talk is a tool, but statistically not a very good tool. Storaska and others advocate that people should "treat the rapist as a human being." Treat the rapist as what he is—an assailant who may or may not act like a human being. Chapter Four presented the case for trying to talk an assailant out of an assault before resorting to violence. That still remains a reasonable initial approach; but when it comes to rape, do not invest too much time in negotiation. Where assault is generally an escalating affair, subject to being discouraged, diffused, controlled, or otherwise influenced at several critical points along the way, rape involves an attacker with one very specific and willful intent: sexual violation. Too much concern for the rapist as an individual and too much talk risk valuable time and escape opportunities in exchange for little chance for success.

When an attacker is wielding a weapon, it is time to consider *all* your options. Rapidly assess the situation. Look for an escape route, attempt to distract the attacker long enough to get away, but above all, ask yourself if it is worth losing your life by resisting. I cannot make that determination, nor can anyone but you. Rose Olivieri, an officer with Chicago's rape prevention program says of facing an armed rapist,

> If you feel confident that by hurting the person, giving him some type of pain, you can get away, then by all means try that. On the other hand, if you wake up in the middle of the night and someone is kneeling on top of your head with a weapon, use your head (Kotulak 1).

Remember that no one avoidance strategy is effective for all people in all situations. And, quite frankly, there are some criminals out there so determined to commit a crime, so physically overpowering, and so insensitive to reason, fear, or disgusting physical display, that they will not be deterred by any form of resistance short of killing them. It is just such an individual that offers the most compelling argument for Jim Carmichael's (*The Women's Guide to Handguns*) version of gun-toting self-defense. Only deadly force is going to stop such an assailant, and if you are not trained to render it with your hands, you had better find some kind of equalizer or resolve right now to submit and hope for the best.

"What are the chances I'll run into someone like that?" you may ask.

Slim—but not nonexistent. It only takes one. The anti-gun-at-all-costs and pacifist pressure groups will likely stop reading right here, for they prefer to deal in folklore and ideology rather than fact. Using a gun or a knife is the most effective form of resistance for preventing completion of a rape (Kleck & Sayles 158).

"Yes, but will I be hurt if I resist a rapist?" many women ask.

Rightly concerned about personal injury, women have sometimes chosen to do nothing rather than resist. But unlike assault victims, rape victims who forcefully resist do not significantly increase their chance of injury (see Table 7.3). Usually injury preceeds resistance, rather than results from it. Still, some rape counselors and rape prevention advocates continue to suggest that resisting a rapist will only anger him and drive him to harm you further. Since you do not know what you are dealing with, they claim, you cannot be certain you will not antagonize your attacker. But advising people not to resist so they may avoid injury makes two false assumptions about the rape situation: (1) that by not resisting you somehow ensure you will not be injured; and (2) that injury occasioned by fighting back is somehow more grievous than the completed rape. Hundreds of women have the physical scars to prove the first assumption wrong, and hundreds more still carry enough psychological scars to refute the second.

TABLE 7.3. Does Self-Protection against a Rapist Bring about Injury
in Addition to the Rape, or Prevent the Rape Itself?

	Injured (%)	Uninjured (%)
All rape victims	56	44
Victims who took self-protective measures	58	42
Victims who took no self-protective measures	46	54

Note: With the figures this close, protecting yourself against a rapist basically boils down to
trading a slightly higher degree of personal injury by resisting for a better chance of foiling the
criminal in his act. It is a personal matter and a hard choice for most women, who must
ultimately decide if suffering the traumatic injury of the rape itself is worth the slight risk of
additional suffering that accompanies fighting back.
SOURCE: *Sourcebook—1990*.

> Only 7.7% of the additional injuries experienced by rape
> victims could be described as serious, i.e., involving a gun or
> knife wound, broken bones, teeth knocked out, internal
> injuries, or loss of consciousness. . . . In short, the most
> serious injury the victim faced, in all but 3% of the rapes, was
> the rape itself (Kleck and Sayles 160).

Atkeson, Calhoun, and Morris found in a 1989 study on victim
resistance to rape that victims who showed greater resistance were
more likely to be verbally threatened, physically restrained, and
injured. They also admit that "victims appeared to resist *because
they were being injured*, as opposed to *being injured because they
resisted*" [italics mine] (505). And these researchers also found that
women who resisted were less likely to be subjected to any
number of humiliating sexual acts beyond vaginal rape. So even if
you resist and enrage your attacker, the odds are still with you that
you will (a) avoid the rape and (b) not suffer an injury greater than
the rape itself. Al Marrewa, who runs a rape prevention program
in Los Angeles says,

> Most women hesitate [to strike or kick an assailant]
> because they've been taught that if they fight back, they'll
> make an attacker angry. I explain that if they know how to

> fight back correctly, they will seriously hurt him. Once they
> hear that, they go all out (Caminiti, *Working Woman*).

"Women finally are beginning to know that it is possible to resist and survive," says Pauline Bart. Advising women to learn self-defense, Bart says proper training is good for a woman's self-esteem and forces her to realize that danger is lurking in the real world. With training she says you can avoid being "so stunned that . . . you can't do anything" (Kotulak 1).

While those techniques that successfully thwart a stranger will generally stop an acquaintance, there are some differences between the two rape situations. Acquaintance rapists are more likely to act alone and likely to be less violent than strangers. Women who are raped by strangers or casual dates are more likely to have used alcohol prior to the crime. In a 1988 issue of *Psychology of Women Quarterly*, researcher Mary Koss states,

> sexual violence is more likely to occur in the context of drug
> and alcohol use when the parties are strangers or casually
> acquainted . . . it is possible that the disinhibition subse-
> quent to alcohol use is needed to excuse or rationalize the
> forceful sexual conduct (20–21).

"I was drunk. I didn't know what I was doing." Such a claim never has been, nor shall it ever be, justification for sexual assault.

Some research suggests another important difference between stranger and nonstranger rape—that women tend to hesitate in the use of active avoidance strategies when the assailant is someone they know, and they seem to be less prepared psychologically to render an active defense than they might against a stranger. This hesitancy often enables the assailant to complete his crime, or as Amick and Calhoun put it,

> the stimulus, or cue, to elicit self-protective behavior is much
> less ambiguous in the case of an armed stranger in a dark
> alley, than in the case of a boyfriend in a dimly lighted living
> room.

But the Atkeson et al. findings (1989) call that notion into question. It was discovered that a victim's prior relationship with her attacker did not affect her willingness to offer resistance; and specifically, 78% of women assaulted by acquaintances resisted physically, and *all* offered some kind of resistance.

Koss indicates that stranger rapists were more likely to threaten with bodily harm, engage in hitting and slapping, and use a weapon; but both stranger and acquaintance rapists about equally resorted to twisting the victim's arms, holding her down, choking her, or beating her (10). As to avoidance strategies, there were few significant differences between acquaintance and stranger rape victims. Both groups about equally relied upon turning cold, reasoning or pleading, crying or sobbing, running away and fighting (12). What is perhaps more revealing in Koss's research, however, is that women more often hesitated to use two of the more effective deterrents—yelling and running away—when they were assaulted by someone they knew. Koss sounds a warning that echoes Hazelwood and Harpold's imperative about being prepared.

> No group of victims used these strategies as often as their demonstrated effectiveness warrants. Preparation for the use of active avoidance, especially in potential acquaintance rape, may need greater emphasis than in rape prevention programming (21).

A final difference in these situations of rape is the social support a victim may expect. Successfully stopping a stranger rapist is not only accepted within the social community, it is usually applauded. But resisting an aggressive boyfriend or husband, with all its ambiguous feelings, frequently elicits a different response from the community and friends of the victim. Both instances of rape are equally threatening, equally frightening, and equally dangerous; but in the first situation society will call the woman a hero and in the second situation call her a bitch. Victims sense this inconsistency and frequently pattern their response to rape accordingly.

With rape, as we learned with assault, one of the best ways to stay out of trouble is to trust your instincts. There is a direct correlation between the sense of foreboding, which many rape victims experience prior to the event, and the actual occurrence. The 1976 Queens Bench Study, one of the earliest foundational studies of rape victims, indicated that victims felt uneasy during the casual conversation that immediately preceded their attack, but they failed to act upon those feelings (Amick & Calhoun 154). "Women who have gotten out of rape situations felt early on that there was something weird going on and acted on that feeling right away," says professor of psychology Stephanie Riger (Kotulak 1). Yes, some rapes are impulsive acts, but many rape situations are characterized by a gradual escalation. Be alert for strange statements, attitudes, long glances, an unaccounted for presence or interest, odd activities, strange twists in a conversation, or a preoccupation with sex as a topic of discussion. Some women who have thwarted a potential rapist had actually been able to see the rape coming.

CHARACTERISTICS OF THE RAPIST

Just as victims and rape circumstances differ, so do the rapists themselves. That is the unfortunate factor making panaceas ineffective. Rapists range from one-time offenders who repent, pay their debt to society, and proceed to lead productive lives, to serial rapists and murderers who take life after life until they eventually lose their own. Techniques that may be effective against one rapist may not only be ineffective against another, but could motivate him to do greater harm. While the serial rapist gets most of the press attention and tends to generate fear in the community, he is not the individual most women are likely to encounter. By understanding some of the motivations of the various types of rapists, we can get some clues as to what may or may not work in a given situation and we can recognize the dangers in across-the-board solutions. The problem inherent in interviewing rapists to determine the advice they can offer a citizen is the problem of which rapist do you believe? The advice is often contradictory, and to assume that all rapists behave the same way and respond similarly to avoidance techniques is at best naive, and at worst lethal.

The Three P's

The Behavioral Science Unit (BSU) at the FBI Academy in Quantico, Virginia, has experience in the study of sexual violence in over 1,000 rape cases. Through interviews with the criminals, the BSU has put together some parameters of sexual assault situations, which may be useful in helping a potential victim choose a course of action. These parameters include the confrontation environment, the personality of the victim, and the type and motivation of the rapist (Hazelwood & Harpold 1–2). Special agents Hazelwood and Harpold compare preparing yourself to deal with a rape situation with an athlete preparing for a major sporting event. You assess your individual strengths and weaknesses and prepare to play at different locations. This allows you to size up your competition on the spot, and adjust your defensive strategy accordingly. "To survive one must prepare himself for the unexpected. Similarly, potential victims have an excellent chance of surviving a rape confrontation if they are prepared in advance" (5).

Preparing for rape involves playing "What if . . . ?" What if I came home and found a man hiding in my garage? What would I do? Would I scream? How would I escape? Is there a door I could use? Are any weapons within reach? Cindy Miller, a policewoman formerly with undercover vice operations in Los Angeles, agrees that women should think about being mugged or raped.

> If she just thought about it one time, she'd be much safer. Just so that she has something to fall back on. If you've thought about it before, your thought will flash into your mind. If you haven't thought about it before, nothing will come to mind and you'll do nothing or you'll panic (Arnold 136).

Anticipating a rape scenario and planning for possible actions involves considering the three P's: *place*, *personality*, and *perpetrator*.

Place.   Many experts recommend that women make noise to frighten away the attacker, and in some situations that is sound advice. But those situations are tied to the location of the crime. A whistle or any other noise-making device (including personal alarm sirens) is only effective if someone is around to hear it. If your car breaks down on a country road where the nearest house is two miles away, and you are confronted by an assailant, you can blow your whistle until you pass out before anyone comes to your aid. However, if the same attacker were to confront you on a city street and push you into an alley, the noise-making defense would likely draw the attention of a bystander, either bringing help or possibly frightening the attacker away. But the success of this technique is strictly location-dependent. In the example of the college student, we saw that she was attacked on a dark street in the early morning hours. This is a favorable crime location primarily because of the absence of bystanders (guardians), so screaming at the top of her lungs may or may not have alerted anyone. There are not too many people roaming the streets at 1:30 A.M.; after all, that is why the rapist chose that spot to commit his crime.

Many women opt for chemical sprays, and, as we have seen, Mace and weapons like it can be useful; but there are places where chemical sprays can be just as dangerous to you as they are to your assailant. If an attacker forces you to the ground on a windy day, your chemical spray may end up in your own face. Also, the close quarters of an automobile make it difficult enough to fight off an attacker, and if you try to spray a chemical in those close quarters you are likely to receive more of it than your assailant does.

Being attacked in your home creates other restrictions on your response. Depending upon where you live, screaming for help may not draw the desired attention. Are there others in the house whose safety may be determined by what you do, for instance, children, elderly people? Sometimes you can be effective in stalling the rapist, as one woman did by insisting she needed a cigarette to calm her nerves. This act was designed to buy time for her to think of a way to escape. Some experts have suggested that if you are caught alone in your home you can claim that your brother or your father is on the way over. Perhaps you can convince the rapist to move the attack somewhere else. You haven't stopped the rape, but you have bought time. If you can get him to take you outside, there is a greater chance of a bystander being alerted to the crime. Another woman indicated to her attacker that she would cooperate if he would only take her somewhere where she could buy a birth control device. The trip offered her a chance to get away (Booher 78). None of these are guaranteed to always work, but they become yet another entry in your log of possible responses.

Another location that influences rape response is the shopping mall. According to Lisa Sliwa, victim advocate, author of a rape prevention book, and wife of Guardian Angel founder Curtis Sliwa, malls draw a disproportionate number of women—women with jewelry, credit cards, and cash. Because malls appear to be safe, boasting broad, well-lit corridors, crowds of shoppers, and security guards, women are sometimes lulled into a false sense of security. And once inside the mall, one can feel relatively safe. But you have to get inside first, and then you have to get back home. Since rape sometimes accompanies robbery or mugging, malls offer a target-rich environment for the criminal. The lighting in the parking lot is usually inadequate, no matter how large the mall, so women are particularly at risk to someone stepping up and forcing them into an automobile (Sliwa 90–91). Park as close as possible to the mall entrance and always try to find a spot under a streetlight. This can be difficult during Christmas shopping days, but it would be well worth driving around a few more minutes if it would discourage a rapist. Whether the site of the attack is a city street, a public restroom, your home, or a shopping mall, you must constantly remain alert and ready to respond. Atkeson and colleagues discovered that the location of the assault or the time of the assault seems to have no effect on the willingness of a woman to resist her attacker (501).

Personality.   A second variable to consider when choosing a rape avoidance technique is your own personality. Your attitude and bearing has an important effect upon the type of resistance you can best apply. In an article, entitled "Reactions to Assaultive Rape," for a 1978 issue of *The Journal of Communication and Psychology*, J. Selkin used the California Personality Inventory (CPI) to discover some of the personality characteristics that differentiated successful resisters to rape from those who were unsuccessful. Selkin discovered that many effective resisters exhibited dominant personalities, exuded social presence, and demonstrated sociability in their CPI scores (Amick & Calhoun 154). A woman with a dominant personality, or what Lisa Sliwa calls "attitude," is more likely to engage in an active measure of self-defense rather than a passive one, and we already know that active measures are generally more effective. Still, each woman must examine her own personality to decide what method of resistance is best for her. It is the old "know thyself" routine all over again. A long-standing rule among those of us who are old self-defense teachers goes like this:

> If you know yourself and you know your enemy, you will
> win most of the time; if you know yourself but you don't
> know your enemy, you will win some of the time; if you don't
> know yourself and you don't know your enemy, you will lose
> most of the time.

A passive individual is going to have a difficult time using physically aggressive confrontation techniques against a rapist who is bigger and stronger than she is, even though that might be the best choice in a given situation. It will be just as hard for someone who is domineering, forceful, and assertive to adopt a strategy of submission, even when the situation calls for it. This means that the relative effectiveness of a particular type of resistance depends entirely upon the victim's willingness and ability to apply it. Again, this suggests preparedness as a central factor in deterring rape. Police officers who have survived encounters with deadly felons frequently attribute their success to planning and rehearsing of possible scenarios.

Perpetrator.   Understanding the type of rapist you are facing and what is motivating him to conduct an attack is the most difficult of all the variables you must assess in choosing a resistance strategy. Is your attacker someone who just hates women and needs to dominate them? Is he a sex addict who seeks an emotional high? Is he mentally deranged with no purpose other than to make you suffer? Unlike the criminologists and psychologists, you do not have time to indulge in a thorough study of the problem. Unlike the sociologist, you cannot spend weeks and months evaluating your attacker. Unlike the scholars, you cannot afford to just say, "Oops! I guess I made the wrong choice." When facing a rapist you will be compelled to make an immediate assessment of your attacker, and you had better be right the first time.

> To assume that all rapists are alike in type and motivation demonstrates a lack of knowledge and experience. As Groth and Burnbaum note, "physical resistance will discourage one type of rapist but excite another." If his victim screams one assailant will flee, but another will cut her throat (Hazelwood & Harpold 4).

Rapists are not the most stable, predictable people in the world, and their behavior, coupled with the public misconceptions about who rapists are, can make it very hard to assess the threat.

Frequently rapists are loners, having suffered some emotional, physical, or sexual trauma as a child. Having never fully recovered from that trauma, they are now immature adults unable to cope with the stress of adult life in an often uncaring society (Olson 9). A 1977 Harris Poll found that 87% of Americans think only sick, perverted men rape. But if you are looking out for some lonely-homeless-psycho-ex-con, you are looking in the wrong place.

- 43% of rapists are married.
- Most rapists are 15–24 years old (the 1989 figures show the perceived age of 58% of all rapists was 15–29).

- A rapist will almost always attack someone of his own race.
- Most rapists first choose the location of the crime, then attack whoever is unlucky or unwise enough to come along.
- 58% of single rapes are planned.
- 90% of group rapes are planned. (Booher 64)

Some of the most compelling information about rapists comes from Dr. A. Nicholas Groth, who interviewed over 1,000 jailed rapists during 16 years of research. His work, coupled with FBI interviews of 41 jailed serial rapists, confirms what we learned about vincibility. Most rapists pick their targets based upon "availability, vulnerability, and physical characteristics other than sexual allure" (Olson 9). Dr. Groth classifies offenders as either *power*, *anger*, or *sadistic* rapists. Power rapists want to force their victims to submit. It is not so much about sex as it is about control. By initially appearing to grant the assailant his control over you, you may be able to gain his confidence and create an opportunity for escape. Often these attackers are on an ego trip. Lacking self-esteem, they believe they can show their power and prowess by controlling another person. Often they have feelings of sexual inadequacy and will go to great lengths to prove themselves. They may be brutal or, as in some cases, they may be "gentlemen rapists," as with the 17-year-old woman abducted from a parking lot.

> After he [the rapist] had stripped her and she complained of being cold, he took off his jacket and gave it to her. He rolled the sweater he wore into a pillow for her head (Booher 68).

When he finished his deed, he even drove the woman where she requested to be driven and offered her telephone money.

Anger rapists often commit unpremeditated attacks, spur-of-the-moment assaults than can be savage and brutal. By their own admission to therapists and institutional counselors, these men frequently rape because they hate women, and seek, in their own way, to pay back someone for a perceived wrong. You can neither know or influence why or who the rapist hates, but if you recognize that your attacker seeks revenge for a few brief moments, you may be able to tailor your defense accordingly. I seriously doubt you will be able, in a few seconds, to talk him out of the anger that has built up over a lifetime; but you may be able to deflect it long enough to respond effectively. The anger rapist may be an impulse attacker, who usually has not set out to commit a crime, nor stalked a victim and planned a location. Some unsuspecting female just happens to be in the wrong place at the right time, and finding her vulnerable, the rapist strikes. Acquaintance rape often occurs under such circumstances. The victim is a substitute for the real object of the rapist's anger, and frequently that anger is fueled by alcohol and other drugs (Olson 9). Our old nemesis, alcohol, is never far removed from the causal factors of crime. Alcohol continues to claim its share of the blame in rape as well as assault. According to the Kinsey Institute for Sex Research, 39% of all rapists are drinking prior to their crime. I would be very surprised if that figure were not on the low end of the scale.

The celebrated case of the Central Park jogger in New York reminds us of the potential for gang rape. In this instance, a woman was running alone at night in Central Park. She did not deserve to be raped, yet her choice of location did send her vincibility factor through the roof. What made these young men so brutally rape and assault her? *Opportunity* and the need for peer approval consistently appeared as major factors throughout the investigation into this case. Usually in gang rape the group prede-termines where they will commit the act and then goes looking for a convenient victim. Testimony in the Central Park jogger case seems to indicate a spur-of-the-moment act against someone who presented herself as a soft, opportune target. Rather than stalking the jogger and staking out an intercept point and a concealed location for the attack, the group, in the words of Kevin Rich-ardson, a 14-year-old who participated in the assault,

> . . . started chasing her . . . and then, like, they caught her and pulled her shirt off. And like, she fell. Like, they pushed her down . . . they ripped it [her bra] off . . . she was screaming, like, "Stop!" yelling "Help!" (Pearl & Furse)

The *New York Post*, in its November 17, 1990 edition, quoted
another of the assailants, 16-year-old Kharey Wise, saying, "Ray-
mond [Santana] picked up a rock and hit her in the face. That's
what knocked her out . . . they were punching her face . . .
punching her face." Thus, it appears that the boys who assaulted
the Central Park jogger simply took advantage of the young
investment banker as she passed near them. They overtook her,
incapacitated her, and engaged in their demeaning criminal act.
While the jogger cannot and should not be blamed for getting
raped, her behavior should be scrutinized for how it enhanced her
vulnerability. Did she have the right to go jogging alone in Central
Park? Absolutely—but there is a difference between the right to
do something and the right thing to do.

Sadistic rapists usually resort to bizarre behavior, including
bondage and sexual torture. They also tend to be rather methodi-
cal, plotting detailed and even ritualistic crimes (Olson 9). An
element of sadomasochism runs throughout these assailants' actions, with prostitutes being frequent victims. Hazelwood and
Harpold tell of a 39-year-old white male who "sexually mistreated
his wife over a number of years, even binding her and assaulting
her with a hair brush. Additionally, he had raped several women
and molested his two daughters, two nieces, and the daughter of a
female acquaintance" (5).

When he was interviewed about one of the rapes, he was
asked what his response might have been had his victim resisted
with either physical or verbal abuse. The man considered the
question for a few moments, then answered, "I don't know. I
might have left, but then again, I might have killed her. I just don't
know" (5). It is precisely this kind of unpredictable behavior that
makes it absolutely imperative that women have more than one
option for dealing with an attacker. If one technique fails, or
appears to enrage the assailant, it is time to try something else.
But as hard as it may be to make an evaluation of your attacker's
attitude and motivation, it is infinitely more acceptable than doing
nothing. Most of the women I have dealt with over the past 20

years were not willing to accept victimization without some attempt at resistance.

POSSIBLE RAPE RESPONSES

Choosing a response to a rapist is not an issue of right and wrong. You cannot say that a person was raped because she made the wrong response. Sometimes you make all the recommended moves and still get sexually assaulted. It is more accurate and useful to talk in terms of effective and ineffective measures.

Here are some effective alternatives, both active and passive, for rape avoidance. Use them to build a database of responses, or a game plan, from which you can select appropriate actions. These responses fall into four categories: physical resistance, attention-getting maneuvers, repellant actions, and verbal resistance.

Physical Resistance Techniques

Execute self-defense techniques by learning when, where, and how to strike vital body targets. *Requirements*: Proper training, normal physical strength, aggressiveness, and some of Lisa Sliwa's attitude. *Dangers*: If you do not learn to do it right, you may place yourself in greater danger by enraging your attacker and compelling him to seek retribution. Kleck and Sayles tell us this method is most likely to result in injury to the victim (151). *Advantages*: The basic survival instinct in all human beings can drive us to physical feats we never believed possible.

Use chemical sprays or odor repellants to incapacitate or discourage the attacker, buying time for your escape. *Requirements*: Purchase the equipment, get trained in its use, and keep it with you at all times. *Dangers*: Used in the wrong place, or with inadequate training, it may disable *you*. *Advantages*: It is easy to carry, relatively easy to operate, and when properly used, it is generally effective in stopping an assailant.

Many rapists are armed (Table 7.4); thus, another option for a woman is to use a gun, knife, or club to defeat her attacker or disable him long enough for her to escape. *Requirements*: Purchase the weapon, get trained in its use, obtain a permit (in some cases) to carry it, and keep it with you at all times. *Dangers*: You had better not miss. If you lose the weapon to your assailant, expect to have it used on you. If you take someone's life, be prepared to prove you were acting in self-defense. *Advantages*: Properly used, weapons can stop an attacker dead in his tracks, or just plain dead if the situation demands it. Carrying a weapon provides some people with a sense of confidence and security. Kleck and Sayles indicate that resistance with a gun or knife is the most successful means of thwarting a rapist (157).

Attention-Getting Maneuvers

Scream "Fire!" or use a whistle or personal siren to draw attention to what is happening to you. *Requirements*: Purchase the equipment and have it with you at all times. *Dangers*: Noise-

TABLE 7.4. Weapons Rapists Use against Women (figures for 1989)

Weapon[a]	All rapes (%)	Strangers (%)	Nonstrangers[b] (%)
Handguns	26.4	19.6	100
Knives	39.7	43.4	0
Sharp object	6.3	6.8	0
Blunt object	14.0	15.3	0
Others	13.6	14.9	0

Note: What all this means is that if you confront an armed stranger who intends to rape you, he will most likely be carrying a knife.
[a]In some cases, more than one weapon may have been used.
[b]This category represents 10 or fewer samples in the survey; thus, it may not be indicative of a true distribution.
SOURCE: *Sourcebook—1990*.

making devices are effective only if someone is around to hear them. *Advantages*: These devices are usually low-cost and readily available; they are easy to carry and require no training.

Repellant Actions

Claim you are pregnant or that you have a venereal disease or AIDS, or vomit, urinate, or otherwise foul your attacker in hopes of frightening or repelling him. *Requirements*: Basic acting ability and on-call bodily functions. *Dangers*: Some attackers are so insensitive that they will continue the rape regardless of your efforts. Others may be so mentally unbalanced as to be unaffected by your display. *Advantages*: Against a relatively nonaggressive rapist, these methods can sometimes be effective; and you do not have to physically injure anyone to employ these tactics.

Verbal Resistance

Use voice, tone, manner, and attitude to convince your attacker to abandon his effort. *Requirements*: Patience, extreme self-control, and good interpersonal skills. *Dangers*: Statistically, this is the least effective method of preventing a rape, and spending too much time negotiating or threatening a rapist can waste valuable time better spent in a more aggressive response. *Advantages*: You avoid violence and *may* be able to deter your opponent from escalating his level of violence.

Instruction in all of these skills is usually available from law enforcement agencies, women's organizations, or rape crisis/awareness centers in your community. Many major companies, like Time Warner, HBO, and Sony provide rape education and prevention workshops in support of their employees and families. If your employer does not offer such seminars, discuss it with him or her and try to bring in a professional. Al Marrewa, a 33-year-old director of Powerflex USA, a rape education and prevention center in Los Angeles, offers such a workshop—a six-hour program that companies often schedule between noon and 3:00 P.M. over a two-day period. Marrewa, who has a graduate degree in public health and a black belt in a Chinese martial art, keeps his classes small— no more than eight women—and charges anywhere from $99 to $129 per student, depending upon the number of participants (Caminiti).

AFTER THE RAPE

Let us assume the worst. Despite preparedness, alertness, and several attempted actions to resist, you are raped. What now? First of all, the battle is not over. Though violated and most likely feeling powerless, you still have some cards to play. Number one action—call the police and report the crime and/or get medical attention, whichever priority demands to be first. You will receive crisis intervention and rape counseling support from either law enforcement, medical providers, or both. Do not shower, douche, or change clothing. As defiled as you feel, these actions will destroy valuable evidence that can help you turn the tables on your attacker. Call a friend or relative for emotional support, and be prepared to describe the incident in minute detail.

If you can gather your wits, write down everything you can remember about the encounter, including particular statements the attacker made or anything else you can recall. Don't worry if it seems insignificant at the moment. It may become crucial later. Give a physical description of the rapist, concentrating on his weight, height, hair and eye color, scars, clothing, and anything else you can remember. If he used a car, write down what it looked like, for instance, the model, style, crunched fender, mobile phone. Also note down the location of the attack, which direction the rapist came from, which way he left, and approximately how long the assault took place.

Medical personnel are not only going to treat you for your

injuries, they are going to assist the police in gathering evidence. Be prepared to be asked hundreds of questions, photographed, and quizzed again and again. But just remember that every rapist on the street is a threat to some other woman, and your cooperation and timely reporting could save someone else from the horror you have just experienced.

The role and value of DNA testing to identify rapists has received much attention in the press over the past five years. Since the DNA (deoxyribonucleic acid) configuration is unique to each person (except identical twins), and since it is found in nearly every cell in the body, there is a good possibility that a rapist will leave his signature at the scene of the crime. But lest the breakthrough in DNA technology lead a victim to a cavalier attitude about preserving physical evidence, remember that DNA testing and resultant use in rape cases is a two-edged sword. While only a tiny drop of dried blood or semen, or a hair, or the clawed skin from beneath fingernails is often enough to paint a DNA portrait of a rapist, the DNA test results are often grounds for freeing the accused rather than convicting him (Dillion D3). From 1990 to 1992 the FBI conducted DNA screenings for 6,000 criminal cases, predominantly rape cases and sexual assaults. These were cases where the subjects were already arrested and charged based on other evidence, such as eyewitness identification. According to John Hicks, director of the FBI laboratory in Washington, D.C., many of "the suspects' DNA failed to match evidence from the crimes and charges were dropped" (Dillon D3). Thus while DNA testing has helped to convict rapists, it is certainly no panacea; and its capacity to exonerate in spite of eyewitness testimony has led some, like Leslie Wolfe, executive director of the Center of Women Policy Studies in Washington, D.C., to suggest that "[DNA testing] will have a chilling effect on women reporting rapes when only 10 percent to 20 percent report it now" (Dillon D2).

Chapter Eight

THE THREAT TO CHILDREN

I met Mike Burnside in May of 1985, when his mother brought him to his first self-defense class. Mike was a bright-eyed, intelligent, young man of average height and weight. He had just turned 11. The chief instructor at our school introduced me to Mike's mother and I took a few minutes to talk to her before the class began.

"You know, this is Mike's first lesson," she began, "and he's a little nervous."

"I'm sure he is," I said, "most of the children are anxious about the first few classes, but as they get into the program and see that they can learn to protect themselves, they get more and more confident."

"I've been meaning to start him for almost a year, now. I finally got around to where I could do it," she explained.

"Is Mike here primarily for the physical workout or is the emphasis going to be the actual self-defense skills?" I asked.

The mother hesitated for a moment, looked down and away, but then turned to face me again.

"Mike had a bad experience about six months ago," she began. "Frankly, he hasn't been the same since. We live over in the Forest Meadows area, about two miles from here. Mike was coming home from school one afternoon, alone, when a man in a car stopped by the curb to ask Mike for directions. Mike tried to explain how to get there, but the man said he didn't understand and asked him to get in the car and ride with him to show him where it was."

"I think I see where this is going," I said. The mother nodded.

"Mike told him that he didn't think his mother would want him to do that, so this guy opened the car door and reached for him. Luckily, Mike was far enough away to be out of reach, so he took off running. This guy drove along after him, but I guess he figured he couldn't catch him, so he disappeared. When I got home after work that afternoon Mike told me about it and I called the police. He was terrified. I really wasn't sure what I should do, but some of my friends recommended that I bring him down here and have him learn to protect himself. I just keep asking myself, 'What if that man had gotten his hands on Mike?' I'm not sure he would have known what to do to get away."

Mike was a bright, young man. He already knew many of the right things to do, but the mother's concern was well founded. Many children—and a number of adults for that matter—do not know how to respond to the threat of physical assault or abduction. I appreciated Mike's mother sharing the background with me, and I told her it would help me to fashion a program with Mike's particular concerns in mind.

"He's excited about getting started," the mother added, "and I just hope it will be good for him. I think it will. I just don't want him to be in a situation like that again and feel unsure of what to do. He might not be so lucky next time."

Over the next nine or ten months I watched Mike grow in physical and mental ability through his training, and I saw a young man replace his uncertainty about protecting himself with a cautious confidence in dealing with threatening situations.

Mike's story is not unusual. Thousands of other children across the country experience their own confrontations with criminals. The threat of stranger violence against children is similar to that which exists for adults. The figures for violent crime against children, as reported in the *Sourcebook of Criminal Justice*

Statistics—1990, show a 26.8 victimization rate (per 1,000) for 12- to 15-year-olds, and a 40.3 rate for 16- to 19-year-olds. Compare that to an average victimization of 17.7 for people 20–64 years of age and you see that our children have a serious threat to their safety (266). Our children are subject to a wide range of criminal confrontations, including abduction, molestation, and lunch money "shakedowns" and threats from the neighborhood bully. While each of these situations represents a different level of danger, all are very real in the mind of the child, and they may result in anxiety, frustration, and fear that can influence the child's outlook on life for years to come. As parents, we try to raise our children with the skills to handle these varied situations, but we often are at a loss for exactly what to do.

While child victimization is nothing new in our society, its prevalence is increasing; and although the public is becoming more aware of the problem, we as citizens are not necessarily more willing to take preventative measures to prepare our children to deal with the threat. In spite of the growing public interest in the problem, many parents either fail to recognize the threat against their children, fail to take their child's fears seriously, or fail to take precautions until it is too late. But it's too easy to blame any problem a child has on something parents didn't do right, and such actions disenfranchise children from personal responsibility. Still, we parents are the primary guardians of our offspring and it is our attention to the facts surrounding crime against children that ultimately has the most impact upon curbing that crime.

One myth we Americans must overcome is the notion that elderly people are the most likely victims of violent crime. It is our young people who make the most likely targets of violence. The 1989 figures on violent crime victimization among young people indicate a rate of 62.9 per 1,000 persons. Note how in Table 8.1 the demographic grouping of people under age 20 virtually swells in proportion to the rest of the chart. Young people have twice the chance of being victimized as the person 25–34 years of age, and three times the chance of a person 35–49 years of age (*Sourcebook—1990* 260). But the threat of crime is no news to the children,

TABLE 8.1. Teenage Victims Comparing Crime against Teenagers with Adults in 1989 (victimization rate per 1,000 persons in each age group)

Crime	Age				
	12–15	16–19	20–24	25–34	35–49
All crimes of violence	62.9	73.8	57.8	34.9	20.8
Assault	52.3	61.5	47.1	27.1	15.7
Rape	1.1	1.8	1.6	0.8	0.5
Robbery	9.5	10.4	9.1	7.0	4.5

SOURCE: *Sourcebook—1990*.

it is news only to us adults, who have not paid close attention to the figures; children live with the threat every day and their attitudes reflect their accompanying fears. In her book, *Street Smart Child*, Grace Hechinger tells of a study done by Nicholas Zill, a psychologist and president of the nonprofit research organization Child Trends, for the Foundation for Child Development. Zill found that 68% of the 2,000 7- to 11-year-olds he surveyed feared an intruder might enter their home. Over one-fourth feared someone would hurt them when they went outside, and more than half had been harassed by other children or by adults while playing outside (4). Some of this fear is most certainly big-kid–little-kid, or the unfortunate but rather natural law of childhood that teaches us social interaction; but much of it is a greater threat than simple childhood rivalries. Some of it is serious business.

When asked the question, "Have you ever been punched or beaten by another person?" some 44% of the 18- to 20-year-olds answered "yes" in 1990 (*Sourcebook—1990* 292). How much of this reflects a mild scuffle between friends and how much of it is street assault is uncertain. But when you consider the statistics, it is not hard to see why a study by the Institute of Social Research at the University of Michigan found that the biggest worry of high school seniors was not finding a job or going to college—it was crime (Hechinger 5).

Parental lack of understanding of the threat to children should not be confused with a lack of concern. Few parents would wait until their children step in front of a city bus and are run down before warning them about the dangers of crossing the street. Few parents would wait until their house is burned to the ground before instructing children not to play with matches. Even toddlers are warned not to touch a hot stove before they receive second- and third-degree burns on their hands. It just makes good sense to warn your children of the dangers that face them instead of waiting until they have been victimized. But you must be aware of those dangers to responsibly warn your children. The two categories of crime against children most likely to affect your child are street crime and school/playground crime. While I shall talk about these categories separately, it is important to note that preparation is the key to stopping victimization in both of these areas.

Parents, *talk to your children*!

You should be less concerned about frightening them than about what will happen if they are left to their own devices when confronting an assailant.

> Children should be taught about crime as soon as they are allowed out of the house by themselves. The idea of this instruction is not to terrify them or to make them distrustful, but to train them to take the proper precautions. Most parents have found that if children develop a habit at an early age that habit will stay with them through adolescence. Thus, it is important for children to be exposed to crime instruction while they are still young (Griffith 161).

Helping children plan strategies for various threatening scenarios will ultimately pay off in increased confidence and the awareness necessary to control fear and panic. That is not to say that a little fear is not a good thing; for, as we have seen, fear, in limited degrees, keeps both children and adults on their toes. The parent's biggest job is balancing a child's fear against the realities of the crime-ridden world, while trying to enable the child to live a rich, engaging, and fulfilling life. Psychologist Steven Levenkran of the Montefiore Hospital in New York says the two biggest fears of children and teenagers are death and humiliation.

> When kids or adolescents come into a hospital these are their two main fears. We think of them as street fears—and they are—but I don't think kids are as aware of them on the streets as they are if you put them into a hospital; yet the fears are present whether they are expressed or not . . . It's not just teens and kids. In fact, most of us have fears of being left alone or being physically harmed or humiliated or killed. These are the fears we can identify with (Hechinger 20).

Levenkran indicates that many of the power struggles between young peers that seem silly or pointless to adults are actually expressions of a child's sense of powerlessness in the adult-dominated world. We should view those struggles in the context of the child's attempt to influence his or her environment wherever possible (Hechinger 20).

The popular conception that the elderly comprise the most crime-frightened element of our society has been recently challenged by Purdue University sociologist Kenneth Ferraro. In a 1,100-subject nationwide telephone survey that asked respondents to rate their level of fear for ten different crimes, Ferraro found that young people were more fearful than elderly persons. And according to an August 1992 issue of *USA Today*, high-risk groups (for instance, young people) show a correspondingly higher fear of being victimized, with 18-year-olds being the most afraid. The bad news is that children are already scared, the good news is that by teaching them conflict avoidance techniques we can channel their fear into a tool to help keep them safe.

STREET CRIME

This broad category encompasses stranger assault, robbery and abduction/molestation. Street crime is different from school/

playground crime in that in the former, most often the perpetrator is a stranger to the child. Instead of a peer out to make an image for himself, or some bully from down the block, the criminal in a street crime situation is out for something more. It may be money or sex or just a deviant form of kicks, but the potential for harm to your child is generally greatest in this category.

Stranger Assault

This aspect of street crime against children is not unlike the assault we have been examining throughout the book, except that the victim and the perpetrator are likely to be younger and smaller. Most crimes against young people are committed by other young people. Some kids just pick on other kids—kids they do not even know. They do it for the thrill, or for status within their group, or for something as scary as stealing a pair of brand-name sneakers. The closer that group is to an organized gang, the more the violence will escalate; and if you allow your child to be in a gang or to run with a crowd that associates with gang members, you can just plan on spending some time at the local emergency room.

The same advice that works to keep adults out of compromising situations will work with children, for instance, staying out of high-crime areas at high-crime times, avoiding the appearance of affluence, or recognizing the inherent dangers of alcohol and other drug use. But for all their avoidance efforts, children are going to get into fights with strangers. If you can show your child that saving face at all costs is both a dangerous and unnecessary response when challenged by another child, you will be well ahead in the game; but that is a tall order for an age group in our society for whom image means virtually everything. We will see, under the heading of school/playground crime, a suggestion about how to accomplish that tough task—a suggestion that should be easier for the child to carry out when faced by a stranger than when faced by someone he or she knows.

Robbery

Once again, what is true for adults is also true for children. You are worth more than your possessions. There is nothing in the possession of fifth-graders that their parents would want them to give their lives for. Teach your children to resist an armed mugger only if they are absolutely certain they will be severely injured or killed regardless of their response. Escape should be the goal, not fighting off an attacker, for it may be entirely possible that your child has neither the physical skill nor the mindset to resort to forceful retaliation. If he or she is robbed by an adult, certainly he or she is at a physical disadvantage; but even child-on-child robberies can offer some wide disparities in size and prowess. Just take a look at a class of middle-schoolers (sixth to ninth grade) if you have any doubts about nature's often tardy endowment of body maturity. Grace Hechinger, author of *Street Smart Child*, suggests that we as parents should not lecture our children on what to do in such a situation, but rather, we should share with them our own feelings and experience to lead them to their own conclusions (58). While all of us have had confrontational experiences we can share with our children, all of us are not equally equipped or comfortable sharing our views with our children. The public library is a valuable source of youth primers on everything from premarital sex to avoiding abduction or abuse. Once attitudes and possible actions are internalized by the child, they are more likely to be used effectively and less likely to be seen as rules to rebel against.

"I'll show Dad. Nobody can mug me," is not the response most of us want to hear from our children. Personally, I would settle for a nod of the head and some mild attention that hopefully would allow my suggestions to sink in later. Above all else, I would suggest you remind your child of these basic notions— which apply to adults as well—when they are faced with an armed robber:

1. Give up the goods. Your life is more valuable than your basketball shoes or your jacket or your watch. In January of

1991, the *Washington Times* reported how trendy sports-team jackets are becoming the target of thieves and armed robbers. Be careful what you dress your child in. You may inadvertently make him or her a target.

2. Remember that the last thing a robber wants to do is hang around—he or she is out for a grab-and-run encounter.

3. Try to remain calm, and keep your voice and mannerisms as controlled as possible. Particularly when facing an armed robber, your excitement will only make your attacker more nervous and therefore more dangerous.

4. Memorize your attacker's appearance and report the crime to the police immediately. You are looking for hair color, eye color, race, build, and peculiar characteristics of voice or manner.

The June 4, 1993 *Columbus* (Ohio) *Dispatch* reported on the trial and sentencing of 18-year-old James George, Jr., who admitted to stabbing to death 14-year-old DeWayne Williams just to steal his name-brand Los Angeles Raiders jacket. George was sentenced to life in prison with no possibility of parole for 30 years. The father of the slain youth, apparently recognizing the involvement of alcohol in the crime, said that the state of Ohio should crack down "on just one law—selling beer to minors," which he indicated "could go a long way toward reducing violence" (Karsko C1).

Abduction/Molestation

From 1983 until 1985 there was an 80% increase in sexual molestation, according to the House Select Committee on Children, Youth, and Families. One in eight boys and one in four girls are sexually abused before age 18 (Wooden 150). The National Committee for Prevention of Child Abuse estimated that in 1991 approximately 400,000 children under age 18 were reported to have been sexually abused. That figure reveals a 6% increase over 1990; and considering the FBI estimates only one out of ten molestations is reported, this is likely only a fraction of the true number (Whiteley 76). Most of these sex crimes against children are committed by people they know, love, or trust. Among the sexually abused persons under the age of 18, we know that 47% are abused by someone within the family, and another 40% are abused by nonfamily members who are acquainted with the family. That means that 87% of the cases of sexual abuse among children under 18 years of age are committed by people with whom the child has at least a passing relationship. Only 10% of such cases in this group are committed by strangers (Hertica 12). The National Institute of Mental Health profiles the average child molester as a white male with one year of college, working a full-time job. Often, those previously convicted of sex crimes against children continue to offend, since we lack any kind of effective national tracking system for molesters. Senator Mitch McConnell of Kentucky is working on a bill that will force national registration of all child sex offenders (Whiteley 80). Senator McConnell says,

> I find it ludicrous that for years we have been able to trace stolen cars and jewelry across state lines, but we have not been able to track convicted sexual abusers of our nation's children. It's time we took sexual crimes against children as seriously as we take auto theft (Whiteley 80).

In Delaware, Patricia Forbes and Darlene Sullivan, leading advocates for child sexual abuse victims, administer Action For Children Today, a nonprofit organization that helps to rewrite laws in the area of child abuse. They were successful in getting state legislator David Sokola to sponsor a bill requiring registration of all convicted pedophiles in Delaware (Soulsman). Their work is an example of what other states can do to confront this threat to children.

Sexual abuse is not the only street crime against young people, for assault and robbery also occur at an alarming rate among children. The key to protecting children from sexual abuse, abduction, assault, or intimidation by their peers is educating them on their options in dealing with such a situation. Many of the techniques that are effective in dealing with strangers can be effective in dealing with threats from people the child knows. Victimologists and psychologists agree that it is only through effective education (examples of which we will see later) that we can raise the awareness of our children to a level where we can be reasonably confident that they will make the right choices when confronted by a stranger or a relative who seeks to harm them. But it is not only important that we educate them on what they can expect in dealing with assault, it is also critical that we provide such education in a rational, factual manner that does not promote anxiety and cause undesirable by-products in the learning process. In this book, the definition of children has been kept intentionally broad, realizing that while parents recognize different ages and levels of maturity in their own offspring, the law and the realm of criminal justice research generally views anyone under age 18 as a child. Obviously, some of the discussion applies specifically to younger (preteen) children, but the context of the remarks will make their applicability apparent.

There are numerous programs designed to help children develop survival skills, sometimes referred to as "street-proofing." The goal of any program to protect your children must have as its basis the idea of minimizing your child's fear while enhancing his or her awareness. Just sitting down and telling your children all the horror stores you have ever heard about child molesting and abduction will not protect them. Simply making your child afraid will not reduce his vulnerability. One of the greatest disservices parents can do to children is to terrorize them into believing that all strangers are evil and that everyone is out to get them. Not only will that interfere with their socialization skills, but it may also cause some long-term psychological effects.

Whether you handle the training of your own children or enroll them in a program specifically designed to impart survival skills, you must pay particular attention to messages the child is receiving. A 1986 Roper survey reported that 76% of the children interviewed said they were "worried that they might be kidnapped" (Kraizer et al. 70). No one questions the importance of making a child aware of the threat of abduction, for education is the first step in deterrence. The problem is the use of the word "worried." A child has the right to be a child, and as such, should not be forced to grow up too soon. We must be careful that we do not create children who are walking around 24 hours a day in constant fear of being abducted.

Some parents have told me, "I don't care if my children are worried, just as long as they are safe." Of course parents are concerned about the safety of their children, but they need not necessarily trade safety for fear and anguish. Through proper training, we can have our children safe with confidence and understanding, instead of fear and apprehension. S. K. Kraizer, in a 1988 article for *Child Welfare*, "Programming for Preventing Sexual Abuse and Abduction," says we should avoid placing our children in a frame of mind where they respond to the definition of a stranger with something similar to what is described below.

> Strangers are people who kidnap you, poison you, cut off your head, and you never see your mommy and daddy ever again . . . concern has been expressed that messages of this kind may be damaging to children, that children may be more afraid and anxious after prevention programs are presented than before, and that these programs may not be effective in teaching the desired prevention skills (70).

It is not enough just to be concerned that your children might be victimized, and to tell them what happened to little Johnny who lived down the street. The instruction must be presented in such a way that the child draws positive lessons about his or her own abilities at handling a threatening situation, instead of negative images that result from a steady diet of anxiety-producing stories that may do more to terrorize than inform. Teaching children the dangers of sexual abuse and abduction involves behavioral strategies in addition to theory. Discussions alone do not guarantee that children will respond properly to a given situation. Correct answers on paper are not predictive of success in a real situation. The most effective means of teaching children to handle criminal confrontation is through behavioral circumstances involving role-playing, specifically providing the successive refinement of their skills as they progress. No matter how good your slide-show may be, or how nicely your workbooks are printed, they will not be as effective without the addition of behavioral exercises. The National Committee for the Prevention of Child Abuse says "behavioral assessment strategies . . . represent the only means of estimating the strength of the behaviors being taught" (Kraizer 74).

Effective behavioral learning can be something as simple as the role-playing game of "What if . . . ?" It can be practiced within the family unit.

> Sarah, what if a person you didn't know were to come to the front door before Dad got home one day, and ring the doorbell. You look through the peephole and see a person you don't know. What if they said to you, "I really need to come in and use your telephone. My car broke down in the middle of the street, and I need to call the service station to get someone to fix it." Would you let them in to use the telephone? What if that happened, Sarah? What would you do?

Beginning a discussion like this, you might have the child explain how he or she would handle the situation. You now have the opportunity to listen to his or her response and evaluate its strengths and weaknesses. Then you might act out the scenario to reinforce the learning situation. You can emphasize attitudes and behaviors that are conducive to survival in an atmosphere that approaches the threat through fact, instead of through fear alone. These kind of activities promote faster learning and allow the children to retain the information for longer periods than do strictly informational approaches. Hechinger (40) suggests these other "What if" questions for young children.

WHAT IF . . .
1. we are separated in a shopping center, in the movies, at the beach?
2. you are lost in a department store, in the park, at a parade?

3. a stranger offered you candy or presents to leave the playground?
4. a stranger wanted you to get in his car?
5. a stranger started fussing with your clothing?
6. someone you did not know asked your name and phone number?

Parents are often unsure when they should begin to train their children in self-protection. Children as young as 3 or 4 years of age have benefited from some programs, but the broadest level of success seems to be the period of kindergarten through second grade. Children at this age have the mental abilities to assimilate the information and they are developing the physical skills necessary to execute some of the avoidance measures they will learn. Thousands of young children have learned conflict avoidance and self-defense, and they tend to learn it much easier than do their older siblings. They are successful because they have fewer preconceived ideas and misconceptions that get in the way of learning (Kraizer 77). You are not always going to be around to protect your child. The older the child gets, the less you will be available to offer protection. So beginning at an early age just enhances your child's survival. Since children are most vulnerable between the ages of 9 and 12 years (Wooden 150), it makes sense that we should begin training them early.

One program that teaches personal safety strategies for young children is the Red Flag/Green Flag People program. This national program offers a workbook-based curriculum emphasizing sexual abuse prevention concepts, and it has been used and evaluated in both home and school settings. Using a coloring book, the program highlights both verbal and physical communication, including proper and improper touching, to enable children to recognize unwanted sexual advances. A film, "Better Safe Than Sorry II," augments the coloring book and further defines and explains various sexual assault situations (Kolko et al. 31). Studies of the Red Flag/Green Flag People program have demonstrated that children who undergo the program have both short-term and long-term retention of the skills, and that a child's awareness of the potential for sexual assault is enhanced. In a comment about this effective program, but equally applicable to all educational formats that seek to make children less vulnerable, Kolko et al. indicate

> . . . follow-up impact may be bolstered if programs include parents and teachers, are extended in length and comprehensiveness, incorporate booster or review sessions, provide behavioral rehearsal of preventive strategies and performance feedback, and offer continued assistance once the program has been terminated (42).

In other words, whatever the chosen curriculum, a *team* effort involving all those adults significant in a child's life, such as parent, teacher, coach, policeman, doctor, is the best approach to safeguarding our children. A program does not have to be elaborate, employ dozens of psychologists and criminologists, or be expensive to be effective. Springfield, Missouri, was the site of a test program that used a robotic McGruff the Crime Dog to deliver a safety message to children. Of the 291 students participating in the program, some 85% said they understood McGruff's message warning them about drugs and advances from strangers. Since McGruff was familiar to the children as a symbol of safety, the students indicated that the robot's presence made the police officers' message more understandable; and after all, communication is the first step to crime prevention among children (Bell & McDowell 20–21).

Rules of the Game.   It is important that parents set up some basic rules for children to follow when dealing with strangers or family members who might attempt to violate them. Being able to recognize the various ruses that child abusers and molesters use, you can prepare the children to meet these situations. A program entitled "Children Need To Know: Personal Safety Training Program," developed in 1981, offers several fundamentals for protecting children (Kraizer 69). I have reproduced these rules below, but

I have expanded the discussion of each one so you can better explain them to your children. By reviewing these rules with your child, you can get off to a good start in street-proofing them.

RULE ONE: *A stranger is anyone you don't know.* That sounds obvious, but many children have never met a stranger, particularly very young children. There is a tendency for young children to be friendly to everyone. We raise our children to be sociable and encourage them to sit in the laps of people we have barely met. But there has to be a limit to even a child's sociability, and that means reinforcing their understanding of exactly who strangers are and how to act around them.

RULE TWO: *Most people are strangers and most of them are nice.* It is important to emphasize to children that everyone who is a stranger is not out to get them. This is the hardest balance to achieve. You want a child who is friendly and able to interact among new acquaintances, yet you do not want to develop such a sense of trust that would make him or her vulnerable to a criminal. You cannot tell by looking who is nice and who is not. We have seen in the chapter on profiles of offenders that outward appearance can be deceiving. One of the most successful ruses used by child abductors/abusers is to create a disarming sense of confidence in the child. Molesters often fake the appearance of authority, such as that of the police, clergy, etc., to gain access to the child. Children must understand that just because a stranger wears a uniform, that doesn't make him or her "nice." Some child abductors even drive black or blue cars, since they resemble police vehicles. Again, the parent must draw a tedious line between respect for authority and blind obedience to anyone wearing a uniform. One technique to help a child validate a uniformed stranger's instructions or request is to have the child let another adult verify the authenticity of the stranger.

RULE THREE: *When you are with an adult who is taking care of you, that adult is principally responsible for making decisions about strang-*

ers.   Children must understand this concept to walk the fine line between autonomy and respect for adult authority. It is the decisions that adults make in the child's presence that frequently set the example for the types of decisions the child will make when he or she is alone. That makes it all the more important that parents know the rules for dealing with criminal confrontations.

RULE FOUR: *Whether by yourself or with your friends, you should follow the rules with all strangers.*   This encourages the child not to take chances and not to gamble on the veracity of a stranger. Through effective discussion and role-play, the child will develop a good idea of how to handle a given situation; for the ultimate test comes when you, the parent, are not around to make sure the child chooses correctly.

RULE FIVE: *Remain farther away than an arm's reach from someone you don't know.*   Maintain a "Circle of Safety" around yourself. If this idea sounds familiar, you will recall the concept of personal space in the chapter on conflict avoidance. Age is not a determiner of the need for personal space. That small safety zone that children maintain around themselves can mean the difference between abduction and freedom. For Mike Burnside (my young student mentioned earlier), the distance he kept between himself and the stranger's car allowed him to escape and outrun his assailant.

RULE SIX: *Don't talk to someone you don't know. Don't answer their questions.*   On the surface, this may appear to be an extremely antisocial behavior to demand of a child. There is an element of unfriendliness involved, but when you consider the price your child may pay for being too friendly to a stranger, you may be ultimately saving the youngster considerable grief. Better some adult get slightly offended by your child's lack of responsiveness than to have your child abducted or molested. As Linda Meyer teaches in *Safety Zone*, her excellent read-aloud book for preventing child abduction, "You don't always have to be polite to a big person. Your safety is more important" (17). A question–answer lure was the very approach Mike Burnside faced. By engaging him in casual conversation, the offender hoped to gain Mike's confidence long enough to get him inside the car.

RULE SEVEN: *Don't take anything from someone you don't know, not even something that belongs to you or your family.* Most children of my generation were drilled in the old adage, "Don't take candy from a stranger." While it was a simple approach, it was effective for many children. Child abductors/abusers frequently offer children candy, toys, money, or other inducements to accompany them. The older the child, the bigger the inducement, for instance, skateboards or radios. Not only is it important to warn your child of the possibility of bribery lures, it is also necessary that the child inform you if one of these incidents takes place.

RULE EIGHT: *Don't go with someone you don't know, unless (for children 6 and up) the individual knows your predetermined family code word.* Parents sometimes become annoyed at the suggestion of using a family code word. "Our society can't be bad enough for that!" a mother said to me one evening. "Has it really come to this?" another parent asked. Many adults react in disbelief because they did not sense the problem was this bad when *they* were children, so they wonder how it could be this bad now. It is normal for parents to evaluate their child's environment in terms of what they experienced; and they are correct in the sense that few families felt the necessity to use a code word as a recently as 20 years ago. But times have changed and they have brought with them changing approaches to the problem of child abduction/abuse. The principle behind the family code word is to give the child the sense of security in knowing that the person picking him or her up is a bona fide representative of the parent. The code word need not be intricate or difficult, but may be any word that the child can immediately recognize and associate with safety. Even if you decide that a family code word is unnecessary, you must ensure that your child accompanies no one until he or she has made an effort to check the person out with you or your spouse. A fact-based, made-for-television movie depicted how a young boy was abducted from a daycare facility by a stranger. The child's body was found several weeks later—a victim of sexual abuse. How could this happen? The child believed the individual who picked him up was an authentic representative sent by a parent, so he willingly accompanied him. This particular lure is commonly connected to the creation of a false emergency situation, where someone arrives to pick up a child from school or home, with some story that the child's parent has been injured. The abductor tells the child he will see the injured parent if he or she comes along quickly. Phrases like, "Your daddy had a car accident and he wants me to pick you up from school today," are common ploys. An appeal like this is extremely powerful to a young child who has been led to respect the authority of adults and who senses that his or her father has been hurt. The family code word can help to prevent such a lure from being successful, for its absence immediately alerts the child that something is wrong with the situation. The child may then be inclined to check out the story by calling home or asking a teacher to intervene. If you tell your child, "Under no circumstances do you go anywhere with a stranger," and if you prepare a contingency plan for emergency notification, you can reduce the risk that your child will be victimized.

Programs That Teach and Protect.   Children have a strong, instinctive sense of right and wrong when it comes to violation of their bodies. If a loved one, family member, acquaintance, or a stranger has taken liberties with a child, the child will often give signals that this has occurred, sometimes using lines like "She touched me in a bad place." It is then up to the parents to be observant and to trust their own instincts as well as their child's.

Parents who lack confidence imparting the skills necessary to protect their children from assault or abduction may find it effective to enroll them in various programs designed to teach survival skills. These programs, some of which were previously mentioned, should provide not only avoidance measures to keep the child out of potentially dangerous situations, but also basic instruction in self-defense. Not all programs that offer counseling and education about the threat to children will provide self-defense as part of the curriculum. Unfortunately, some parents have been led to believe that self-defense training for children promotes aggressiveness and antisocial behavior. That has not been my experience. Over the past two decades, I have seen hundreds of children receive training in self-defense, and with few exceptions, those children demonstrated no abnormal aggressiveness or socially unacceptable behavior. In most cases, their aggressiveness diminished, or was at least channeled into a healthy activity. Anxiety was usually replaced with quiet confidence. The fear that self-defense training creates little monsters and bullies is unfounded and unsupported by any serious scholarly research. A good self-defense program teaches children when *not* to fight as well as how to fight if they must. Exposing children to the philosophies and theories of criminal avoidance without emphasizing the criticalness of self-defense is leaving the job half done. Yet despite the best training in the world and the diligent efforts of young people, it is sometimes impossible for a child to talk his or her way out of a situation and escape untouched. Without the basics of self-defense training, a child's options are limited. Survival and protection programs like Red Flag/Green Flag People effectively improve a child's self-esteem and confidence. When such an approach includes self-defense as an integral element of the curriculum, the result is a more balanced, useful, and effective course.

Another program that teaches conflict avoidance skills is called Stop Child Abuse Through Education (SCATE), a Maryland-based enterprise that was developed jointly by the Prince George County Police Department (Child Abuse and Community Relations Divisions) and the Prince George County General Hospital Sexual Assault Center. Evolving from the "Dangerous Stranger" program of the local law enforcement community, it is a good example of what the combined efforts of local service organizations can produce. It reaches out to students through PTAs, and has been offered in the local schools for over ten years (Flaherty 9).

SCATE seeks to replace children's fears with awareness, through education and sensitivity to the criminal threat. Officials have taken great care to produce a curriculum that informs without terrifying or making the children paranoid. Instructors profile the offenders and advise students what to look for in a potentially dangerous situation. They offer advice on how to handle conflicts and provide parents with indicators to look for in the behavior of their children.

A slightly different approach to street-proofing children is the Safety and Fitness Exchange (SAFE). This organization provides a synthesis of counseling, self-defense instruction and assertiveness training. As in SCATE, the instructors come from varied backgrounds in community service, including social work, counseling, education, and the martial arts (Burns 24). SAFE was initiated in 1981 when some parents sought help for their children who had been victimized. From the first ten sexual assault victims, aged five to twelve, SAFE expanded to offer a broad range of instruction to meet a growing demand within New York City communities. The founders of SAFE call their organization a consulting firm that specializes in conducting crime avoidance seminars and self-defense classes (Burns, 24). Much of the material they present to children was created from evaluating the various needs the children themselves expressed. Hundreds of children have completed the SAFE program and both the children and their parents feel more confident about their ability to handle an assault situation. One mother noted that if her son "got into a situation before, he never would have screamed. Now I think that would be his first instinct," she said. "It's been a tremendous asset for his self-confidence, his awareness. Now he's aware of his environment, which is very important to me" (Burns 53).

The SAFE curriculum is a good example of an approach to safeguarding your children, which includes information, role-playing, and basic self-defense instruction. Check with your local community service organizations to see if they offer a program like SAFE. If there is no program available, you might be able to start one by drawing together professionals from law enforcement, mental health, child welfare, and the martial arts. In the case of SAFE in New York, both the Girl Scouts and the Girls Club became actively involved in the program, and several grants were obtained to cover the cost of operation. If you are interested in more information about SAFE, you can write to SAFE, 541 Avenue of the Americas, New York, New York 10011.

Children are both willing and able to learn how to avoid trouble and how to escape from people intending to harm them. Pamela McDonnell, one of the cofounders of SAFE, put it this way:

> Most people don't believe that children can physically defend themselves . . . We're one of the few groups that believe that children can defend themselves against Daddy, or the babysitter, or the softball coach, or the scout leader, if necessary (Burns 25).

But unless parents are willing to teach children avoidance strategies at home, using the "What if . . . ?" scenario or some recognized curriculum, or enroll them in an organized program, children will be as vulnerable as ever to the criminal element in society.

SCHOOL/PLAYGROUND CRIME

A 1991 nationwide survey of 12,272 high school students conducted by the Centers for Disease Control showed that 42% had been in at least one fight during the last year, and discovered a ratio of about 140 fights reported per 100 students. Some 26% admitted they had carried a weapon during the month prior to the survey, with 11% of those most often carrying a handgun (Neergaard 3D). If that is not enough to make a parent sit up and take notice, what will? Most of us, Baby Boomers and beyond, can recall those halcyon days when we went to school to learn—or to goof off at the worst. A fist-fight after school by the smoking rail in back of the gymnasium was a big deal, sure to draw a crowd of curious onlookers; but we were all reasonably sure it would not get out of hand. Either one guy would get the best of the other and render him to the point of humiliation and/or tears, or the principal would step in to break the whole thing up. That kind of action can still be found at a public or private school, but the whole business of student conflict has taken on a more ominous and potentially deadly nature. If one out of four students is carrying a weapon as the above survey suggests, what happens when the armed student begins to lose by the *Marquis De Queensbury* rules? The answer is clear when you discover that the murder rate among children under 15 has doubled in the last five years (*CBS Evening News*). But what is a parent to do?

According to *USA Today*, in an article entitled "High School Girls Face Harassment," almost 40% of Wisconsin girls had experienced physical harassment from their peers by the time they were high school seniors, with one-third admitting they were subjected to undesired sexual intercourse (12). The National Institute of Education says that 11% of all secondary school children in this country have something stolen from them every month (Hechinger 111), and who can forget the celebrated case of the youngster who was killed for his state-of-the-art basketball shoes?

Two-thirds of the junior and senior high school students in St. Paul, Minnesota, public schools indicated they had been the victim of crimes or threats at school, according to the *St. Paul Pioneer Press-Dispatch* (December 1, 1992). This survey of 2,500 students, in which they indicated cafeterias, hallways, stairs, and restrooms as the "most dangerous school areas," reflects what is likely the situation in many schools across the nation. Driven by their fear, 29% reported carrying a weapon to school at least once during the year—usually a knife or razor (Livingston 5A). Superintendent Curman Gaines said:

> People who raise their eyebrows at these statistics are not living in the real world, . . . We have to instill in our children the value of nonviolence. We as a community have to take more responsibility for what is happening in our community. We cannot look the other way (Livingston 5A).

What do the students say is the answer? Make staff changes, strictly enforce rules, and remove problem students. The larger the school, the greater the capacity for crime, with your child's chances of being a victim highest during the middle of the week. A seventh-grader is most likely to be robbed—a senior the least likely. His or her classroom is ultimately the safest place on campus (Hechinger 112).

Role Models

Schools are a microcosm of society and playgrounds tend to reflect the personality of a given neighborhood. Your child can be at risk from a criminal act in either location unless he or she learns some ground rules early. No child I ever knew has come through 12 years of education without encountering some kind of physical threat at school; and I cannot imagine a child who has not run afoul of at least one of his or her peers during neighborhood play. How your child handles these normal confrontations of life depends on the example he or she has observed through your personal role model, as well as the instruction you have provided. If Daddy gets drunk and wants to fight on the slightest provocation, then his little Johnnie can almost certainly be expected to bloody the lip of some other child who happens to get to the merry-go-round first. If Mommy—red-eyed, high, and reeking of the sick-sweet odor of marijuana smoke—cusses out her next door neighbor for playing the stereo too loud, no one should be surprised when little Sandra becomes profane, abusive, and threatens one of her classmates in middle school. Yes, these are extreme examples, but they are unfortunately very real. How you as a parent handle a threatening situation—your degree of self-control, compassion, and common sense—is the controlling factor in how a child will respond to a threat. Some social psychologists and Ph.D.'s in child development may disagree, but *your* example is even more important in influencing your child's behavior than the powerful, ever-present specter of peer pressure. In the 1991 study of Wisconsin girls mentioned earlier, as cited in *USA Today*, those reporting harassment and sexual exploitation also demonstrated the following factors that increased their risk of being victimized:

- A history of sexual abuse by an adult
- Parents who did not closely monitor their behavior
- Low self-esteem or a feeling of having no future
- A family that provided few opportunities for them to develop good decision-making skills (12)

Notice the absence of peer pressure as one of those factors. Parents must not only tell their children what constitutes appropriate behavior, they must *demonstrate* that behavior.

Fear and Reporting

It is sad but true that students are not the only ones afraid to go to school nowadays. Over 110,000 teachers suffered attacks at the hands of students, according to the 1978 *Safe School Study Report* sponsored by the National Institute of Education, and a 1980 study found that when "teachers were asked to describe their fears, apprehensions, and concerns related to teaching, student discipline usually head[ed] the list" (Dworkin et al. 160).

On January 18, 1993, a 17-year-old high school student named Scott Pennington shot and killed his teacher, a custodian at the school, and held 20 of his classmates hostage in the small town of Grayson, Kentucky. Pennington, described by students and school officials as a loner, was "among the last ones you'd choose" to commit such a crime, according to Ray Tussey, his high school principal. Other than having a stutter, which occasioned some derision from fellow students, there was little to tip off teachers to Pennington's penchant for violence. For reasons the psychologists will likely spend years trying to sort out, the young man just walked up to his last period English teacher and gunned her down with a .38 caliber pistol. When the janitor heard the shot and came to investigate, the boy killed him too (Voskuhl 1). Why did he do it? That's a good question. It is on everyone's mind. But a more important question is, "What's he doing there with a gun in the first place?" Grayson is a small country town. Unlike many major cities, it is not ravaged by gangs that threaten and intimidate young people. No student at that high school should have so feared for his life as to need a gun; however, that was precisely the reason given by a young Los Angeles teenager who two days later accidentally discharged a .357 Magnum in a classroom. According to an Associated Press story appearing in the Louisville *Courier-Journal*, the boy's mistake took the life of one fellow student and severely wounded another (Gun A2).

"I'm sorry. I didn't mean to do it," he mumbled, as he stared at the child he shot. But it was a bit too late for apologies. Prior to the incident, the young man had been showing the weapon off and claiming it was protection against gang members. No wonder many teachers are so intimidated, so frightened by unruly students, that they refuse to confront the discipline problems for fear of being victimized themselves. Now, if teachers are afraid, you can bet your child will be. So it only makes sense to teach conflict avoidance skills as soon as your child is old enough to understand them.

A tremendous number of crimes by children against other children are never reported to the police. Whether the crime occurs in school or on the playground, many children will not report the incident or tell their parents for fear of retaliation. Often it is hard for a parent to understand how anyone could be afraid enough of a 10- or 12-year-old child to not admit he or she has been victimized. But you must remember that the bully, or the budding strong-arm robber that looks so small and harmless, may be of equal size as or bigger than your child. If that is not enough, the perpetrator may possess the ultimate power in the eyes of pubescent youth—he or she may be *cool*—and everyone knows you don't anger the cool people. Remember that your child has to face his nemesis daily. You don't. Your child has to dodge the wrath of a juvenile perpetrator who will often avoid punishment even if he or she is found out. Also, many youngsters fear their parents' reaction if they admit they have been beaten up or shaken down for their lunch money.

"I didn't want Dad to think I'm a wimp," Carl Melton, an embarrassed 14-year-old told me in self-defense class one night. He'd been relieved of his allowance. A petite, 11-year-old young lady named Jennie didn't want her parents to know she had been in a fight over her sweater at school.

"My mother will say that's not ladylike," she confessed. A clique of female bullies had been bothering her for more than a month, but she wouldn't breathe a word of it to her parents.

Some children think they will be blamed for allowing an assault to happen, or in some way ridiculed for not standing up for their rights. And there are few actions more embarrassing to a child—particularly a teenager—than having your parents come to school to solve your problems. Teenagers are embarrassed enough by their parents, even when their parents are just walking near them in the mall. It only gets worse when they are made to feel less than the perfect and mature creatures they have come to view themselves as.

Danger Areas

Liddon R. Griffith, in his book *Mugging: You Can Protect Yourself*, lists several school danger areas to warn your children about: lunchrooms, staircases, restrooms, and the playground (157). But do not be alarmed if they act unsurprised when you sit them down to talk. Chances are they already know the danger areas because they have either experienced them, seen others confronted, or heard rumors. And remember that it is just as important to listen to what your children tell you about the school as it is to impart information to them. While you will probably remind your child of the usual safety precautions—for instance, do not leave valuables unsecured in lockers, keep your belongings in sight when you are changing clothes, do not remove your rings when washing your hands in the lavatory, stay with a larger group whenever possible—make sure you communicate to your child the importance of reporting to *you* any frightening incidents or situations that make him or her uncomfortable. With a little effort, the two of you can probably figure out a way to handle the situation that will neither escalate the problem nor embarrass the child.

Talking to children about "danger areas" at school seems foreign to many parents, but unfortunately, it has come to that. A student's best insurance against assault in school is the presence of teachers and other students he or she trusts. In other words, urge your children to make upright friends and to remain in their company as much as possible. Also, keep in mind that the more a child is present at school long before or after normal school hours, the better target he or she becomes. The decrease in guardianship by teachers and peers, plus the increased likelihood of people present who are not affiliated with the school, such as drug dealers, gang members, and street thugs, combine to create a threatening environment. Extracurricular activities are important to a child's educational and social development, but parents must make sure their children are protected.

As parents know, it takes significant parental sacrifice in money and time for young people to effectively participate even in high school sports. But the late departures from school after practice, and the late arrivals back at school after away-games, create an environment ripe for crime against a child. The school should do its best to ensure safety, offering an activities bus for those who stay later after school, and providing sufficient teacher and parental supervision of the activities themselves. But parents can make sure children aren't standing alone in the dark on the steps of the school, and that someone is there to pick them up at 9:00 P.M., when the bus returns from an "away" game. And when it comes time for children to drive themselves, make sure you know when they leave and when they should arrive home; and if they are late, start looking. The key is to make sure you do *something* to verify and monitor the security of your child's school activities.

Whenever possible, have your child travel to school with friends or in a car pool with parental supervision, and use the notion of guardianship to discourage those who would take advantage. Unfortunately, many parents face the difficult challenge of raising a child alone, where they must often deal with latch-key arrangements and can only dream about car pools and group security for their child. Still, young people must be prepared for the dangers they face, and reinforced in the same confrontation avoidance habits discussed in the earlier chapters. Students who are untutored in the realities of life are little more than prime targets for the young criminals at the local school.

"[Children] need to know how to communicate what they do and do not want, and how to protect themselves from potentially harmful situations," says Donell Kerns, a doctoral student at the University of Wisconsin-Madison. The study of Wisconsin youth that identified victimization of female high school students says the best action parents can take to safeguard their children is to "monitor their activities, take an interest in their lives, and know where they are and who they are with . . ." ("High School Girls" 12).

Reacting to a Threat

Liddon R. Griffith's advice to young people who are confronted by a potential assailant is grounded in common sense, courtesy, and inner strength. He suggests that parents should make children aware of adult values such as courage, and how values may be measured differently by adults. "Everyone admires the person who is strong and brave, but it also takes a courageous person to say, 'Excuse me' or 'I'm sorry,'" argues Griffith (161). This response to a threat mirrors the advice presented in the chapter on self-defense, that is, apologizing for some perceived offense if it means avoiding trouble. The bully who blocks your child's path in the hallway may not be looking to rob him or her for lunch money, or to take some jewelry. The perpetrator may be looking for status or image among his selected group. Learning to say "excuse me" before attempting to pass gives the assailant an opportunity to save face without forcing a fight. Also, that simple act puts the moral responsibility of any ensuing violence clearly upon the shoulders of the aggressor—a point not to be taken lightly if the matter ends up in the principal's office. Many of us have experienced the blind sweep of school justice that sometimes penalizes an entire class or group for the actions of one. When your child demonstrates self-control and courtesy, and attempts to resolve a potential conflict short of violence, he or she not only appears more mature than the aggressor, but creates a virtually unassailable position of socially acceptable behavior. But this response pattern is grounded in a previously discussed idea: what we do, how we behave, and our value system *as parents* are the strongest indicators of a child's response to the threat of crime. If you are not willing to demonstrate similar behavior in your own response to confrontation, then you are wasting your breath trying to teach your child to resolve conflict in this manner. Your child will imitate what you do, not what you say.

It is hard enough to get children to adopt this approach to a threat even when parents provide a solid example, for children are prone to mistake kindness for weakness. Sometimes reinforced by short-sighted parents who indignantly declare to a bullied child, "Why didn't you punch the bum's lights out?" children often feel they must fight to create an image, to be a tough guy, or to be cool. Some even feel guilty for not standing up to an assailant (Griffith 161).

A Case Study.   There had been some comments passed at school between two ninth-grade girls, Wendy and Anna. Finally, one day Anna and three friends confronted Wendy and one of her friends down the street from Wendy's house. More words were exchanged and Anna threatened Wendy and challenged her to fight. Wendy, who was smaller than Anna, said she didn't want to fight her and that she wanted to be left alone. As is often the case in a situation like this, Wendy could not be certain that Anna would be her only opponent should she have to fight, and she wisely attempted to talk her way out of it. Unfortunately, Anna seemed determined to have some satisfaction in the matter, so she struck Wendy, sending her to the ground, and continued to pressure her to fight. But Wendy resisted the temptation to start punching and wrestling around, and she simply refused to stoop to the other girl's level. As Wendy walked away, more words were hurled in her direction, but she eventually got home with no further harm. Wendy felt confident and trusted her parents enough to tell them what happened. She realized they were not going to go out and do something stupid and embarrassing. But her parents were concerned about what happened, and they were particularly bothered by the fact that Wendy was visibly afraid of going to school the next day. They might have chosen to ignore the matter and "let the children work it out," but physical violence was their trip wire. Words between children, and even adults, are one thing; but when someone strikes your child, the matter escalates to the level of intervention.

After hearing Wendy's version of what happened (and with children it is important to recognize that the two sides to a story can be widely disparate), her father contacted Anna's father and had a talk with him on the front porch. Before arriving, Anna's father had determined that the incident went down substantially as Wendy had described it, and he did not deny that his daughter had struck Wendy.

"John," Wendy's father said, "if they want to argue between themselves, that's one thing. But when someone hits my child, I get upset."

John began to say how he had grown up in a rough neighborhood, and while he was sorry for what Anna had done, he believed a certain amount of that was to be expected; but the other parent was not satisfied with that response.

"Let me put it to you like this. In my family, we don't hit other people. If we have a disagreement with someone, we don't settle it with violence unless we have no other choice. Now, I think we have the fundamental right to be able to walk down the street of our neighborhood without being punched or kicked or knocked to the ground."

Anna's father agreed with that statement.

"And what's more important," Wendy's father continued, " is that this *isn't* a rough neighborhood and I don't intend for it to become one. So my feeling is this: Let's put this incident aside, I'll have my daughter keep her distance from Anna and you do the same. But if Anna strikes my daughter again, I will involve the police and I will press charges."

Now, some parents will say that Wendy's father overreacted to the situation; but anytime an altercation between children escalates to violence, it is time for parents to get involved. He sternly warned Wendy about not inciting Anna with hurtful language and keeping her distance, and as of now there have been no further incidents. In fact, Anna and Wendy are on speaking terms again and that is good.

*   *   *   *   *

While the above example of nonforceful reaction to a physical threat worked out satisfactorily, many times it does not. As with adult confrontation, there are times your child will be unable to avoid a fight. If such a situation occurs, let me first of all urge you not to rush your child to a psychotherapist to see what is wrong with him or her. That is the opposite end of the spectrum from the parent who asks, "Why didn't you punch her lights out?" There is a limit to how far a child should have to go to avoid violence.

Most of the world's major religions have some teaching about when it is appropriate to protect oneself. Christians, for example, are raised to pay particular heed to these words:

> But I say unto you which hear, Love your enemies, do good to them which hate you,
> Bless them that curse you, and pray for them which despitefully use you.
> And unto him that smiteth thee on the one cheek offer also the other; and him that taketh away thy cloak forbid not to take thy coat also. (Luke 6:27–29).

While that is sound advice for life, remember: You have only *two* cheeks. There is a limit to what a child (and an adult for that matter) has to take from another person before responding in self-defense. According to the rules of my household, if my daughter strikes another child in retaliation, then my child had better come home with the moral equivalent of two red cheeks; otherwise, she did not go far enough to avoid trouble. The rules and occasions of self-defense for children are not much different than for adults, though the law views tumbling around in the playground as considerably less important than a fist-fight between 40-year-old men at the mall. Sometimes your children will have to fight. You cannot protect them from that. Some psychologists suggest helping your child to feel the motivation of his or her aggressor. What makes the bully bully? Is he the child of a divorced parent and just looking for attention? Is he being beaten up at home? Such a suggestion is ridiculous. Your child has no business trying to psychoanalyze an assailant. One New York psychologist says, "Your child may then feel stronger in relationship to that youngster because he or she can see the bully himself as a victim in another setting" (Hechinger 119). That kind of advice is too far removed from reality to be effective. Just try your best to teach them that fighting is a last alternative, and even then it should be over something significant. Yes, fighting can be dangerous; but capitulation has hidden costs—many of them psychological—that can affect a child for years. That is why it is important to demonstrate and teach adult values, so that a child can be both mature in avoiding physical violence, and confident that if he or she must resort to violence, it is appropriate for the situation.

In an interesting and disturbing twist to parental intervention in child violence, a 33-year-old single mother in Lubbock, Texas, faced assault and disorderly conduct charges because she confronted the teenage boys who allegedly raped her daughter. Reiko Phillips reportedly waited at a school bus stop until a young man exited the bus, then grabbed the youth by the collar, pointed Mace at him and "threatened to kill him in an alley" ("Mom Is Charged" 5A). The woman's daughter had accused the boy of raping her and the boy had reportedly been bragging about it at school.

"He was harassing her on the school bus, making fun of her

Figure 8.1. After school security. If your child hangs around the school for extracurricular activities, make sure he or she is supervised. Students left alone can be the target of undesirables who inhabit schoolyards after most students and faculty have left for the day.

and telling everybody that they raped her, that she liked it," Phillips said. "It made her cry" (5A).

Most parents would sympathize with the righteous indignation and anger Ms. Phillips felt toward the alleged assailants. And at least on the surface, there seems to be a certain justice in the

Figure 8.2. Have children supervised both going to and coming from school. A parent's best insurance policy for a child's safety at school is talking to the child about the potential threats, urging the child to cultivate and stick with a set of well-behaved friends, and monitoring the child's travel to and from school.

confrontation. But the district attorney saw things differently. Allowing such parental retribution, says Lubbock County DA Travis Ware, "has folks taking the law into their own hands and complete anarchy" (5A). Ware also indicated that Phillips did not let the system work because she refused to allow her daughter to cooperate with prosecutors. She called the police but never brought her daughter in to file charges or make a statement.

Parents cannot claim higher moral authority and circumvent the system if they never allow the system to work. Although Reiko Phillips faced a misdemeanor assault charge and four counts of disorderly conduct, the district attorney eventually dropped the charges when the young man involved failed to come forward and testify against Phillips.

Chapter Nine

THE THREAT TO THE AGING

Growing old should be a period in life when people can enjoy the respect they have earned over a lifetime. The elderly are entitled to live peacefully and safely in their homes, and they should have the chance to watch their children and grandchildren grow up. But far too many older Americans are cheated out of that opportunity because of crime. They live in fear of being the victim of violent crime, and instead of coming and going freely in the neighborhood they have helped to build, whole segments of our nation's aged are literally prisoners within their own homes. Not only are many of them afraid to walk the streets, or afraid to visit a grocery store, they are also terrified that some street thug will kick down their front door and attack them in their living room.

Part of growing older is recognizing and dealing with increased physical limitations, for instance, slower reactions, reduced agility, and seeing or hearing degradation. Decreased capacity carries with it an increased sense of vulnerability.

"Could I really outrun some young hoodlum?" an older person may ask. "Do I see well enough to be able to identify a purse snatcher?"

Because of a sense of increased susceptibility to assault and/or robbery, many older Americans have altered their lifestyle to

215

minimize risk; but they have paid a price in opportunity costs. George B. Sunderland, Manager of Criminal Justice Services at the American Association of Retired Persons (AARP), says that the quality of life for many of our elderly has been eroded by the paralyzing fear of victimization (Lent & Harpold 17).

We know from Chapter One that violent crime has increased over the past three decades, and as law enforcement agencies are stretched more thinly, many of the elderly in our society have lost confidence in "the system's" ability to protect them. Their fear has its basis in the knowledge that they, as older persons, are much more vulnerable to criminal acts. They know what the bad guys know: Old people are good targets. Yet despite the attractiveness of the elderly as criminal targets of opportunity, and the overall increase in crime rates, senior citizens in the United States are actually victimized *less often* than most other age groups in our society (Table 9.1). The public has misperceived that older persons are the most common target for criminals, but the statistics simply do not support such a notion. In 1981 the U.S. Department of Justice found that the elderly victimization rate had only modified slightly, with no significant change in the rate of rape, a slight downward trend in robbery, and virtually no change in the rate of

TABLE 9.1. Victimization Rate for the Elderly
(per 1,000 persons)

	All violent crimes	Assault	Rape	Robbery
54–64 years	7.9	5.5	0.0[a]	2.4
65 years and older	3.5	2.2	0.0	1.5
16–19 years	73.8	61.5	1.8	10.4
35–49 years	20.8	15.7	0.5	4.5

[a]The studies do not suggest that no one in this age group was raped, but the estimate was based on 10 or fewer sample cases. The point here is the comparison of rates, or the likelihood of victimization. The elderly are clearly at a statistically less probable risk of victimization.
SOURCE: *Sourcebook—1990* 260.

assault. Herbert Covey and Scott Menard's 1988 study, "Trends in Elderly Criminal Victimization from 1973 to 1984," found that the elderly (defined as those aged 65 and older) were "proportionately less likely to be victims of violent crime as opposed to property crime over the period 1973–1984" (335). While simple assault rates were rising for the general population, they were declining for the elderly. So, why the decline? Some have suggested that as the population reflects fewer young people—the group that commits a high percentage of the crimes—there have been fewer bad guys to victimize senior citizens. Others suggest that older persons may be more likely to take precautions against criminal assault/robbery; therefore, they may be chosen as a target less often (Covey & Menard 337). Better programs designed to inform the elderly of the criminal threats against them may be working to keep them mentally alert. But reduced victimization may also be a result of senior citizens choosing to limit their activities, and as some theorize, reduced exposure may be responsible for reduced victimization (Khullar & Wyatt 105). Then if older persons are being attacked less, why all the concern and attention on this particular group?

Our society is beginning to pay more attention to the plight of older persons, partly because the American population that is 65 years of age or older is steadily increasing. At the turn of the century only about 4% of the population was 65 years of age or older, but by 1950 some 8.1% were within that age category. The U.S. Census Bureau estimates that 13% of our population will be 65 or older by the year 2000 (Lent & Harpold 12). As a larger percentage of our population reaches advanced age, we can expect the victimization rate for that age group to increase accordingly. In the July 1988 *FBI Law Enforcement Bulletin*, agents Lent and Harpold encourage more people to become aware of the victimization of the elderly, saying, "Crime against the aging should not be an issue of concern for only law enforcement and elderly persons; it is a problem that at some point affects everyone" (13). We know from our study of victims that the young male in his late teens and early twenties is at high risk to becoming a victim of crime. But the statistics do not fully reflect the degree to which older people are suffering at the hands of criminals.

Just because the victimization rates among the elderly are lower than that of the general population does not mean that older persons fear crime less. In fact, the fear of crime seems to be inversely proportional to the risk in the case of the elderly. Clemente and Kleiman, in their 1976 article "Fear of Crime Among the Aged," as well as Cook et al. (1978), also writing for *Gerontologist*, found that the perception of rampant crime and the fear of being the next victim are significantly higher among older persons than among the rest of the population. This fear, while statistically unfounded, is nonetheless real and ever-present in the minds of America's senior citizens. Vulnerable to the psychological price of fear, many older persons have radically modified their previously active lifestyles to keep themselves out of a confrontation with a criminal. Even in their own neighborhoods, the elderly are more likely to feel unsafe and vulnerable—a feeling that begins a cycle of withdrawal—forcing the person to remain alone and locked up inside his or her home. The more they remain alone, the more they fear; thus, the more they stay isolated. "Fifty-three percent of all older people interviewed in the National Crime Survey said that they had limited their activities as a result of crime" (Khullar & Wyatt 102). Another 59% said they feared walking in their own neighborhood, whether day or night. Such fear takes a precious toll in opportunity costs and abbreviates the chances of an older person living a full, happy life. So, will a proud grandmother pass on the opportunity to attend her granddaughter's piano recital because it is being held downtown after dark? Will an elderly gentleman just suffer through a headache rather than risk going to the corner market after 8:00 P.M.?

Some of the fear shown by older persons reflects the fact that a crime committed against them is often more damaging than the same crime committed against a younger person. The physical result of an aggravated assault is quite clearly more damaging to an older person, for the elderly take longer to heal and often do not heal as completely as do younger men and women. But there are other crimes that we often take for granted, or at least fail to see in terms of their true cost to the senior citizen. Take robbery, for example. If a young businesswoman is robbed of the contents of her purse, she may lose anywhere from $50 to $200, depending upon her location and destination. If she loses the higher amount ($200), and she makes $4,000 a month, she has lost 5% of her income for that month. On the other hand, if the same thief takes $200 from a 69-year-old woman living only on a social security check of $600 a month, the thief has deprived her of 33% of her monthly income. Living on a fixed income is difficult enough for older persons, but try it without a third of your normal amount. Obviously, the hardship wrought upon the senior citizen is greater than that caused to the young businesswoman.

While the *Sourcebook of Criminal Justice Statistics* tells us that such incidents happen less often to older persons than to the rest of us, those statistics may not be telling the whole story. Many older persons are unwilling, unable, or too scared to report a crime against them. Some crimes against older persons are of a nature that makes them difficult for the aged to discuss, for instance, sex crimes and the sense of taboo that many older people have about discussing such matters. The shame of having been taken by a scam or having been overwhelmed or outsmarted by an assailant often forces other elderly victims into silence.

"I'm older," they reason to themselves, "I should have been smarter. How can I admit being taken like that?"

The combination of anger, outrage, and shame sometimes compels older persons to just try and forget the crime ever happened—to put it out of their minds—and to pretend it never occurred. But psychologically, this can be a dangerous option, leaving the victim even more violated by the memories and tormented by the constant reminder of what occurred. Second-guessing by well-meaning friends and relatives, and anticipating what others might think, often fuels the guilt of a victim—for example, "Why were you outside alone at that time of night?" or "Didn't you think to lock your doors?" The elderly person will keep silent and let the crime go unreported rather than run the gauntlet of stupid, embarrassing questions. Thus, many crimes against the elderly may go unreported as the victim remains stoic about the deed and the perpetrator, or if reported, the details necessary for successful investigation may be missing.

Other older crime victims may not report crime for fear of retaliation.

"What if that guy gets out and comes after me again?" they reason. "Maybe I won't be so lucky next time. I'll just let it go and maybe he'll choose someone else next time around."

Such an attitude does not help get the criminals off the street, you argue? Put yourself in the mindset of an older person for a moment. Picture yourself as suffering some physical malady as do many older people, and recognize that you cannot run as fast as you used to or react to a threat as quickly. Imagine you have had someone break into your home, assault you, rob you, or beat you up just for the thrill of it. Your attacker then leaves with your month's food money and some of your jewelry. Your lip is bleeding and your shoulder aches. You hope it's not broken. Now it is time to call the police. Before you do, think about this. In testimony before the House Select Committee on Aging in 1978, an assistant chief of police testified:

> The majority of our violent crimes are committed by people under 20 years old and most of them under the age of 18, which classified them as juveniles. Time after time, we arrest the same person and we end up, three hours later, giving them a ride home because there are not sufficient facilities for them and the programs are oriented toward rehabilitation (Khullar & Wyatt 102).

Is there any doubt why many crimes against the aged go unreported?

Sometimes older people die only to have their death ruled as due to "natural causes," when it may have been crime-related. Older persons frequently die alone, in the absence of witnesses. If a 75-year-old woman, the frequent victim of armed robbery, or burglary, or threats upon her life, dies from a heart attack, how much of her heart trouble can one attribute to the stress of criminal menacing?

In 1982 Cora Bentley hired a young man to rake leaves in her front yard. Physically disabled, Cora constantly relied upon temporary help to keep the grounds around her home in order. Upon completing the yardwork the man came inside Cora's home to be paid. He demanded more money than the amount they had agreed upon and Cora refused to pay it. The man got angry and demanded that she tell him where she had all her "hidden loot." She had no money in the house and she tried to tell him that, but he didn't believe her. He proceeded to ransack her home in search of money, destroying many of her valuable antiques while she watched. He did not assault her but he did threaten and terrorize her throughout his stay in the home. Cora was afraid to try to call the police or attempt to attract the attention of a neighbor. The offender eventually tired of his search, took the ten dollars in Cora's purse and left the scene.

Three months later Cora died. The medical officials ruled the death a result of "natural causes" brought on by old age, but her family and close friends have a different version of what caused Cora's death. They believe the anxiety and stress of an encounter with a criminal was directly responsible for bringing on her death. You will not find these types of incidents reflected in the crime surveys and statistics, but older people like Cora frequently die such crime-related deaths.

Because older persons often use the services of temporary employees whom they do not know, and because many of the aged do keep money on the premises to pay for such services, they become a likely target for criminals. Offenders perceive many of the aged as helpless and extremely vulnerable. They sense the fact that many of them live alone and do not have access to other people who can act as guardians against crime. Thus, the factors of isolation, the appearance of ineffectual resistance, and the possibility of money on the premises work together to draw criminals to the aged.

According to Gurdeep Khullar and Burt Wyatt, in their article, "Criminal Victimization of the Elderly," there were 18,976 homicides committed in the United States in 1985, and 12% of those were committed against victims 55 years of age or older. While overall crime rates for elderly persons are lower, personal larceny with contact and muggings occurs most frequently to persons 65 years of age and older (103), with up to 90% of bunco (confidence scams, "Pidgeon Drop" scams, etc.) crimes being directed against the elderly. Who are these people victimizing the elderly? The offender profile looks like this:

- Young male in his late teens or early twenties
- Little education, usually unemployed
- The same race as the victim and living in the same neighborhood
- Motivated to seek money or just "put the hurt" on someone
- Frequently operates with a partner
- Has a criminal record, that is, assault, burglary, etc.
- A sloppy offender, leaving considerable physical evidence behind (Lent & Harpold 14).

A 1975 study of housing projects found that 39% of the elderly residents were victimized in projects that also housed younger people, but only 14% were victimized in age-segregated housing (Khullar & Wyatt 101). That is a strong argument for finding a secure retirement community; unfortunately, it is an option many cannot afford.

Many crimes against the aged that begin as burglary end as sexual assault. The deviants in our society often use the opportunity of a burglary entry into a home to compound their offense. Since many older persons were raised during a time when sex was not openly discussed, there is a tendency for them not to report the crime to police. That hesitancy is based upon fear of the loss of reputation, concern for the loss of independence, concern that the offender might retaliate if the crime is reported, and sometimes a concern that law enforcement officials will not believe their story. "Who would believe that anyone would want to rape an old woman like me?" is an all-too-common attitude among the elderly. Yet the police will listen to an older person's story *if* they ever get a chance to hear it. Criminals know this when they choose the aged as their victims. For, while the Department of Justice 1981 figures indicate that an older woman only has a one in 10,000 chance of being raped, when a sexual assault does occur, it may be more debilitating and have a longer emotional effect on an older person than on a younger person. Fear is a predominant emotion in any sexual assault, but particularly among the aged, since their fear is often magnified by the fact that the assault is committed right there in their home. Long after the offender has gone the victim is faced with a daily reminder of the crime, and the sense of violation and the loss of the security of their home is reinforced every time the victim looks around the room. All of this reminds the victim of just how vulnerable he or she may be.

The key to protecting older persons from the threat of crime involves (1) educating them in the confrontation avoidance techniques we've already learned, (2) aiding law enforcement in their efforts to control crime, and (3) showing them the positive, physical measures, such as door locks, personal alarms, telephone security networks, and escort services, they can take to safeguard themselves. Social organizations, community groups, and families offer the best means of getting information to the elderly. Church groups for older citizens, travel groups, or continuing education groups can sponsor lectures, demonstrations, or informal discussion sessions with law enforcement or personal security consultants. Through these organizations we can raise the awareness of the elderly and reduce the aspects of their daily life and behavior that make them attractive to criminals. Conflict avoidance procedures, such as traveling in groups and avoiding the overt display of money, work just as well for older persons as for anyone else. Families can play an important role in adopting a program of safety checks and periodic communication with the aged to insure they are not being terrorized by criminals. These concepts combined with effective law enforcement can help to reduce the fears many elderly Americans face. The police can

intensify their patrols in communities where the elderly are frequently victimized, but the police are limited in numbers and you
must remember that every time they concentrate their efforts in
one area, it means another area is less guarded against crime. A
good example of positive police action to protect the aged is found
in the South Senior Citizens Unit (SCU) of New York City's
Manhattan area. The organization was founded in 1974 with a
mission to investigate the instances of assault and robbery committed against older persons. It had the additional community
relations mission of reducing fear in the community. The effectiveness of the organization is best viewed in how it handled a case
involving two holdup men who committed over 100 robberies.
This duo had the nasty habit of biting the fingers off its elderly
victims in order to obtain their wedding rings. The SCU arrested
one and shot the second during a stakeout (Lent & Harpold 15).

We all understand that the police can't be everywhere at one
time, and that funding limits how many units like the SCU can be
available in different localities. Still, by urging the elderly to report
crimes—*all crimes*—and by getting involved in Neighborhood
Watch organizations to keep surveillance high in the communities
of the aged, and by urging families to watch out for their aging
members, we can round out the effort of the law enforcement community.

It is not uncommon for the elderly to retreat into further
isolation when they have been victimized, indirectly making
themselves more vulnerable. Once isolated, the elderly often
suffer continued intimidation. Older persons must be shown that
law enforcement is on their side and they must be encouraged to
join community efforts to control crime. By educating the aged
and reducing their attractiveness to criminals we can reduce the
crime against them.

We can go a step further in preparing the aged to deal with
the threat of crime by not making the judgment that many criminals make. Society should not treat the elderly as though they are
helpless, hapless, and doomed to be victims. Older persons,
acting within the limits of their health and abilities, can learn to

protect themselves from many assault situations. An individual who has been active during the better part of his or her life, can be active in later life. People who refused to be intimidated at age 25 can still refuse to be intimidated at age 65. The basic principles of self-defense are available to older persons, who, while they may not be as strong or as fast as they once were, are a lot smarter. Older people are likely to think more carefully about the risk involved in various actions. Nature has an interesting way of balancing off our strengths and weaknesses as we grow older.

There are certain physical factors that must obviously be taken into consideration in teaching older people to protect themselves, such as the effect of aging on the bone structure. The techniques that an older person might use to fend off an assailant bent upon taking his or her life are different from those a young person would use, but we must never discount the option of self-defense simply because someone is older. A man in his eighties may not be able to wrestle a 20-year-old assailant to the ground, or punch hard enough to stop him with one blow, but the older person could, with proper training, learn to apply a less forceful blow to a pressure point that might render his attacker incapable of continuing. Through proper instruction that emphasizes redirection of an opponent's force rather than facing it head-on, as a 20-year-old might, we can offer the older person some options other than capitulation at all costs.

It is only through the careful combination of improved law enforcement tailored to the needs of the communities inhabited by the aged, the dissemination of information about conflict avoidance through community organizations, and instruction in the fundamentals of self-protection geared to their age and ability that we can expect to help the elderly prepare themselves to meet the potential dangers of crime. The American Association of Retired Persons (AARP) has done a great deal to inform its members of the risk to their generation, and many police agencies make officers available to speak to community groups about safeguarding residences. These safety seminars and services that deal with protecting the aged are available if we only ask for them.

Group activities that work to limit the opportunities for crime in a neighborhood also serve to lower the anxiety of the residents and reduce the fear of crime, particularly among the elderly. The answer to the problem of crime against the aged is not to wring our hands and say that old people are just doomed to be vulnerable to crime and unable to protect themselves or to be protected by the system. We owe the elderly more than that.

The following story is an excellent example indicating that just because a person is older does not mean he or she cannot protect himself or herself. Mr. Shimabuku, an Okinawan well into his seventies, was visiting the United States in the 1970s. He had earned the respect of generations of Americans who studied the art of Isshin-ryu Karate. Mr. Shimabuku, or Sensei (teacher) Shimabuku, had come to this country to see the progress of his art, and he was visiting several different organizations and offering encouragement and demonstrations to his loyal students and instructors. In spite of his advanced age, Shimabuku maintained considerable quickness and a mental intensity and concentration that was greatly admired.

Mr. Shimabuku was preparing to catch a taxi to go to the airport in New York City when he was accosted by two young hoodlums. They figured it would be a simple matter to rob this old man, for he did appear to be rather small and vulnerable. They followed Shimabuku to the corner and seized him by each arm, demanding that he give them his wallet. They said they would beat him up if he didn't comply. Shimabuku's command of English was not good enough to convince the assailants to release him, so he was forced to extricate himself. Both of the young assailants were immediately disabled and they eventually required hospitalization at the hands of this vulnerable-looking, small, aging man. They had made the mistake of choosing a victim who, in his prime, drove nails with his fists, and who, in advanced age, still maintained the heart of a warrior.

Chapter Ten

SOME FINAL THOUGHTS

Americans are frightened of crime and they are specifically concerned about stranger assault. Like a huge monster, stranger
crime has risen within our society and now casts its shadow over
an entire generation. While the population was increasing 13%
between 1960 and 1970, reported robberies were increasing 224%,
purse-snatchings 332%, larcenies 245%, and residential burglaries 337% (Lent & Harpold 17). Although crime has its genesis
in the misguided, antisocial, and evil designs of the criminal
mind, it is frequently nurtured and nourished by an odd combination of public fear, apathy, and a sluggish criminal justice system.

A national poll conducted in 1987 by the AD council found
that most people believe:

- Crime is inevitable
- Nothing can be done about crime
- Crime is a police problem
- Crime is not "their" problem (Lent & Harpold 17)

These four myths about crime must be overcome and public
attitudes must be modified if we expect to offer substantial resistance to the monster. By sharing with you the facts about stranger

crime, coupled with my interviews and experience dealing with victims, this book proves that crime is not inevitable in your life and that you can do something about it. Now that you understand the threat of crime and have some idea of who the criminals are and what they look for in a victim, you are better prepared to meet the challenge of a stranger assault. Knowing the principles of confrontation avoidance and having confidence in your ability to handle a situation gives you a sense of personal security that moves beyond fear and out of the shadow of crime. By understanding the statistics that show your chances of success if you are forced to confront a criminal, you perceive options you did not recognize before, which helps you understand the trade-offs of nonresistance and resistance and the advantages and disadvantages of forceful and nonforceful resistance. Now you can make decisions based upon fact and preparation, rather than spur-of-the-moment assessments or media-induced bravado.

Assess yourself for vulnerability, keep a sharp eye out for criminals, apply the principles of confrontation avoidance, and fight only when you have no other alternative to serious injury or death. Eduard Ziegenhagen and Deloris Brosnan said in their study, "Victim Response to Robbery and Crime Control Policy," in *Criminology* (1985):

> Individuals may know what is best for them but are ignorant of how to interpret accurately the likelihood of outcomes for a given situation. Nevertheless, the assumption that individuals are capable of exercising some level of judgment seems to be accepted generally. Individuals attempt to know how best to use available resources to make the choice that is in their best interests (693).

Roughly translated, what that academic jargon is trying to communicate is that you, the average citizen, are ultimately the best judge of what to do when facing a criminal. Your action or inaction is the most critical factor in dealing with stranger assault. Take what is offered in this book and supplement it with advice from your local law enforcement agencies and you will stand a good chance of keeping yourself out of the crime statistics.

But it takes more than individual effort to put up a good fight against this creature of crime that robs us of our liberty. Citizens must work together in a myriad of community organizations to take advantage of their total strength. Everyone need not rush out and join the Guardian Angels or become Neighborhood Rangers. That may be an option for some, but most of us will have to contribute in a less glamorous manner. By sharing information about crime prevention and by watching out for each other, we can reduce the number of available victims of crime and begin to starve the creature that stalks us.

GUARDIANSHIP PROGRAMS

Numerous organizations have surfaced over the past decade to help citizens focus their efforts in the contest against crime. By calling the crime prevention unit of your local police department, you can get information on the kind of programs your city or local area offers. Neighborhood or Citizen Watch groups have been successful in reducing residential burglaries and assaults by forming a communication chain to alert each other of unusual or suspicious activities. Acting as the "eyes and ears of the police," Neighborhood Watch organizations have broadened the scope of guardianship, and have, in effect, become a mass-deputized body of observers—an extension of the guardianship the police could normally provide (Marx 515). Some police departments will even furnish community organizations a map of where burglaries and other crimes are taking place, and the frequency and time of day for these incidents. But while you may be interested in preventing crime in your neighborhood, your neighbors may be less informed about the threat, and thus less inclined to get involved. How can you go about enlisting their help?

First of all, you cannot make people care about crime prevention. You can share facts with them, voice your concerns, but ultimately they must want to get involved for their own reasons. Unfortunately, nothing gets neighbors interested in a community crime watch quicker than being a victim. If you decide to organize a crime prevention program in your area, there is no substitute for leading by personal example. Talk to your neighbors one-on-one, explaining to them that what you have in mind is not a new idea, it is as old as our country. Neighbors watched out for neighbors long before we had well-organized police and broadened law enforcement authorities. Tell them how a program like Citizens Watch works to strengthen a neighborhood, bringing families together in ways that go beyond stopping criminal activities. One by-product of your program, you might explain, is that neighbors will get to know each other, and will be there to help one another in cases of flood, or fire, or tornados. Explain to them that it will not take a crime against someone for them to see how much better their community can be. Block parties, street dances, potluck suppers are just a few of the activities that can enable people to come together as a family of families. As coordinator/captain of your community effort, you will distribute crime prevention literature, interface with local law enforcement officers, work with other watch groups in the surrounding area, and provide a place for people to meet and talk about crime concerns. It is a big responsibility, but a tremendously satisfying activity that gives you the knowledge that you are doing your best not only for yourself and your family's safety but for your fellow community members as well. Gary T. Marx puts it well in his 1989 paper, "Commentary: Some Trends and Issues in Citizen Involvement in the Law Enforcement Process," appearing in *Crime and Delinquency*:

> The case for [community watching and reporting] is clear. Police cannot be everywhere. In large diverse areas they depend on citizens for information about wrongdoing and wrongdoers. In some ways this is a continuation of the citizen-based policing that is the hallmark of the Anglo-American tradition. In its ideal form it contrasts with the imposed police of colonial and totalitarian societies (516).

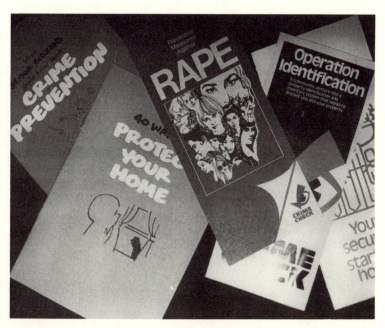

Figure 10.1. Looking for help.   Your local law enforcement agency is ready and willing to provide you with brochures, lectures, and other information to help you reduce your vulnerability to criminals. But you have to ask.

Programs like Neighborhood/Citizens Watch are most effective when they are part of a comprehensive community organization that is working to solve other problems, and when they are employed in changing neighborhoods where local crime problems are caused by outsiders trafficking in and through a neighborhood (Marx 501). These programs have improved community-police relations, and other community efforts, like Crime Stoppers, have helped to solve a number of "dead-end" cases that have baffled police. But whether you work to form a broader organization, like Citizens Watch, or just informally gather some interested friends and neighbors, some of the behaviors that police suggest neighbors watch out for are:

- Anyone coming to your door who appears to be lost, or who, upon asking to consult your telephone directory, appears to be looking around or "casing" the area.
- Anyone hanging around a neighbor's house when that neighbor is away. (It's better to be a bit inquisitive of strangers than to have to explain to your neighbor how thieves walked away with their possessions while you watched. There have even been cases of so-called good neighbors actually helping burglars cart away people's belongings.)
- Service or repair persons who show up uninvited.
- Cars that arrive on your street, park in front of a home, yet no one ever gets out, i.e., the driver appears to be waiting for someone but no one ever comes (especially at night).
- Anyone walking along your street looking into windows or into parked vehicles.
- People you do not recognize loading high-dollar items, such as computer or stereo equipment, into a car or truck.
- A neighbor's dog, who is usually kept indoors or on a leash, running free in the neighborhood. (This was the first clue we had that a family member's home had been burglarized while they were away—their *house* dog running up to meet our car.)

PROPERTY IDENTIFICATION AND SECURITY

Programs like Operation Identification help citizens to mark and later identify stolen property by etching ID numbers on valuables. Since police cannot prosecute a robbery suspect without a complainant, these ID programs have helped to link the perpetrator with the stolen goods. Burglars know that if they are apprehended with marked goods, the case against them is much stronger. Also, buyers of stolen property are less likely to handle a thief's goods if they are marked. With Operation ID, not only may you get your valuables back, but you can help put the criminal away as well. The window sticker that will identify you as an Operation ID participant might just make a criminal look for another target. And keep in mind that a burglar, once in your home, may commit other crimes; so Operation ID may well serve as a preventative measure against assault, rape, or even murder.

The FBI's C.R.I.M.E. Dog has helped raise public awareness and may be available to teach young people to be security conscious. In addition to offering helpful literature, many local police departments welcome your calls to survey your home or apartment, examining lock capacity, window security, and lighting, to make your living quarters more secure; and most any law enforcement organization is willing to give seminars and classes designed to teach security skills.

NEIGHBORHOOD PATROLS

Some communities face tougher crime challenges, and have subsequently fostered groups like Curtis Sliwa's Guardian Angels, who literally patrol the streets as a deterrent to criminals. What began in 1979 as "The Magnificent Thirteen Subway Safety Patrol," has since evolved into a national organization with local chapters in over 40 cities (Perry 129). While I was disappointed to hear Mr. Sliwa admit on his weekly radio show in November 1992 that some of the Guardian Angels' early rescues had been staged to gain public acceptance and support, he has earned my respect for having the courage to tell the truth. Perhaps it was his near-fatal shooting in a New York City taxi that convinced Curtis to make this revelation; at any rate, those unfortunate incidents during the founding days of the Guardian Angels in no way take away from the good they have done since. A 1984 survey in Toledo, Ohio, found (quite logically) that areas of greatest victimization, that is, high-crime, inner-city neighborhoods, had the highest level of support for Guardian Angels activities, with lower income persons being most supportive (Perry 130). Beyond the deterrent effect of the Guardian Angels' patrolling is the program's positive role model for young people and the opportunity it presents for community service (Marx, 502). But the police have not always been pleased about the Guardian Angels and organizations like them. Many predicted they would not last, and feared their tendency toward intervention in a criminal act might lead to injuries or death. But their success can be attributed to the personal determination of Curtis and Lisa Sliwa, a clear definition of their purpose, guidelines for the behavior of their members, and wide-based community support.

During the 1970s and 1980s, other groups have emerged who attempt to expand the reach of law enforcement agencies. Some of them are "escort services" that provide citizens, particularly the elderly, with a trustworthy companion to take along on a shopping trip or a visit to the doctor or other necessary travel. Police appear to be endorsing, or at least tolerating, escort organizations, primarily because they are not adversarial. Nothing makes police agencies more nervous than the notion of some vigilante organization that has declared itself judge, jury, and executioner for all crimes within a neighborhood. Guardianship—not retaliation—is the key to a successful program that will garner police support.

Age is not a factor in becoming a neighborhood patrol member, for in some retirement communities, senior citizens band together to look out for one another. One such organization, the Sun City Posse, which boasts over 250 members, helped to reduce vandalism and burglary in Sun City, Arizona (Persico 126). But a citizen patrol will be successful only if it works in cooperation with local law enforcement agencies; and by obtaining information and guidance from those agencies during the formation of your guardian group, you will only enhance its effectiveness. Should you desire to organize some type of neighborhood patrol, contact one of these organizations for information: The National Institute of Justice, the National Sheriff's Association, the National Crime Prevention Council, or the Eisenhower Foundation.

While some people may not have the time or the skills necessary to contribute to such guardian enterprises, there are other effective organizations that can help disarm the crime beast in different ways. Police-sponsored programs like Home Safety, Business Watch, and Traffic Safety provide ample opportunities for citizens to affiliate with law enforcement; and the increasing popularity of television shows like *Crimestoppers* and *FBI Most Wanted* also encourage people to pay attention to what is happening around them. Law enforcement agencies are constantly looking for civilian participation, and they have long since realized how important public involvement is to the common task of crime prevention (Gales 6).

As previously mentioned, citizens watching out for each other is nothing new. Back in the early 1800s, before the emergence of a police force, major cities like New York employed "citizen watches," consisting of citizens who strolled around all night and kept an eye out for fires or burglars or vandals. They would sound an alarm or ring a bell to warn their sleeping neighbors of trouble (Persico 123). Just keep in mind that there is a big difference between being vigilant and being a vigilante. Both words are based upon the root word *vigil*, taken from the Latin, meaning to be awake. A vigil is also a watch kept during night hours, or a surveillance. Each of us should be *vigilant* in our homes and communities, in that we should keep watch against crime and help each other avoid becoming a victim. The word *vigilante* means one who is a member of a vigilance committee—an organization that takes upon itself the power of pursuing and punishing criminals. We, citizens, are not and should not be in the business of dealing out punishment, but we had better be in the business of watching out for criminals and alerting the authorities of their activities.

You will note that this book is concluding on a communal note, for while we must certainly employ the techniques of confrontation avoidance to protect ourselves, our best defense against stranger assault comes not from two million individual efforts, but from the synergy obtained when we work together and look out for one another. Read this book and internalize its concepts, then have your family members read it and talk over strategies for self-protection. Practice those strategies, remind each other of dangerous situations, and watch out for one another. Then get your neighbors involved. Share the tenets of this book with them and develop a community effort to put a stop to victimization. Remember that in the shadow of stranger crime, many of us become lax and inattentive in our daily activities, allowing ourselves to fall within an offender's grasp. Those who remain cautious and mentally alert will keep themselves out of reach. And while the criminal may change his shape or vary his approach, alert citizens will still recognize him and be prepared to deal with a confrontation. Our mind is our best weapon against criminal assault, for our rational facilities can warn us of its approach and enable us to choose the proper response. Our hands, our feet, and our voices are all weapons we can use against criminals; but our community and personal weapons are powerless unless used, and ineffective unless we know *how* to use them. We would all like to stop crime instantly, but no one of us can deliver a single, killing blow. It is only by the cumulative effort of each individual citizen, each doing his or her best to reduce his or her own vulnerability, that our society can truly confront and overcome the threat of stranger assault.

REFERENCES

Abbey, A. "Sex Differences in Attributions for Friendly Behavior: Do Males Misperceive Female's Friendliness?" *Journal of Personality and Social Psychology*. 42: 830–838.

"Alcohol Topics in Brief." Division of Substance Abuse Drug Information for Kentucky, Frankfort, KY.

"Alcohol Use and Criminal Behavior." *Chicago Tribune*, July 8, 1984, Sec. 6.

Amick, Angelynne E. & Calhoun, Karen S. "Resistance to Sexual Aggression: Personality, Attitudinal, and Situational Factors." *Archives of Sexual Behavior*. 16.2 (1987) April: 153–163.

Amir, M. *Patterns in Forcible Rape*. Chicago: University of Chicago Press, 1971.

Arnold, Peter. *Lady Beware: A Practical Guide to the Physical Safety of Women*. Garden City, NY: Doubleday, 1974.

Atkeson, Beverly M., Calhoun, Karen S., & Morris, Kim T. "Victim Resistance to Rape: The Relationship of Previous Victimization, Demographics, and Situational Factors." *Archives of Sexual Behavior*. 18.6 (1989) December: 497–507.

Bard, M. & Sangrey, D. *The Crime Victim's Book*. New York: Basic Books, 1979.

Bart, P. B. & O'Brien, P. H. *Stopping Rape: Successful Survival Strategies*. New York: Pergamon, 1985.

Bart, P. B. & O'Brien, P. H. "Stopping Rape: Effective Avoidance Strategies." *Signs: The Journal of Women in Culture and Society*. 10. 83–101.

Barkas, J. L. *Victims*. New York: Scribner's, 1978.

Behan, Cornelius J. "Fighting Fear in Baltimore County—The COPE Project." *FBI Law Enforcement Bulletin*. November 1986.

Bell, E. & McDowell, D. "McGruff Robot Teaches Kids." *FBI Law Enforcement Bulletin*. 60, October 1, 1991: 20–21.

"The Bodyguard." *Home & Auto Security*. May/June 1993, p. 63.

Booher, Dianna. *Rape: What Would You Do If . . . ?* New York: Julian Messner, 1981.

Brady, J. S. "Perceptions of Date and Stranger Rape: A Difference in Sex Role Expectations and Rap-supportive Beliefs." *Sex Roles*. 24 (1991) March: 291–307.

Brewer, James D. "Martial Arts Weapons and the Law." *Taekwondo Times*. May 1985.

Bridges, Judith S. & McGrail, Christine A. "Attributions of Responsibility for Date and Stranger Rape." *Sex Roles*. 21. 3–4. (1990) August: 273–286.

Bureau of Justice Statistics. *Report to the Nation on Crime and Justice*. March 1988, pp. 24–25.

Bureau of Justice Statistics. "The Fear of Crime." *Report to the Nation on Crime and Justice*, U.S. Department of Justice. March 1988, 24–25.

Burns, J. "A Safe Place for Children." *Victimology: An International Journal*. 9.1 (1984): 23–65.

Caminiti, Susan. "A Lifesaving Seminar at Work." *Working Woman*. April 1992.

Carmichael, Jim. *The Women's Guide to Handguns*. Indianapolis: Bobbs-Merrill, 1982.

Castleman, Michael. *Crime Free: Stop Your Chances of Being Mugged or Burglarized by 90 percent*. New York: Simon & Schuster, 1984.

CBS Evening News. November 5, 1992.

Clemente, F. & Kleiman, M. "Fear of Crime Among the Aged." *Gerontologist*. 16 (1976): 107–210.

Cook, F., Skogan, W., *et al.* "Criminal Victimization of the Elderly: The Economic and Physical Consequences." *Gerontologist*. 18 (1978): 338–349.

Covey, Herbert & Menard, Scott. "Trends in Elderly Criminal Victimization from 1973 to 1984." *Research on Aging*. 10.3 (1988) September: 329–341.

Dillon, Karen, "Paradox of Rape Cases: DNA Convicts, Frees." *Kansas City [MO] Star*, March 13, 1993.

Dworkin, Anthony, Haney, C. A., and Telschow, Ruth. "Fear, Victimization, and Stress among Urban Public School Teachers." *Journal of Organizational Behavior*. 9 (1988): 159–171.

Facts on File, 1992. New York: Facts on File Publication, 1992.

Flaherty, Michael J. "Stop Child Abuse Through Education." *FBI Law Enforcement Bulletin*. January 1986.

Frankel, Valerie, "How to Crime Proof your Life." *Mademoiselle*. January 1992, pp. 98–99.

Gales, Daryl F. "A Partnership Against Crime." *FBI Law Enforcement Bulletin*. August 1986.

Gamecock, the Student Newspaper of the University of South Carolina.

Goodstein, Lynne. "The Crime Causes Crime Model." *Victimology* 5 (1980): 133–151.

Griffith, Liddon R. *Mugging: You Can Protect Yourself*. Englewood Cliffs, NJ: Prentice-Hall, 1978.

"Gun Fired by Accident in Class Kills 1." *The Courier Journal*. January 22, 1993.

Hazelwood, Robert R. & Harpold, Joseph A. "RAPE: The Dangers of Providing Confrontational Advice." *FBI Law Enforcement Bulletin*. 51 (1986) April: 1–5.

Hechinger, Grace. *Street Smart Child*. New York: Facts on File Publications, 1984.

Herrington, Lois. "President's Task Force on Victims of Crime." U.S. Government Printing Office. 1982.

Hertica, Michael A. "Police Interviews of Sexually Abused Children." *FBI Law Enforcement Bulletin*. January 1986.

Hindelang, Michael J. *Victims of Personal Crime*. Cambridge: Ballinger, 1978.

"High School Girls Face Harassment." *USA Today*. 121: August 12, 1992.

Hoose, Shoshanna. "Carrying Courage in a Canister." *Maine Sunday Telegram*. March 8, 1993. p. C11.

Kadish, Sanford H. *Encyclopedia of Crime and Justice*, Vols. I–III. New York: Free Press, 1983.

Kalette, Denise. "The Untold Story: Campus Crime." *USA Today*. January 13, 1988, pp. 1A–2A.

Karmen, Andrew. *Crime Victims: An Introduction to Victimology*. Monterey, CA: Brooks/ Cole, 1984.

Karsko, Bernie. "'Jacket' Killer Gets 30 to Life." *Columbus Dispatch*. June 4, 1993. p. C1.

Kaylin, Lucy. "Home Alone?" *Mademoiselle*. January 1992. pp. 98–99.

Keenan, Marney. "The Female Fear." *Chicago Tribune*. April, 1989, Tempo section, p. 1+.

Khullar, Gurdeep S. and Wyatt, Bert. "Criminal Victimization of the Elderly." *Free Inquiry in Creative Sociology*. 17.1 (1989) May: 101–105.

Kleck, Gary & Sayles, Susan. "Rape & Resistance." *Social Problems*. 37.2 (1990) May: 149–162.

Kolko, David J., Moser, Joanne T., and Huges, Judith. "Classroom Training in Sexual Victimization Awareness and Prevention Skills: An Extension of the Red Flag/Green Flag People Program." *Journal of Family Violence*. 4.1 (1989) March: 25–45.

Koss, Mary, Dinero, Thomas, & Seibei, Cynthia. "Stranger and Acquaintance Rape." *Psychology of Women Quarterly*. 12 (1988): 1–24.

Kotulak, Ronald. "What You Can Do to Take Back the Night." Chicago Tribune. April 16, 1989, Tempo section, p. 1+.

Kraizer, S. K. *et al.*, "Programming For Preventing Sexual Abuse and Abduction." *Child Welfare* 67 (1988) January/February: 69–78.

LeBeau, J. L. "The Journey to Rape." *Journal of Political Science Administration*. 15 (1987): 129–136.

Lashley, James R. & Rosenbaum, Jill L. "Routine Activities and Multiple Personal Victimization." *Sociology & Social Research*. 73.1 (1988) October: 47–50.

Lent, Cynthia, J. & Harpold, Joseph A. "Violent Crime Against the Aging." *FBI Law Enforcement Bulletin*. July 1988.

Levine-Macombie, Joyce & Koss, Mary P. "Acquaintance Rape: Effective Avoidance Strategies." *Psychology of Women Quarterly*. 10 (1986): 311–20.

Livingston, Nancy. "Two-thirds of St. Paul Students Victims of School Crime Threats." *St. Paul Pioneer Press-Dispatch*. December 1, 1992.

Martinez-Schnell, Beverly & Waxweiler, Richard. "Increases in Premature Mortality due to Homicide—United States, 1968–1985. *Violence and Victims*. 4.4 (1989) Winter: 287–293.

Marx, Gary T. "Commentary: Some Trends and Issues in Citizen Involvement in the Law Enforcement Process." *Crime and Delinquency*. 35.3 (1989) December: 621–640.

Mason, Janet. "Women Who Fought Back and Won." *Black Belt Magazine*. November 1987.

Maxfield, Michael G. "Lifestyle & Routine Activity Theories of Crime." *Journal of Quantitative Criminology*. 3.4 (1987) December: 275–282.

McKee, Robert. "Fear: Your Best Friend and Worst Enemy." *Inside Kung Fu*. October, 1987.

Miethe, T. "Citizen-based Crime Control Activity and Victimization Risks: An Examination of Displacement and Free-rider Effects." *Criminology*. 29: 419–439.

Miller, Bill. *Washington Post*. December 27, 1992.

Mills, Steve. "Violent Crimes Scar Victims' Minds." *Democrat and Chronicle*. February 26, 1989, p. 1A+

"Mom Is Charged After Confronting Boy Accused of Raping Daughter." *Columbus Dispatch*. June 4, 1993, p. 5A.

Neergaard, Lauran, "Surveys Illustrate Teenagers' Main Risk for Death Is from Injuries." *The News Enterprise*. October 18, 1992, p. 3D.

Olson, Dean. "Myths of Rape." *Sunday World-Herald*. June 26, 1988, p. 8+.

Parrot, Andrea. *Coping with Date Rape and Acquaintance Rape*. New York: The Rosen Publishing Group, 1988.

Pater, Alan F. & Pater, Jason R. *What They Said in 1990: A Yearbook of World Opinion*. Palm Springs, CA: Monitor Book Co., 1991.

Pearl, Mike & Furse, Jane. "Jogger's Attackers 'Felt Good' Afterward: Defendant." *New York Post*. November 11, 1990.

Peden, Lauren. "What Every Woman Needs to Know About Personal Safety." *McCall's*. May 1992, p. 72+.

Pernanen, Kai. "Alcohol and Crimes of Violence." *Social Aspects of Alcoholism*, 1976.

Perry, Joseph B. "Public Support of the Guardian Angels: Vigilante Protection Against Crime, Toledo, OH." *Sociology & Social Research*. 73.3 (1989) April: 129–31.

Persico, J. E. Keeping Out of Crime's Way: *The Practical Guide for People over 50*. Washington, DC: AARP, 1985.

"Physiological Effects of Alcohol." *Alcohol Topics in Brief*. Drug Information Service for Kentucky. Frankfort, KY, 1982.

Pineau, Lois. "Date Rape: A Feminist Analysis." *Law and Philosophy*. 8.2 (1989) August: 217–243.

"Police Programs." *Glamour*. 90:140, September 1992.

Poyer, Joe. "Carjacking: The Nation's Newest Crime Wave." *Home & Auto Security*. (1993) May–June: 12–16.

Purdum, Todd S. "The Reality of Crime on Campus." *New York Times*. April 10, 1988, Sec 12, pp. 47–52.

Read, Katy. "Rape Counseling with a Difference." *Times-Picayune*. February 11, 1992.

Reilly, Brian. "Gay-Bashers Beware." *Washington Times*. February 24, 1993, p. C4.

Riedel, Marc. "Stranger Violence: Perspectives, Issues, and Problems." *The Journal of Criminal Law and Criminology*. 78.2 (1987).

Roiphe, Katie. "Date Rape's Other Victim." *The New York Times Magazine*. June 13, 1993, pp. 26–40.

Room, Robin. "Behavioral Aspects of Alcohol and Crime." *Encyclopedia of Criminal Justice*, Vol I. Sanford H. Kadish, Ed., Free Press. New York: 1983.

Rossi, Melissa. "Annie Got Her Gun." *Mademoiselle*. June 1992, p. 66+.

Rubin, James H. "Overall U.S. Crime Rate Barely Changed in 1991." *The News Enterprise*. October 27, 1992, p. 9A.

Sampson, Robert J. "Personal Violence by Strangers: An Extension and Test of the Opportunity Model of Predatory Victimization." *The Journal of Criminal Law and Criminology*. 78.2 (1987).

Seipei, Tracy. "Mace Not Always The Best Defense." *Denver Post*. February 7, 1993, pp. C9–C10.

Selkin, J. "Reactions to Assaultive Rape." *Journal of Communication and Psychology*. 6:269–274.

Siegel, M. "Crime and Violence in America: The Victims." *American Psychologist*. 38 (1985) January: 1267–1273.

Silberman, C. "Criminal Violence." *Criminal Justice*. 11 (1978).

Skogan, Wesley G., & Block, Richard. "Resistance and Injury In Non-Fatal Assaultive Violence." *Victimology*. 8.3 (1983): 215–226.

Sliwa, Lisa. *Attitude—Commonsense Defense for Women*. New York: Crown, 1986.

Soulsman, Gary. "War On Child Sexual Abuse." *News-Journal* (Wilmington, DE). January 5, 1993.

Sourcebook of Criminal Justice Statistics—1990. Edited by Kathleen Maquire *et al.*. Hindelang Criminal Justice Research Center, Washington, D.C. 1991.

Sourcebook of Criminal Justice Statistics—1991. Edited by Kathleen Maquire *et al.* Hindelang Criminal Justice Research Center, Washington, D.C., 1992.

Steffensmeier, D. J. & Harer, M. D. "Is the Crime Rate Really Falling?" *Journal of Research in Crime and Delinquency*. 24 (1987): 23–48.

Storaska, Frederic. *How to Say No to a Rapist and Survive*. New York: Random House, 1975.

Sussman, Vic. "A Can of Self-defense." *U.S. News and World Report*. September 28, 1992, pp. 82–88.

Tanoika, Ichiro. "Evidence Links Smoking to Violent Crime Victimization." *Sociology and Social Research*. 71, October 1, 1986: 58.

Treen, Joe *et al.* "Striking Back at Crime." *People*. August 24, 1992.

Uniform Crime Reports for the United States—1991. Federal Bureau of Investigation, U.S. Department of Justice. Washington, D.C., 1992.

"Victims of Crime." *US News and World Report*. July 31, 1989: 16–19.

Voskuhl, John. "Scott Pennington: A New Kid, a Loner." *The [Louisville, KY] Courier-Journal*, January 20, 1993, p. 1.

Ward, S. K., Chapman, Kathy, Cohn, Ellen, & Williams, Kirk. "Acquaintance Rape and the College Social Scene." *Family Relations*. 40 (1991) January: 65–71.

"What Women and Men should Know about Date Rape." South Carolina Educational Resource Center for Missing and Exploited Children. Greenville Technical College. Greenville, S.C. 1986.

Wheeler, B. Gordon. "Are You an Easy Mark?" *Woman's Day*. June 29, 1993, p. 63+.

Whiteley, Elaine. "Nightmare In Our Classrooms." *Ladies Home Journal*. October 1992, pp. 74 +.

"Who Is Most Afraid of Crime?" *USA Today*. 121:12 August 1992.

Wooden. "Common Lures Used By Child Abductors/Molestors." excerpt published in *Readers' Digest*. June 1988.

Wozencraft, Ann. "Self-Defense Strategies." *Woman's Day*, June 29, 1993. p. 66.

Ziegenhagen, Eduard A. *Victims, Crime and Social Control*. New York: Praeger Publishers, 1977.

Ziegenhagen, Eduard A. & Brosnan, Deloris. "Victim Responses to Robbery and Crime Control Policy." *Criminology*. 23.4 (1985): 675–695.

Appendix

SUPPORT GROUPS

Throughout the United States, support groups have arisen to meet the needs of citizens who have been victimized by criminals. Some organizations provide counseling, medical and psychological advice, and even legal assistance to victims, while others offer crime prevention programs as well. To provide a state-by-state, city-by-city listing of all the telephone numbers and addresses of various victim support organizations would require a volume hundreds of pages thick. In my state alone (Kentucky), rape crisis volunteers must consult a 65-page resource book to find all the possible contact points for rape counseling and intervention. In rape crisis counseling, as well as child abuse and crime victimization, the support is generally decentralized, with each state, and sometimes each county, raising funds and setting up its own support network. Many victim assistance groups receive some federal money, but because heavy dependence on local and state support may allow for autonomy, such reliance tends to frustrate national coordination efforts. Sometimes these groups interface and sometimes they do not.

Not only does the set-up and support vary from state to state, but the training the counselors receive varies as well. In Kentucky, for example, all Crisis Intervention volunteers are required to have

40 hours of training, and each rape crisis counselor is afforded the same confidentiality privilege as a lawyer or a minister; for instance, their counseling records can't be subpoenaed. Most states require only 20 hours of training and some even less.

I have chosen to list some telephone numbers and addresses of national organizations that can either support you directly or that can put you in touch with a representative organization in your state or local area.

CRIME VICTIMIZATION (GENERAL)

One of the first places a citizen can turn to for victim advocacy or support is the state Attorney General's Office, usually listed in the yellow or blue pages of the telephone directory under "State Government." Most are listed as "(Your State) Victim's Advocacy Office."

The Federal Government also provides a victim support service funded by the U.S. Department of Justice, Office of Justice Programs, Office for Victims of Crime. A representative here can be reached by writing or calling:

NATIONAL VICTIM RESOURCE CENTER
Box 6000
Rockville, MD 20850
(800) 627-6872

In addition to sponsoring victim-related studies, this office provides the names, addresses, and telephone numbers for the various state victims compensation programs. Not only does the National Victim Resource Center provide free subscriptions to the *National Institute of Justice Journal* and the *NIJ Catalog*, but it also offers over 7,000 victim-related books and articles that address issues of child abuse (physical and sexual), domestic violence, victim-witness programs, and general victim services.

Several privately operated victim assistance organizations are open and actively supporting crime victims. If one of these is in your local area, it can support you and refer you to someone who is closer.

NATIONAL VICTIM CENTER
309 W. Seventh Street
Suite 1001
Fort Worth, TX 76102
(817) 877-3355

NATIONAL VICTIM CENTER
2111 Wilson Blvd.
Suite 300
Arlington, VA 22201
(703) 276-2880

Jerome J. Radwin is Executive Director of both offices of the National Victim Center, which offers public education programs, legislative advocacy for crime victims, and training and assistance to law enforcement and legal professionals, as well as information and referrals for victims. The Center's quarterly publications, *Networks* and *Crime, Safety and You*, are available by contacting either office.

Another private organization that offers a broad-based information and support source is:

NATIONAL ORGANIZATION FOR VICTIM ASSISTANCE
1757 Park Road NW
Washington, DC 20010
(202) 393-6682

Maintaining a 24-hour national Crisis Information and Referral Hotline, this organization renders assistance to victims of all types of crime. In addition to monitoring the progress of various victim legislation packages nationwide, the National Organization for Victim Assistance specializes in crisis intervention and crisis response. Its monthly *NOVA Newsletter* costs about $30 a year for an individual subscription, and keeps citizens up to date with on-going victim legislation, research and support programs.

Another proactive group that can help citizens avoid criminal assault is:

NATIONAL CRIME PREVENTION COUNCIL
1700 K Street NW
Second Floor
Washington, DC 20006
(202) 466-6272

A frequent cosponsor of conferences, this organization also provides victim information and referral, legislative advocacy, and public education.

RAPE VICTIMIZATION

Within each state is a Rape Crisis network, the telephone numbers for most of which are listed in the telephone directory or can be obtained from directory assistance by asking for the "Rape Crisis Hotline" or the "Rape Counseling Center." There are, however, a number of national organizations that can channel information or referrals for rape victims or for citizens who just want more information on how to prevent rape.

THE NATIONAL CLEARINGHOUSE ON MARITAL AND DATE RAPE
2325 Oak Street
Berkeley, CA 94708
(510) 524-1582

This organization offers information and referral, public education focused on college campuses, professional associations, and the media, and consultation to crisis centers and other support organizations.

CENTER FOR THE PREVENTION OF SEXUAL AND DOMESTIC
   VIOLENCE
1914 N. 34th Street
Suite 105
Seattle, WA 98103
(206) 634-1903

The Center's quarterly publication, *Working Together to Prevent Sexual and Domestic Violence*, costs $420 a year, and offers worthwhile public information, as well as contact points for training the religious community and the general population. This group maintains a current film and video library available for public rental.

CHILD ABUSE

While each state has its own support network, you can find the closest local child abuse counselor and reporting activity by calling:

NATIONAL CHILD ABUSE HOTLINE
(800) 422-4453

Another organization that provides information and referral, and acts as an advocate for sexually exploited children, missing children, runaways, and abducted children, is:

NATIONAL CENTER FOR MISSING AND EXPLOITED CHILDREN
2101 Wilson Boulevard
Suite 550
Arlington, VA 22201
(703) 235-3900
(To report missing children, call (800) 843-5678.)

This group, in addition to providing crisis intervention services, training programs for law enforcement officials, and legislative advocacy, publishes three times yearly *At the Center*, a primer for parents and professionals.

Another group that supports children is:

ADAM WALSH CHILD RESOURCE CENTER, INC.
319 Clematis Street
Suite 244
West Palm Beach, FL 33401
(407) 820-9000

This center publishes the "Kids and Company: Together for Safety," a child abduction/street-proofing curriculum created for kindergarten through sixth grade. The center also monitors child abuse/exploitation legislation at both the federal and state levels.
Still another source of information and referral is:

AMERICAN ASSOCIATION FOR PROTECTING CHILDREN
63 Inverness Drive East
Englewood, CO 80112-5117
(303) 792-9900 or (800) 227-5242

This division of the American Humane Association conducts research in the field of child abuse and neglect, sponsors national conferences, and provides a public education program.
Specializing in victim assistance to families of missing children is:

CHILD KEYPPERS' INTERNATIONAL, INC.
P. O. Box 6465
Lake Worth, FL 33466
(407) 586-6695 or (800)-395-5678 (to report missing children)

THE ELDERLY AS CRIME VICTIMS

The elderly in our society who, while not victimized at the rate of younger persons may suffer in greater proportion when they are victimized, have several places to turn to for support.

THE AMERICAN ASSOCIATION OF RETIRED PERSONS
601 E. Street NW
Washington, DC 20049
(202) 434-2222

The AARP is not only a legislative watchdog for the aged, it also provides advocacy for victims of elder abuse, neglect, and domestic violence. This organization, coupled with the organization named below, helps broaden our understanding of the special needs of the aged. Both organizations work to limit the vulnerability of the elderly while maintaining their quality of life.

NATIONAL COMMITTEE FOR THE PREVENTION OF ELDER ABUSE
% Institute on Aging
The Medical Center of Central Massachusetts
119 Belmont Street
Worcester, MA 01605
(508) 793-6166

Index

Amir, Menachem, 27, 146, 156
Anderson, Phillip, 136
Appearance, as invitation to
    assault, 79–80
Armed and Female, 128, 136–137
Ashcroft, James, 137
Assault
  aggravated, 5
    defined, 6
    frequency of, 12
  alcohol and, 18–21, 22t
  attempted versus successful, 13
  versus battery, 5
  against children, 185
    deterrents against, 183–184
  of children, reactions to, 207–214
  definitions of, 4–6
  deterrents to
    behavior as, 83
    companions as, 69–70, 83
    control techniques for, 96
    instinct as, 71–74, 83
    law enforcement as, 45
    lifestyle as, 83
    lifestyle changes as, 46–47
    light as, 70–71, 83
    mental alertness as, 63–66,
      83
    personal defensible space as,
      83
    submission as, 44–45
  of elderly, 217
  as entertainment, 33–34
  frequency of, 3
  incidental, 20
  increase in, 3
  in public places, 68
  resisting
    decision to, 87

Assault (*cont.*)
  resisting (*cont.*)
    effectiveness of, 89t, 89–91
    forceful versus nonforceful,
      88–91
    with justifiable force, 106–109
    versus submission, 85–112
  risk factors for, 6, 8, 10–11
  in schools and playgrounds,
    200–214
  sexual. *See* Rape
  simple, 5
    defined, 6
    frequency of, 13
  stranger, 3
    incidence of, 4
    risk factors for, 39–40, 40t
  threat of, 1–13. *See also* Threat
    options in, 44–47
  time and location of, 66–69
  verbal, legal perspective on,
    87–88
  and victim's loss of control, 36–
    37
  weapons as deterrent to, 45–46
  of women, time of, 68
  of young men, 69
Attacker. *See also* Criminal(s)
  age, sex, and race of, 18t
  appearance of, 27–29
  in groups, 29–30
  law enforcement in deterrence
    of, 45
  lone, 17–18, 18t
  profile of, 15–30
  and routine behavior of victim,
    23–27
  submission to, as viable
    option, 44–45

National Crime Survey, 10
  victim interviews in, 4
National Crime Victimization
    Survey, 11
National Institute of Justice Journal,
    246
National Organization for Victim
    Assistance, 34
  address and services, 247
National Rifle Association, gun
    training classes of, 136
National Victim Center, address
    and services, 247
National Victim Resource Center,
    address and services, 246
NCS. *See* National Crime Survey
Neighborhood patrols, 233–236
Neighborhood Watch, 224, 229
Networks, 247
Nonviolence, in response to
    aggression, 92–96
Norris, Chuck, 124

O'Brien, P.H., 146, 155, 158
Olivieri, Rose, 159
Operation Identification, 232–233
Opportunity Model, 41–42

Pagley, Albert R., 23–24
Parents
  intervention in children's
    altercations, 209–214
  as role models, 202–203
  roles of
    in child safety, 205–207
    in preventing crime against
     children, 183
  value system of, 208
Parrot, Andrea, 149

Patrols, neighborhood, 233–236
Patterns in Forcible Rape, 27, 146
Pearsall, Merri, 69
Pennington, Scott, 203–204
Pepper repellant
  availability of, 129
  effects of, 131
  legality of, 131
Pernanen, Kai, 21
Personal alarms
  advertising for, 128
  effects of, 132
Personal defensible space, 72f,
    74–79
  as assault deterrent, 84
  creating, 75, 76f, 77f, 78f
  defined, 75
  in elevators, 76f
Phillips, Reiko, 211–214
Phrenology, 15–16
Pineau, Lois, 149
Pink Panthers, 70
Police departments, crime
    prevention programs of, 229
Powerflex USA, 176
Poyer, Joe, 111
President's Task Force on Victims
    of Crime, 3
Priest, Carrolyn, 132
Property, identification of, 232–233
Prostitutes, as rape victims, 172
Public places, as crime location, 68
Purse-snatching, increasing rate
    of, 227

Quigley, Paxton, 128, 136–137

Racism, crimes based on, 9
Radwin, Jerome J., 247